Mad Dogs
and Englishmen

PRECEDING PAGE Bulldog breed: the March 1900 issue of *Navy and Army Illustrated* magazine leaves its readers in no doubt as to its stance on British possessions.

THIS PAGE Loyal subjects: on a state visit to Aden in 1921, Edward, Prince of Wales (the future Edward VIII; saluting) is driven past a banner proclaiming the colony's devotion to his father, King George V.

TELL DADDY WE ARE A

Mad Dogs and Englishmen

A Grand Tour of the British Empire at its Height
1850 – 1945

Ashley Jackson

Quercus

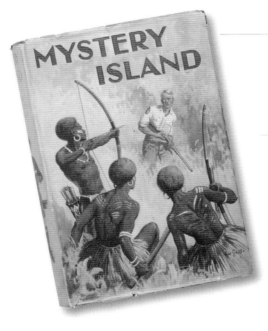

Contents

6–9
Introduction

10–23
The British Empire: Red on the Map

24–41
New Worlds to Settle and Sell To:
The Expansion of the British Empire

42–57
A Light Unto the Gentiles:
Missionaries, Abolitionists and Humanitarians

58–77
The Source of the Nile: Exploration and Knowledge

78–97
Crown Imperial:
The Imperial Monarchy and its Native Allies

98–115
A World to Govern:
District Commissioners, Chiefs and Whitehall

116–141
Soldiers of the Queen:
Gunning for the Empire on Land, Sea and Air

142–153
Steamer to Suez:
Air Routes, Sea Lanes and Ports of Call

Clockwise from top left:
A novel by Major Charles
Gilson; H.M. Stanley;
cigarette card from Wills's
'Arms of the British Empire'
series (1910); programme
from the International
Exhibition, Adelaide (1887);
detail from *Herbert Strang's
Annual;* 1950s stamp from
the British Caribbean

154–165
Colonial Gothic and Narrow-Gauge Tracks:
Architecture and Engineering

166–189
Elgar and 'Chums':
The Empire and Popular Culture

190–199
Elephant Guns and Leather on Willow:
Sports and Safaris

200–213
The Playing Fields of Aligarh and Eton:
Schools, Lodges and the Imperial Élite

214–223
The Imperial Treasure Trove:
Produce and Marketing

224–231
Legacies of Empire

232–235
Further Reading

236–239
Index

239
Picture Credits

240
Aknowledgements

INTRODUCTION

MAD DOGS AND ENGLISHMEN takes as its inspiration the vivid representations of the British Empire conveyed by a wide range of media throughout its 'high noon' in the 19th and 20th centuries. The power of imperial imagery and ideas was immense, reverberating around the globe and defining the way in which millions of people viewed themselves and the world. No nation or international organization could lay claim to such widespread influence or such all-pervasive iconography as the British Empire.

A souvenir from British Columbia commemorating the 60th anniversary of the union of Upper and Lower Canada to form the Dominion of Canada. Around the world, British imperial endeavour created new states and territorial agglomerations.

Between 1860 and 1960 successive generations were thrilled, informed and entertained by reports from the furthest reaches of the British Empire and the waves over which Britannia ruled. They were given a solid grounding in geography and a sense of Britain's imperial heritage through maps, novels and newsreels; through comics in the great public school tradition of Billy Bunter; by visiting museums and imperial exhibitions at Earl's Court or Wembley Stadium; by collecting jubilee mugs and postage stamps showing the monarch's profile set against a multitude of colonial scenes; by poring over pictures of warships in the Channel; and by reading ripping yarns about pith-helmeted youths facing rampaging elephants in deepest, darkest Africa. For many people, the British Empire meant royal tours, exploration, exotic chiefs, safaris, cocoa, gunboats, colourful flora and awe-inspiring fauna. The world was presented as a white person's playground, full of smiling and brightly-dressed natives, breathtaking scenery, elegant hotels and verandahed houses, all there to be set about with a sense of purpose and opportunity.

As the Empire expanded in the 19th century and the British became more

Canada's Diamond Jubilee of Confederation 1867 1927

GREATER VANCOUVER, BRITISH COLUMBIA

aware of their imperial position, Empire was increasingly identified with patriotism and a sense of Britain's unique mission in the world. Imperial imagery and information became more widely available to the public as literacy, leisure and the media expanded. Empire and imperial ideas remained a central feature of British popular culture into the 1960s and even beyond. A multitude of sources directed the mind's eye through which people viewed the world and visualized what Kipling described as Britain's 'dominion over palm and pine'.

Of course, just how accurate the image portrayed was, and how people interpreted it, is open to debate. Yet there is no doubt that the images purveyed were striking and shaped people's understanding of the world in which they lived: just as the Greenwich meridian placed London unequivocally at the centre of the world, so literature, education and a host of cultural references placed Britain at the top of the international tree. The Empire was an indispensable feature of the world and was widely regarded as a powerful engine for peace, progress and security. Empire and *Pax Britannica* were associated with modernity, innovations in science and engineering, travel and global communications, discovery and knowledge and the spread of freedom and the rule of law. Empire, it was widely believed, prevented bloodshed, eradicated barbaric practices and brought good government, education, free trade and civilization to the world.

The British Empire's heyday coincided with the rise of Europe and its dramatic encounter, on unequal terms, with the rest of the world. It carved Britishness into the world, naming lakes and mountains, defining political boundaries and creating transport networks and cityscapes from the Americas to Australasia. The British Empire presented a fascinating spectacle: the largest *imperium* in history embracing diverse peoples, from head-hunting Dyaks to Fulani horsemen, Gulf sheikhs, Canadian loggers, Eskimo hunters, Zoroastrian pilgrims and Indian maharajahs riding high upon bejewelled and caparisoned elephants. It was a public show on a palm-fringed global stage, gilded with ceremony and grandeur, the vibrancy of Bombay street life contrasting with the serene mystery of the Empty Quarter, all perfumed by the scent of spices, rum and molasses. 'And over all', wrote one traveller to the South China Seas, 'there spans the enormous Asian sky; nostrils fill again with the renewed peaty, fruity reek of Asia and the heart once more throbs with excitement'. Reigning over this worldwide realm sat an omniscient, imperialized monarchy represented on the ground by men in shorts and pith-helmets.

The King Tiger Hunting in India, 1875.

Colman's Starch

A Colman's Starch advert from the early 20th century showing King Edward VII (then Prince of Wales) tiger hunting during an 8-month tour of India. His liberal attitude towards non-Europeans was noted during the trip, and he complained of racial discrimination in letters home.

Imperial settings were commonplace in literature, both factual and fictional. A 1950s paperback of Pierre Boulle's classic about British and Commonwealth prisoners of war building the Burma–Thailand Railway (the notorious 'Death Railway'). The famous David Lean film of the book was shot on location in Ceylon (Sri Lanka).

The public encountered imperial messages and a shared world-view in missionaries' and explorers' journals, popular music, Coronation souvenirs, patriotic poems, board games, cruise advertisements, museum guides and mail-order catalogues. Empire was a constant theme in novels of derring-do, coffee, soap and tobacco adverts, popular art stimulated by military feats, and youth movements such as the Boy Scouts. Imperial and patriotic images were also conveyed by everyday objects such as ashtrays, bookmarks and tea caddies, as well as stamps, postcards and the collectable cards given away with packets of cigarettes and tea.

To a large extent the British Empire created the modern world – its racial demographics, business, financial and legal culture, its linguistic and religious composition and its political boundaries. It is important, therefore, to understand the attitudes and beliefs that shaped it and to recognize its legacies in the modern world. Of course, while Empire as a 'Good Thing' was a prevalent view at the time, it was always a contested one. Although school history books, 'penny dreadfuls' and jingoistic media might pump out material claiming that the Empire was the best thing since sliced bread and of benefit to all mankind, anti-imperial voices were constantly audible; though 'the sun never set' on the British Empire, the Chartist Ernest Jones declared, 'the blood never dried'. In the 20th century these views found powerful support in the polemics of Lenin, the troubled voice of George Orwell and works of fiction such as E.M. Forster's *A Passage to India* (1924). As empire was increasingly discredited and the right to self-determination became a universal law, voices of dissent grew ever more clamorous.

But until the 'Swinging Sixties' the British Empire was considered by many to be a vital force for good in the world, a champion of liberal values, peace and good government. The rule of Europeans over non-Europeans was viewed as a barrier to the spread of evil and an engine of world progress. Empire was presented as a glamorous and dynamic frontier where there was fun and adventure to be had, riches to be won and souls to be saved, for commerce and civilization as well as for Christ. Indeed, a supreme irony of the 20th century was that, while millions of people of British descent grew up believing that the Empire was a beacon of civilization and progress in a world that would otherwise have descended into barbarism, by the end of that century it had become associated with human suffering and oppression, and the word 'Empire' mired with pejorative connotations. Given all of this, we need to understand the components of this world-view and the manner in which Britain acquired and ruled its Empire.

What follows is an attempt to capture these manifold representations of the British Empire which were so familiar to generations of people, and to offer an insight into the way in which the Empire was run, the way in which it was acquired, the way in which it was perceived by Britons, its trade and communications networks, and the way in which it was protected. While some Britons were out in the wider world doing things, the vast majority never left Britain's shores. Yet they were familiar with a host of imperial themes and attitudes, the result of a myriad references to Empire and non-Europeans embedded in popular culture. Millions of people around the world were brought up on a diet of *Girls' Empire: An Annual for English-Speaking Girls all Over the World*, schoolboy annuals and comics such as *Chums* and *Victor* and the inspiring novels of Empire-minded authors such as Rudyard Kipling, H. Rider Haggard, John Buchan and G.A. Henty. This tidal wave of imperial literature and imagery affected not only British children and their white cousins in British Colombia, Cape Town and Queensland; growing up in British Guiana, people of Indian and African descent were exposed to Enid Blyton, *Just William*, Jane Austen and Shakespeare.

Fittingly, *Mad Dogs and Englishmen* opens with that most potent icon of British imperial power, the map of the world shaded British red and displayed in classrooms from Vancouver to the Tasman Sea.

ABOVE AND BELOW 'Flags of the British Empire', a series of cigarette cards printed on silk that was launched by Wix's 'Kensitas' brand in 1934.

LEFT Britons were tempted to emigrate to New Zealand by alluring publications like this early 1930s booklet. The Dominion was often presented as a sunny Britain in the Southern Hemisphere.

The British Empire: Red on the Map

BRITISH RED COLOURED THE MAP OF THE WORLD until the 1960s, growing from modest coastal shadings in 1800 to cover nearly a quarter of its surface just a century later. In 1860 the map of the world still sported blank spaces and uncharted seas, and British explorers were to the fore in exploring them and revealing their discoveries to a spellbound public back at home. Adding detail to the map of the world as they went, they trailed British rule in their wake.

These burgeoning British footprints stretching across the planet were commonly depicted by splashes of red on the map. No wonder the British loved the map of the world, for it stood as eloquent testimony to the nation's power, stimulating pride in the breast of Britons and jealousy in the breast of foreigners as they scoured the globe for a 'place in the sun'* that the British had not already bagged. To borrow a modern analogy, the British had the biggest beach-towel by far, and the sight of it, draped over every continent and peninsula around the world, drove the Germans and the other colonial also-rans to distraction.

Mapping and colonial expansion

Not only did the colour red dominate the map because Britain ruled so many territories, but the British were also responsible for filling in the lion's share of the map's blank spaces and for christening its major geographical features. Bombay, Madras, Salisbury, Lake Victoria, Hudson Bay, Mount Nelson, Queensland, New South Wales, Rhodesia – British names were legion, and the British even coined regional appellations such as 'the Middle East'. British imperial endeavour had, in historian David Cannadine's words, set 'such seal upon the world, in cartography as in command, as no monarch in the history of mankind has ever set before'.

A key technique in this endeavour was the creation of maps and charts. In 1747 George III commissioned a military survey of the Scottish Highlands following the Jacobite rebellion, the beginning of the Ordnance Survey during a period of English colonial conquest. From this moment on, mapping went hand in hand with British expansion, intimately connected as it was to security, imperial defence and the subjection of the world to British knowledge and power.

A political poster of 1901 triumphantly proclaims the unification of South Africa by British force of arms and the appearance of yet more red on the map. The conquest of the Boer republics of Transvaal and the Orange Free State fulfilled Colonial Secretary Joseph Chamberlain's desire for a South African federation under British rule as they were co-joined with Cape Colony and Natal. As well as the monocled Chamberlain, the poster shows Queen Victoria, Colonel Robert Baden-Powell, defender of Mafeking, and Lord Roberts of Kandahar, commander-in-chief of British forces in South Africa.

* In 1897 the German secretary of state for foreign affairs and future chancellor Bernhard von Bülow, referring to the country's belated rush to acquire colonies, famously demanded that she be allowed to take her 'Platz an der Sonne'.

Captain Colombo's map of 1886 is emblematic of Victorian pride in Britain's global reach. Centred upon the figure of Britannia appear symbols of empire such as North American Indians resplendent in their feather headdresses, pith-helmeted soldiers, tigers, caparisoned elephants and half-naked porters bearing heavy loads. At the foot ran the legend: *'Imperial Federation. Map of the World Showing the Extent of the British Empire'.* Appearing just as the 'Scramble for Africa' began, Colombo's map does not yet show Britain's extensive holdings on that continent.

The British Empire was an icon of the modern age; there were few people in the Western world who had not heard of it and formed an opinion of it, and few people in the non-Western world who had not in some way been touched by it. The iconography of empire was most eloquently expressed by the map of the world; every globe or wall map proclaimed Britain's reach in conspicuous colour, usually a deep red or pleasing pink. These maps showed an oversized Britain sitting at the centre of the world, its inflated dominions spreadeagled from east to west, the huge mass of Canada balanced in the east by Australia and New Zealand, the centre suitably populated by splashes of imperial colour in Africa, the solid cone of the Indian subcontinent and the thin finger of the Malayan peninsula, and discrete but significant holdings in Europe and the Mediterranean (including Ireland, Cyprus, Gibraltar and Malta). Connecting British possessions on the world's major continents were a galaxy of islands and atolls over which the Union Flag flew, often providing key strategic bases guarding the entry to oceans or providing fuelling and bunkering bases in lonely waters for the Royal Navy and the

Merchant Navy, responsible for carrying most of the world's trade. These imperial islands and enclaves, stepping stones of British power, also served as links on Britain's global telegraphy chain, the 'All-Red Route' forged by underwater cables connecting cable and wireless stations in major ports via remote islands such as Canton in the Pacific and the Cocos (Keeling) Islands in the Indian Ocean. Thus, through the possession of strategic colonies dominating choke points such as the Cape of Good Hope, the Suez Canal, the Straits of Malacca and the Straits of Gibraltar, Britain possessed 'the keys that locked up the entire world'.

Proudly charting the Empire

All in all, it was a global presence and network worth bragging about. Many publishers found occasion to produce wall maps or atlases, often to commemorate national or imperial milestones. Thus in 1935 the Royal Primrose Soap Works chose the occasion of King George V's Silver Jubilee to publish *The Royal Primrose Atlas of the British Empire*. Maps of the British Empire made clear the importance of sea lanes bridging the oceans as the colonies and dominions orbited the mother country. Maps showed the many trade routes that connected the world and listed the major exports of the Empire's manifold territories, giving people a sense not only of the strategic logic of a maritime system dependent on sea lanes, but of the exchange of raw materials and manufactured goods that was the lifeblood of the British world. Maps often embodied lofty imperial ideas, such as a famous 1886 edition by one Captain Colombo, entitled 'Freedom, Fraternity, Federation'.

Colonel Sir C.E. Howard Vincent's 1902 map of the British Empire was a classic example of the map as a lesson in British global power and prosperity. Its full title was '*The Howard Vincent Map of the British Empire Showing the Possessions Throughout the World of the British People, Their Extent, Population, Revenue and Commerce*'. This vast wall map, measuring over 6 ft square, was commissioned to mark the accession of Edward VII. It was an object lesson in imperial patriotism, power and pride. 'GOD SAVE THE KING-EMPEROR', it proclaimed. Under the heading 'General Imperial Facts' it recorded that:

> *The Area of the British Empire is upwards of 13,000,000 Square Miles, or more than one-fifth of the Habitable Globe. Population (one-fourth that of the world) 400,000,000; Annual Trade £1,400,000,000; Annual Revenue £260,000,000; Merchant Marine, 8,000 Steamers and 4,000 Sailing Vessels of 14,000,000 Tons total burden (that is more than half the shipping of the entire world, and seven times as much as that of the nearest rival) navigating 133,000,000 Square Miles of Ocean.*

The map also made clear the military might that protected this fabulously wealthy global trading union:

> *The British Defensive Power is represented by 500 Ships of War and 2,350,000 Soldiers, Sailors, and Volunteers, from the North, the South, the East and the West, fighting and ever ready, as shown in the South African War, to fight shoulder to*

RECALL WITH PATRIOTIC GRATITUDE THE WISHES OF OUR FOREFATHERS, LARGELY INFLUENCED BY THE IMPERIAL GENIUS OF WILLIAM PITT, FOUNDER OF THAT GIGANTIC EMPIRE BEQUEATHED TO OUR GUARDIANSHIP AS TRUSTEES FOR OUR DESCENDANTS. REMEMBER THAT IF BRITAIN TO HERSELF BE TRUE, THE UNION JACK GUARDS THE GATES OF THE SEAS, AND THAT BRITAIN HOLDS IN HER ARMED HAND THE COAL SUPPLIES AND COALING STATIONS OF THE OCEANS. IF THESE ARE CLOSED TO ANY OTHER NATION, THE SHIPS OF WAR AND SEA TRADE OF THAT COUNTRY BECOME POWERLESS – AND THEN, AS MUCH AS IN THE GLORIOUS DAYS OF NELSON, IF EVERY MAN DOES HIS DUTY BRITAIN RULES THE WAVES.

– Colonel Sir C.E. Howard Vincent, 1902

shoulder for Empire and Liberty, but most of all by the Patriotism and Union, the Brotherly Affection and Mutual Confidence of all Races, Classes, Parties and Peoples, in every part of the Empire, and the unswerving Loyalty of each single individual to the common whole, the common good, and the one Constitutional Sovereign. The British People are One People, animated by One Spirit, and determined to stand together as One Man in defence of their Common Rights and in the maintenance of their Common Interests. 'One For All – All For Each'.

Colonel Vincent's map was strident propaganda for the cause of Imperial Federation – the desire of many influential people to see the British Empire fashioned more self-consciously into an economic and military union in order to better meet the challenges posed by up-and-coming land-based powers such as America, Germany and Russia. 'THE BRITISH EMPIRE', it proclaimed:

… is fifty-five times the size of France, fifty-four times the size of Germany, three and a half times the size of the United States of America, with quadruple the population of All the Russias. It extends over four Continents, 10,000 Islands, 300 Promontories and 2,000 Rivers. The mutual inward and outward trade between the several Possessions of the British People amounts annually to more than £300,000,000 and embraces every single article required for food, clothing, education, commerce, manufacture or agriculture, and for all the pursuits, avocations and pleasures of every one of His Most Gracious Majesty's Loyal and Devoted Subjects in the United Kingdom and throughout the Empire. Their great mercantile interchange is capable, moreover, of such limitless expansion, by reason of the diversities of climate and geological conditions, as to make the British Empire in Europe, America, Australasia, Asia, Africa and Oceania, Federated in Imperial Union – with a due commercial understanding between the several local governments – not less absolutely independent of the productions of every other country than invulnerable against the rest of the world.

Instilled with imperialism

Imperial education through the map of the world was very common – an incidental part of going to school or looking at an atlas or a souvenir pull-out in a newspaper. The 1902 book *King Edward's Realm* made plain this link between Britain and her distant dominions:

A glance at the map of the world in which the parts of the British Empire are coloured red may well fill us with astonishment that the little spot marked England has expanded into an empire that covers one sixth of the habitable globe … The British Empire looks like a sprawling giant with his limbs outstretched, having his head in one sea, and his arms and legs in as many others … The

The 1902 'Coronation edition' of Reverend C.S. Dawe's *King Edward's Realm: Story of the Making of the Empire* was typical of the patriotic history of Britain and its imperial growth. The habit of giving books to children as prizes and to commemorate Royal events was ubiquitous in British schools and Sunday schools.

Continued on page 18

THE PINK BITS

The ubiquitous Mercator projection map helped develop an imperial consciousness among Britons from schooldays onwards, not necessarily a sophisticated view of the world, but certainly an imperial one. In John Boorman's film *Hope and Glory* (1984), an elegant commentary on the British home front during the Second World War, a schoolteacher strikes various parts of the wall map with her cane and asks:

'Pink. Pink. Pink. Pink. What are all the pink bits?'
'They're ours, Miss', replies Rowan.
'Yes', says the teacher. *'The British Empire. What part of the world's surface is British?'*
'Two-fifths, Miss', answers Jennifer Baker.
'Yes. Two-fifths – ours. That's what this war is all about. Men are fighting and dying to save all the pink bits for you ungrateful little twerps'.

BELOW 'Wider still and wider' – the British Empire at its greatest extent, just after the First World War. At this stage, it was literally true that the 'sun never set' on the British Empire, since at any given moment it was daylight somewhere in its far-reaching dominions. Yet appearances were deceptive: by 1900, Germany had already outstripped Britain in industrial output, while the global influence of the United States grew steadily from 1898 onwards.

MAPPING THE WORLD

The growth of British power led to the mapping of remote regions such as India's North-West Frontier, and to the production of nautical charts of distant coastlines and sea beds. In the first half of the 19th century the Great Trigonometrical Survey of India set itself the modest task of mapping the entire subcontinent. Its work had begun in the 1760s and became a single, continent-wide project 50 years later.

Work began in Madras and spread north and south, finally reaching the Himalayas under the directorship of George Everest and his successor Andrew Waugh. This huge undertaking involved surveying every inch of land with chains, triangulations and theodolites, much of it conducted by explorer-spies whose intelligence gathering enabled the Great Trigonometrical Survey to map areas never previously surveyed. Fear of Russian expansion gave this work added impetus, as surveyors in India needed accurate information about the Himalayan region. To do so without arousing suspicion the British employed Hindus trained as surveyors. These pundits (from the Sanskrit pandita, 'learned') ventured into Tibet disguised as Buddhist pilgrims. Trained to walk exactly 2000 paces to the mile with surveying equipment concealed in prayer wheels, they secretly mapped the approaches to Lhasa (intelligence which proved invaluable when Sir Francis Younghusband invaded the kingdom in 1904).

Staking a claim

The compilation of maps, inspired by the desire for knowledge and the need to thwart strategic rivals, was replicated elsewhere in the world. In Egypt, for example, the surveyor-general's department was keen to extend its knowledge of the Western Desert in order to fix the boundary with Italian-controlled Libya in a manner favourable to British interests, and to identify passable vehicle routes and the location of oases in case of fighting in the region.

Many of the men who rose to prominence during the Second World War as specialists in unconventional warfare developed vital skills through their pre-war experiences on the frontiers of empire, mapping, observing and exploring. The career of Orde Wingate [1903–44] brought together many of these global strands. After Charterhouse and Sandhurst came camel patrols in the Sudan, the training of Jewish irregulars in Palestine and desert exploration. The Second World War saw him leading Abyssinian rebels as the British sought to defeat the Italians and reinstall Haile Selassie as Emperor, before his most famous role as creator and commander of the Chindits Long Range Penetration Force in Burma. During his time in the Middle East, Wingate developed a plan to get the Senussi people of Libya to revolt against their Italian overlords, and as a company commander in the Sudan Defence Force he took part in a Royal Geographical Society expedition in search of the lost oasis of Zerzura on the Libyan-Egyptian border.

The *Index Chart to the Great Trigonometrical Survey of India* shows the enormous extent of the mapmaking survey begun by Colonel William Lambton and completed by George Everest between 1802 and 1843. When British surveyors discovered the highest mountain in the world in 1855, they named it Mount Everest in honour of their renowned predecessor, who had spent 20 years of his life superintending the enormous project.

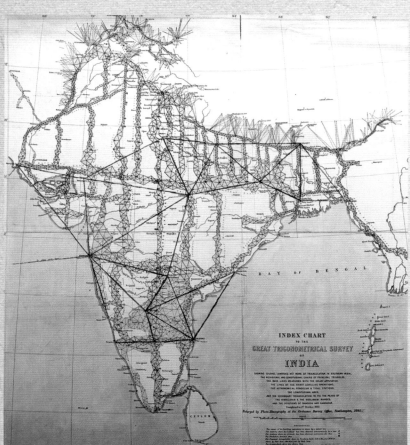

INDEX CHART
TO THE
GREAT TRIGONOMETRICAL SURVEY
OF
INDIA

Surveying the world's oceans

As on land, so too at sea. Britain's growing naval presence around the world led to unparalleled knowledge as the navy furthered its traditional interest in charting new territory and gleaning scientific information, most famously represented by the voyages of Captain Cook in the Pacific. As well as establishing international maritime law and suppressing piracy and slavery (after this trade had finally been abolished in the British Empire in 1807), one of the navy's great services to the world was the provision of accurate charts, for which countless seamen of all nationalities have had occasion to be grateful ever since. By the mid-19th century there were few coastlines between Africa and the Malay barrier that had not been charted by the British. By then the Persian Gulf was a familiar haunt, and expeditions like that led by Captain William Owen, sent by the Admiralty to survey the East African coast in 1821, built an encyclopaedic knowledge of the world's oceans, to be published in the Admiralty Guides.

Owen's career encapsulated several common themes of British imperial expansion – naval power, the quest for scientific knowledge, humanitarianism and a willingness to act unilaterally in the name of the Crown (a factor often referred to as 'the man on the spot'). He intervened forcefully at the court of the Sultan of Oman and Zanzibar to stop his kingdom trafficking in slaves, and declared a British protectorate over Mombasa. Thus the world's oceans were subjected to British knowledge and power. In the early 20th century the work of surveying the world and creating maps was supplemented by aircraft, and little time was lost in harnessing this technology to the cause. Between November 1927 and June 1928 Sir Alan Cobham and his crew made the first circumnavigation and aerial survey of Africa, flying a distance of over 20,000 miles in a Short S.5 Singapore I flying-boat . So the British Empire came to dominate the map of the world, and that map itself became an iconic representation of imperial power and an explanation of the way in which the world 'worked'.

Sir Alan Cobham and his wife Gladys, Lady Cobham in the cockpit of the Short Singapore I flying boat in which they and a crew of four completed their pioneering aerial survey of Africa. Leaving Rochester on 17 November 1927, they arrived in Cape Town on 30 March 1928.

A caricature of the hero of Mafeking and founder of the Boy Scout movement, Sir Robert Baden-Powell, from *Vanity Fair* magazine (5 July 1900).

sundered portions of the British dominions are connected by the sea, and the sea offers a ready-made road to every ship that sails . . . We may rightly regard the seas that come between our shores and the rest of the Empire, not as separating but as connecting its several parts, and enabling the motherland to keep in constant touch with her daughter states in other lands.

Military maps divided the world according to the responsibilities of different geographical commands, such as India Command, Far East Command, Middle East Command, the China Station and the South Atlantic Station. Global strategic awareness was second nature to British political and military policy-makers thanks to the country's imperial heritage. From the grand strategists in Whitehall to British officers and administrators on the ground, these men were versed in the basic tenets of imperial defence and what oft-reprinted textbooks termed 'imperial military geography'. Their knowledge came from British culture and the study of maps, from schooldays to the universities and staff colleges. They knew why Ceylon was crucial for the defence of Australia and how the Shatt-el-Arab waterway contributed to the economic well-being of the British Isles.

The world's policeman

The global extent of British power was often expressed metaphorically through the use of such terms as 'chains of empire' or the 'web of empire', and by likening Britain's world role to that of a policeman. Robert Baden-Powell, founder of the Boy Scout movement, epitomized this imperial strategic awareness and the method by which it was passed on to children through popular literature. Describing a tour of Scout centres in British Africa in the 1930s, Baden-Powell's *African Adventures* included numerous throwaway lessons in imperial defence: 'A great British man-of-war – the *Barham* – lay before us as we came to the mouth of the Suez Canal at Port Said. Nearby was a steamer full of Italian soldiers off to Abyssinia'. Baden-Powell told his young audience that Italy had nearly gone to war with Britain because of the latter's opposition to Mussolini's Abyssinian invasion:

Had she done so, we should have stopped her ships going through the Canal, and the Barham *was there, like a traffic policeman, to stop them if necessary. Also the*

Mediterranean Fleet was close by, in Alexandria, like a lot more policemen in a police-station, ready to come out if wanted.

Continuing his African progress, Baden-Powell travelled through the Red Sea, calling at Port Sudan and Aden before heading off to British East Africa. Here he drew his readers' attention to a tiny volcanic island in the Bab el Mandeb Straits where the Red Sea meets the Gulf of Aden.

These straits are a narrow waterway about eight miles across, with the island of Perim in the middle. If that island were armed with any big guns or warships it could prevent enemy's ships passing in or out of the Red Sea, just as Gibraltar with its guns and warships can stop ships using the Mediterranean. But Perim has got guns, and they are British guns! Also, as our ship rounded the corner of the island, there we saw, above the roofs of the village and the barracks, the towering upper works of two British men-of-war anchored in the inner harbour behind them. But you must not think that Britain holds these posts from any wish to go to war; quite the opposite: Britain has become a sort of policeman of the world and aims to prevent other nations fighting.

In the opinion of Baden-Powell and the imperial élite, the British domination of the world so graphically represented by the map was all about peace and goodwill, noble causes that could not be entrusted to foreigners. Security for the good of humanity was one of the Empire's most compelling justification myths.

What was the British Empire?

As Colonel Sir C.E. Vincent Howard's tub-thumpingly patriotic map of the British Empire boasted, 'Greater Britain – the possessions of the British People over the seas, is 125 times the size of Great Britain'. Establishing political control over this motley imperial estate, and administering the affairs of its multitudinous population, required organizational genius and a large measure of pragmatism. The British Empire may have appeared uniform on the map of the world, every territory neatly shaded red, but this apparent uniformity concealed a gallimaufry of distinct political arrangements, from Crown colonies to Dominions and condominiums. In Australia and Canada local politicians and parliaments directed the affairs of state, though Whitehall remained responsible for their defence, foreign policy and economic wellbeing; in Africa, governors and their district commissioners ruled with the aid of chiefs and a hidden army of indigenous clerks, interpreters and messengers; whilst in Sarawak, a dynasty of British men held absolute authority until the 1940s.

The Empire was, first and foremost, a political entity by virtue of the fact that all of its territories around the world were effectively ruled from London by the British monarch and his government. Power was real; unlike in pre-industrial empires such as those ruled over by the Chinese emperor or the Ottoman sultan, where vast swathes of imperial territory were in fact autonomous and even capable

At the London Conference, held in the Westminster Palace Hotel between December 1866 and March 1867, Canada's status as a Dominion within the Empire was established. Although Canadian delegates wished it to be designated a 'kingdom', the British rejected this proposal lest it anger the United States. Instead, the term 'Dominion' was proposed and accepted; it was an allusion to Psalm 72: *'He shall have dominion also from sea to sea, and from the river unto the ends of the earth.'* The event is commemorated in this painting, *The Fathers of Confederation*, by John David Kelly (1862–1958).

of raising armies to march upon the imperial capital. In the British Empire, whatever the local arrangements for governing a colony's people, the authority of the Crown was real and direct, and rebellion easily crushed. Though a great deal of autonomy reposed in the local representatives of the British monarch, and a degree of real power remained in the hands of local rulers such as chiefs and mullahs, the writ of London trumped all, as was seen during times of world war. Then, whether the fight was against Napoleon, the Kaiser or Hitler, London and its representatives dictated the manner in which every territory contributed, controlling the ships that connected the Empire across the oceans and the troops that defended it, while remaining responsible for all of the Empire's economic and political links with the wider world (even the Dominions did not conclude treaties with foreign powers or maintain their own diplomats and foreign ministries until deep into the 20th century).

Commonwealth, Colonies and Dominions

The British Empire's terminology requires some clarification. 'The Commonwealth' initially referred to Britain and the Dominions of Canada, South Africa, Australia and New Zealand. Newfoundland was a Dominion until the 1930s when it was taken under direct British rule and then became a province of the Dominion of Canada. 'Dominion' was a word used, from the turn of the 20th century, to describe these, the Empire's 'white', self-governing territories. Upon its foundation in 1921 the Irish Free State also became a Dominion, and India was offered 'Dominion status' in an effort to get it to agree to a political relationship that fell somewhere short of total independence. The 1926 Balfour Declaration, and the 1931 Statute of Westminster, enshrined the fact that Britain and the Dominions were equal and free, though in practice Britain remained, by virtue of her much greater military and economic power, *primus inter pares* long into the second half of the 20th century. Britain's relations with the Dominions were, from 1925, managed by a separate Dominions Office and a network of high commissioners and governors-general.

THE TRAVELLER OF 1938 SAW THE WORLD CLOSE TO. IT WAS AN INCOMPARABLE GEOGRAPHY LESSON – AND LARGELY A LESSON IN IMPERIAL GEOGRAPHY. BETWEEN CRETE AND INDONESIA THERE WAS ONLY ONE STOP OUT OF ALMOST A SCORE – IT WAS, IN FACT, BANGKOK – WHERE THE FLYING-BOAT TOUCHED DOWN ANYWHERE NOT UNDER BRITISH RULE OR EFFECTIVELY UNDER BRITISH AUTHORITY. ALEXANDRIA, THE LAKE OF GALILEE, HABBANIYA, BASRA, ABU DHABI, MEKRAN, KARACHI, JAIPUR, ALLAHABAD, CALCUTTA, AKYAB, RANGOON, PENANG, SINGAPORE – ONE WAS WITNESSING THE UBIQUITY OF A POWER ON WHICH THE SUN HAD NOT YET SET. I SAW; I FELT; I MARVELLED.

– Enoch Powell, travelling to Sydney University in 1938 to become the youngest professor in the British Empire

The term 'colonial empire' referred to the Empire ruled by the Colonial Office – in other words, the entire British Empire minus the four Dominions, India and Burma, which was administered by India until 1937 when a separate Burma Office was created. Aden was also separated from India in 1937, becoming a Colonial Office responsibility and thus a part of the colonial empire. This colonial empire consisted primarily of crown colonies and protectorates. Of these, there were in excess of 50 spread around the world, located mainly in Africa, the Caribbean and Southeast Asia and including scattered island colonies in the Atlantic, the Indian Ocean, the Mediterranean and the Pacific.

Special cases

India was a separate imperial entity, an empire within an empire, ruled by a Viceroy and an India Office in London, and responsible for maintaining numerous 'British' interests in areas such as Burma, the Persian Gulf, Nepal and Tibet. The Viceroy of India, though formally subordinate to London, was in fact one of the most powerful men on earth, such was the autonomy customarily permitted the monarch's gubernatorial appointees, and such was the might of the Raj. Southern Rhodesia was in a category all of its own, a self-governing colony. In theory, this made it subject to the Colonial Office, though in practice it was as politically autonomous with regards to internal affairs as the Dominions, one of the reasons why, when Ian Smith declared unilateral independence in 1965, Britain was left with precious little purchase on the colony with which to try and turn it back. In Southern Africa the protectorates of Bechuanaland, Basutoland and Swaziland were run like colonies, but were in fact the responsibility of the Dominions Office because they were ruled through Britain's High Commissioner to the Dominion of South Africa.

In some parts of the Empire the British did not formally exercise sovereignty at all even if, in practice, they were the dominant power. Treaty relations with the 500-plus Indian princely states, sultans in Malaya and Brunei, the queen of Tonga or the sheikhs of Trucial Oman were often the basis of British power and influence. The Sudan, meanwhile, was a Condominium jointly ruled by the British and the Egyptian governments. Britain was the dominant power in the arrangement, and the Sudan was administered by the Foreign Office and a specialist Sudan Political Service. The New Hebrides was also a Condominium, jointly ruled by Britain and France with an appointee of the King of Spain refereeing disputes between the two. Egypt was only formally a British protectorate from 1914 until 1922, though it was an integral part of the British imperial system from the bombardment of Alexandria in 1882 until Colonel Nasser's nationalization of the Suez Canal in 1956.

The Empire's last hurrah

Throughout the Middle East Britain held as 'Mandates' some of the territories of the defunct Ottoman Empire, administered on behalf of the League of Nations. This last significant spurt of British imperial expansion came as a result of victory

By no means everyone viewed Britain's 'web of empire' positively. This 1878 cartoon, from the satirical magazine *Il Papagallo*, depicts the British Empire as a monstrous snake encircling the globe.

in the First World War, though formal British power was limited by the fact that the new territories, established under article 22 of the Covenant of the League of Nations, were 'owned' by that body, with the British merely acting as trustees. The Mandates run by Britain were Iraq, Palestine and Trans-Jordan. From 1922 Egypt and Iraq were officially independent nation-states, though hosting major British military bases and obliged by treaty to allow British forces access and transit rights in times of war. They were not, therefore, fully sovereign and were very much a part of the British world system. In Egypt, for example, the British maintained the largest military installation in the world. Even Iran's independence was compromised by British imperial power, a fact graphically demonstrated in 1941 when, alongside Russian forces, the British invaded the country and deposed the pro-German Shah.

There were yet more Mandates, such as Southern Cameroon and Tanganyika, though they were administered by the Colonial Office. Even colonies had colonies: the Dominions acquired their own League of Nations Mandates following the First World War and the dismemberment of the German Empire, South Africa taking South-West Africa (modern Namibia) and Australia a range of former German territories including northern New Guinea and the Bismarck Archipelago.

The 'informal empire'

The term 'informal empire' was coined by imperial historians to describe parts of the world that Britain did not formally rule but which nevertheless were heavily influenced by British military, commercial, economic and cultural power. Argentina and Shanghai, for example, were not 'red on the map' but Britain still held great sway there. To these corners of the earth must be added Antarctica, a vast region of 'pink ice' that Britain sought to dominate in an imperial fashion.

Finally, in times of war, the territories administered by Britain grew significantly, either as a result of enemy territory being conquered or the territory of allies being taken over. This category included lands such as the Ionian Islands, Italian Somaliland, Java, Libya, Madagascar and Syria. In the Second World War the commander-in-chief of Allied forces in the Mediterranean, General Sir Harold Alexander, became Governor of Sicily and General Sir Henry Maitland Wilson became Military Governor of Cyrenaica on the coast of North Africa. Southern Persia was occupied by the British, and bases were established in Iceland, the Faroe Islands and the Azores. At the end of the war Admiral Lord Louis Mountbatten's South East Asia Command was made responsible for the reoccupation of the Dutch East Indies and French Indochina, Britain's imperial reach swelled to its greatest ever extent on the eve of the decolonization era.

So, the British Empire's red on the map encompassed a vast array of different territories and ruling arrangements. Before considering some of the Empire's most striking features, such as its quest for discovery, its moral and religious impulses and the manner in which it was governed, the building blocks of imperial expansion must be examined. The expansion of the British Empire, therefore, forms the subject of the following chapter.

A TOUR THROUGH THE BRITISH COLONIES, AND FOREIGN POSSESSIONS.

JOHN BETTS, 115 STRAND.

New Worlds to Settle and Sell To: The Expansion of the British Empire

HOW DID A SMALL ISLAND OFF THE EUROPEAN MAINLAND come to dominate so much of the world's land surface, and all of the oceans in between? In short, it did so through industrial and economic power and its thirst for global trade, the entrepreneurship and wanderlust of its people, the global vision of its rulers and through victory in wars against European rivals and native foes alike.

John Betts' board game 'A Tour through the British Colonies and Foreign Possessions', c.1855. Players began the game in London and after a globetrotting journey returned to the imperial capital, landing at St Paul's Cathedral in the centre of the board, affirming London's place at the centre of the world. Leaving England via Heligoland (British territory off the Danish coast) players travelled to India, via the Mediterranean or the Cape route. They visited Calcutta and the Niagara Falls, went around the Australian mainland and, illustrating the game's didactic intent, were allowed to roll again if alighting on Jamaica in order to mark the Empire's role in abolishing slavery.

Together, this led to the construction of a system of world government known as empire, founded upon naval might, commercial prowess and the successful construction of patron–client relationships with indigenous rulers such as the sultans of Brunei, Malaya and Zanzibar, the sheikhs of the Persian Gulf, the maharajahs and princes of the Indian subcontinent and the chiefs of the African mainland. Empire and imperial governance was cemented by an explosion of overseas settlement that created strong British communities in Africa, Australasia and the Americas, where settler societies became junior partners in the enterprise of establishing British power in non-European lands. This chapter describes the reasons for the creation of the British Empire and the main motive factors leading to imperial expansion, including overseas settlement, trade, migration, strategic rivalry and warfare.

The early empire

The British Empire's high noon occurred during the reign of Queen Victoria and, on the surface at least, lasted until the Second World War, as the Empire solidified into a seemingly-permanent, larger than life, feature of the known world. The Second World War brought seismic shifts in global political, economic and military power structures, demoting European powers and their empires just as it lifted up new 'superpowers' and gave unheard of status to previously voiceless nationalists. Nevertheless, it can be said that the long afternoon of the British Empire lasted well into the 1950s, and the mindset and world view associated with the Empire's high noon lasted for decades even after that.

Long before this period, Britain was putting down deep imperial roots and building up the national power that was to drive expansion later on. From the

A 1903 postcard by an unnamed artist shows Quaker William Penn concluding a treaty with Native Americans of the Delaware people at Shakamaxon in 1683. Penn certainly strove to maintain friendly relations with the indigenous peoples, though the treaty signing is not historically attested.

reign of Elizabeth I the British state began to develop its maritime resources. It launched commercial offensives and fought wars against the major imperial powers of the day, often through the employment of privateers or buccaneers, leading to the golden age of piracy in the half century following the Treaty of Madrid (1670), as Spanish trade and settlements were ravaged and terror brought to the high seas. From this period the British people began to develop links with ever more distant places, hunting for fish off faraway shores and claiming sovereignty overseas, as Sir Walter Raleigh did when he declared Roanoke Island British in 1585.

Tobacco plantations sprouted across Virginia and the British began their imperial career in the Caribbean by taking St Kitts in 1624. The Caribbean soon became the Empire's most lucrative real estate. Sugar and tobacco were the early mainstays of imperial wealth, as was the flourishing trade in African slaves linking West Africa, the Americas and Europe in a burgeoning Atlantic economy. The British also began to settle overseas. The first permanent English settlement in the Americas came into being at Jamestown, Virginia in 1607, the product of King James I's grant of a royal charter to the London Company in the previous year. The Pilgrim Fathers established themselves at Massachusetts Bay in 1620 and new colonies grew up on the eastern seaboard, including Rhode Island (1636), Connecticut (1639) and Baltimore (1664). The practice of using colonies as depositories for ne'er-do-wells began when Georgia was founded as a settlement for debtors in 1732. It was in this period that the British also began to acquire colonies through war with rivals; Jamaica became the first colony seized by force in 1653 and, as British power grew in the Mediterranean, Gibraltar (1704) and Minorca (1708) were taken from the Spanish. Colonies were also established by royal favour, as when William Penn founded a colony at Pennsylvania following a royal grant of land in 1681 and when Bombay, a gift to the Crown, was leased to the East India Company.

Thus America and the Caribbean were at the heart of the 'first British Empire'. This first empire was transformed in the late 18th century by the American Rebellion (or War of Independence; 1775–83) and the subsequent creation of the United States, and by the economic eclipse of the Caribbean as new sources of produce and wealth opened up in the East, a burgeoning new field of imperial endeavour and competition. Rather than being an end, however, this point marked a beginning, as the British 'swing to the East' gathered momentum, a movement that was to take British rule to the continents of Africa, Asia and Australasia as the 'second British Empire' spread across the world in the 19th century. In 1788 the First Fleet arrived at Sydney Cove to establish the first permanent British settlements in Australia. The East India Company established a factory at Calcutta as early as 1690, and the Battle of Plassey in 1767 opened Bengal to British domination. In 1819 Stamford Raffles claimed Singapore for the Company and for Britain, and the Napoleonic Wars brought Britain a rich colonial yield as key strategic points such as the Cape, Ceylon and Mauritius were taken from their foes.

Phases of expansion

The growth of the British Empire went through distinct phases, beginning with expansion in the Americas and Caribbean in the 17th and 18th centuries. In the late 18th and 19th centuries British power was extended throughout South Asia and even into Central Asia, as British interests probed the kingdoms of Afghanistan and Persia and sought to thwart Russian expansion. Britain's naval and commercial presence in the Mediterranean was extended in the 18th and 19th centuries as Cyprus, Gibraltar, the Ionian Islands, Malta, Minorca and Egypt were taken and a permanent fleet established there. Southeast Asian lands from southern Siam through Malaya and Singapore and onwards to Borneo, along with numerous islands across the Indian Ocean, also became British during the 19th century. The kingdom of Burma was conquered through wars fought in the 1820s, 1850s and the 1880s. In Arabia, the Red Sea and the Persian Gulf

THE COMMANDER WENT AT THE HEAD, WITH ABOUT TWENTY OTHER PIRATES, WITH THEIR BLACK SILK FLAG BEFORE THEM, WITH THE REPRESENTATION OF A MAN IN FULL PROPORTION, WITH A CUTLASS IN ONE HAND, AND A PISTOL IN THE OTHER, EXTENDED; AS THEY WERE MUCH WOUNDED AND NO CARE TAKEN IN DRESSING, THEY WERE VERY OFFENSIVE, AND STUNK AS THEY WENT ALONG, PARTICULARLY LINE THE COMMANDER; HE HAD ONE EYE SHOT OUT, WHICH WITH PART OF HIS NOSE, HUNG DOWN ON HIS FACE.

– The Boston Gazette, *28 March 1726, reporting the trial in Barbados of Philip Lyne and his crew*

AUSTRALIAN LIFE, A KANGAROO HUNT.

An early 19th-century print showing settlers and Aboriginals spearing kangaroos.

British hegemony was sealed through treaties concluded with sheiks in the early 19th century, the occupation of strategic islands such as Perim and the conquest of Aden in 1839.

In the Far East, war with China brought Britain a permanent foothold at Hong Kong, and until the Second World War the South China Seas and much of maritime China were subjected to British informal empire, the Royal Navy and commercial traffic ensuring British dominance even of major inland waterways such as the Yangtze. Britain had begun to expand in the Pacific region in the 18th century, where the growth of the Dominions of Australia and New Zealand provided a powerful motor for British interests to establish themselves all across the South and Central Pacific.

In Africa at the beginning of the 19th century British holdings amounted to little more than pinpricks on the West African coast, though by its concluding decades had expanded inland so that the most prosperous and populous regions of West, East, South and Central Africa had all succumbed to British suzerainty. Britain's last great period of imperial expansion came in the 20th century when the defeat of the Ottoman Empire brought new colonial holdings throughout the Middle East.

Expansion east of Suez

The dramatic growth of British power in the vast region east of Suez, stretching from Suez and the Swahili coast to the Malay barrier, Australasia and the Far East, illustrates the nature of imperial expansion. It was here that the British developed their Empire in the 18th and 19th centuries after their earlier imperial ventures in the Americas and the Caribbean. The British were parvenus east of Suez, though like many a Johnnie-come-lately, this was not to hinder their rapid rise. Trans-oceanic trade lay at the heart of Britain's interests and operations. The British East India Company created a factory system and administration stretching from the Red Sea to the Persian Gulf, South Asia, the Indonesian archipelago and the China seas. Trade in turn brought an absorbing interest in shipping routes and their defence, and imperial defence concerns brought naval stations, coaling stations, ports and garrisons. These in turn became focal points of power, emitting expansionist sub-waves and driving hinterland expansion as traders, adminis-trators, soldiers, sailors, explorers, settlers and missionaries looked for new horizons of opportunity in Asia and later in Africa.

Settlement and migration

Overseas settlement was a defining feature of imperial expansion. The very existence of colonies and imperial economic and communication networks encouraged migration, both permanent and temporary, all over the world. Slaves were ripped from their homes and dumped on a continent thousands of miles away. As settlers poured out of Britain and into the vast open spaces of the Americas and Australasia, Indian labour migrants reached the Pacific and the Caribbean and the Chinese diaspora spread across the world.

'Ten-pound Poms' – post-Second World War migrants to Australia on assisted passage – religious refugees and dissolute aristocrats all played a part in the peopling of the British Empire. What made the British Empire unique in history – utterly different, say, from the Roman Empire or the French Empire – was that the British, in huge numbers, actually settled overseas. Driven by a whole range of push and pull factors – the need to evade the law, hunger, religious persecution, sexual opportunity, penal banishment, free land grants, a higher calling to work among the heathens – Britons poured out of their native islands and populated the world. In the process, they formed satellites of the mother

An inter-war poster entices young Britons to leave the unemployment and dinginess of industrial Britain for the healthy, wide-open spaces of the Dominion of Canada. Throughout the 19th and 20th centuries all British settler colonies sought to enlarge their white populations.

BRITISH BOYS learn how to own your farm IN CANADA!

Decide on CANADA Now

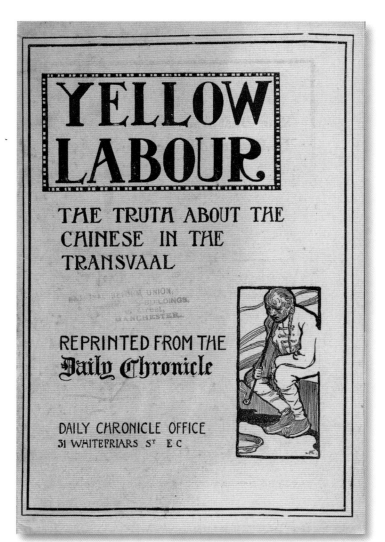

YELLOW LABOUR.

THE TRUTH ABOUT THE CHINESE IN THE TRANSVAAL

REPRINTED FROM THE Daily Chronicle

DAILY CHRONICLE OFFICE
31 WHITEFRIARS ST E C

This pamphlet, dating from the early years of the 20th century, illustrates the political controversy stimulated in Britain by the importation of Chinese labourers to work in the mines of South Africa. While Winston Churchill, a junior minister in the Liberal government, thought the word 'slavery' a matter of 'terminological inexactitude', concern for the plight of the Chinese had been a key factor in the demise of the Conservative government, roundly defeated by the Liberals in the general election of 1906.

country, encouraging the complimentary economics which was a defining feature of the British Empire, the settler Dominions becoming 'ideal prefabricated collaborators' in the project of British expansion, sub-imperial communities pushing forward the frontiers and promulgating British values. The legacy left by this wave of mass emigration was remarkable; the oddity of North American and Australasian continents that are as 'Western' as southeast England, all because of the size and power of the settler communities that established themselves on distant shores.

From a trickle to a flood

In Africa as well as the Americas and Australasia, British settlers forged new communities that would, if their numbers had been greater and indigenous societies not so resilient to imported diseases, have ended up looking like the Dominions. Settlers dominated Kenya until the 1960s, Rhodesia until the 1970s and South Africa until the 1990s. After the world wars, government-approved schemes offered ex-servicemen land grants and the chance of a new life in Kenya or Southern Rhodesia. Enclaves of Cornish and Welsh people sprouted in places such as Patagonia; the Irish formed distinctive communities all over the world; and wherever the British went, Indians followed, as labourers and small businessmen. Even in parts of the world where the British did not form large, rooted, settler societies, transient Britons lived in great numbers, from the Trucial States of the Gulf to the Caribbean, Calcutta and Hong Kong. As late as the 1960s assisted emigration and 'Barnardos boys' (children sent to Canada by the child welfare charity established by Thomas Barnardo in 1867) were strengthening the British strain in the Americas and the Antipodes, as 'white' Dominions and colonies sought to maintain racial purity and increase white numbers. The 'White Australia' policy offset in their minds the threat of the 'yellow peril', just as apartheid was a reaction to the 'black menace'. 'Expat' communities and 'British schools' set down roots all over the world, and from the 1940s, waves of mass migration saw Commonwealth subjects from Asia, Africa and the Caribbean begin new lives in Britain.

A steady stream of migrants, growing into a flood during the 19th century, traversed the world, some as slaves, some as settlers looking for a new life. The burgeoning global economy made huge labour demands throughout the world.

The slave trade flourished between Africa and the Caribbean, between the Swahili coast and Arabia and between Portuguese East Africa and South America, even after William Wilberforce's exertions and the formal abolition of slave trading (1807). The demands of the sugar industry took many Africans from Madagascar and the east coast of Africa to Mauritius and Réunion, and the Clunies-Ross family imported Malays to Christmas Island to work the phosphate deposits. The abolition of the *status* of slavery in the British Empire in 1833 was followed by a massive flow of indentured labour from South India to Mauritius, British East Africa, South Africa, Malaya, Fiji and Trinidad, because the labour that slaves had performed still needed to be done. From 1860 until 1911, about 176,000 Indians were imported into South Africa alone, and in the 1890s over 30,000 Indians built and worked the railway in Uganda (2500 dying in the process).

Sikhs and Muslims from the Punjab were recruited to serve as policemen in Hong Kong, Perak, the Straits Settlements, Nyasaland, Somaliland, Kenya and Uganda. Older migration networks continued to thrive, often conveyed by British shipping companies, as *hajjis* made the annual pilgrimage to Mecca. Europeans also migrated and not just to the Dominions. Europeans formed élite settler communities in places such as Ceylon, Hong Kong, India and Mauritius. Finally, of great significance to the fortunes of the Royal Navy and the Merchant Marine, thousands of men from Asia and China became crewmen aboard British vessels.

ABSENCE OF MIND?

From an ivory tower in Cambridge, Sir John Seeley, one of the founding fathers of British imperial scholarship, set down a Palmerstonian phrase now hackneyed as a description of the piecemeal, unplanned manner in which Britain gained history's largest Empire. In his famous 1883 lectures on *The Expansion of England*, he pronounced that 'the British Empire was acquired in a fit of absence of mind'. His point was that there had been no central blueprint for Empire, no 'Plan of Global Dominance' mulled over and then approved by a British Cabinet, just continual growth on the peripheries. British interests kept stumbling into things and as often as not the result was imperial expansion.

In contrast to Seeley, Harry Flashman, the philandering, gutless, though unfortunately fictional Victorian soldier-hero of George MacDonald Fraser's remarkable series of novels [1969–2005], had quite a different perspective on British imperial expansion,

expressed in typically coarse fashion. 'Absence of mind, my arse,' he declared. 'We always knew what we were doing; we just didn't always know how it would pan out.' His was the view from the colonial coalface, the view of the Empire-builder not the armchair observer. Flashman's point was that it was 'presence of mind' on the part of Britons overseas that led to imperial expansion, even if they could not foresee where their actions would lead. Presence of mind, he said, but also 'countless other things, such as greed and Christianity, decency and villainy, policy and lunacy, deep design and blind chance, pride and trade, blunder and curiosity, passion, ignorance, chivalry and expediency, honest pursuit of right, and determination to keep the bloody Frogs out'.

As a summary of the motive forces of British imperial expansion, MacDonald Fraser's list is hard to better.

Trade, chartered companies and the merchant marine

Global trade was the hallmark of the British Empire and a distinctive feature of British expansion was the chartered company. These private business ventures sought profit across the globe and were often used as tools of the British state's warfare and diplomacy. They were incredible organizations, rather like modern-day companies such as BP or Unilever but granted licence to rule vast tracts of territory, to raise their own private armies and navies, and encouraged to pick fights with any native potentate or European nation that the British government disapproved of. In the earliest years the East India Company, the Hudson's Bay Company, the Muscovy Company and the Levant Company set the trend and the Royal Africa Company shipped slaves from the 1670s. In the 19th century a new generation of chartered companies sprang up, including the British South Africa Company, the Royal Niger Company, the Imperial British East Africa Company and the North Borneo Company.

Imperial expansion fuelled Britain's love affair with silk, tobacco and tea, which earned huge tax revenues for the government, much of it to be spent on the world wars that it constantly waged. It was the levying of exorbitant taxes on the products of the East that encouraged many Britons to choose smuggling as an occupation. Arabian coffee, Argentinian beef, Assam tea, Australian wool, Behari opium, Bengali cotton and jute, Burmese rice, Canadian furs and wheat, Ceylonese

An 1803 aquatint by William Daniell showing the East India Docks. Built at Blackwall just two years before this painting was made, this dock complex serviced the East India Company's thriving trade from the subcontinent and other parts of Asia. Some 250 sailing ships of up to 1000 tons deadweight could berth there to unload their cargoes, which included tea, spices, indigo and silk.

rubber, Chinese silk, East African cloves, Jamaican bananas, Malayan tin, Mauritian sugar, Mesopotamian dates, New Zealand lamb, Northern Rhodesian copper, Palestinian citrus fruits, Virginian tobacco, Pondicherry leeches and South African gold all became standard exports.

The East India Company, a formidable international institution, became a vital arm not just of the British economy but of the British nation at war, and contributed to British success in wars against European and indigenous foes all over the world. East India Company men such as Clive, Hastings and Wellesley (Wellington) were synonymous with British triumph. This unique alliance between the British state and a private company meant, among other things, that from Robert Clive's victory at Plassey in 1757 to the conquest of Oudh a century later, the entire Indian subcontinent came under British rule and Britain's European enemies were left fighting for the scraps that fell from her table.

The private ambitions of individual shareholders in the East India Company, and that Company's aggressive expansion in the markets of the East, were the major engines of British expansion in Asia. Raising its own navy and army, monopoly rights were granted by Elizabeth I and James I, and the security provided by the Company's forces on land and sea drew the silk and spice trade towards it. William Hawkins, sent by James I in 1608 to parley with the Mogul Emperor Jahangir (r. 1605–27), requested permission for the British to trade at

WHILST KING GEORGE FOCUSED ON EUROPEAN DYNASTIC ALLIANCES AND RIVALRY, WILLIAM PITT HAD HIS OWN EYES ON FAR MORE DISTANT HORIZONS. WHILE THE KING FUSSED ABOUT HANOVER, PITT'S IMAGINATION RANGED ACROSS THE FORESTS, MOUNTAINS AND PLAINS OF NORTH AMERICA, THE SUGAR ISLANDS OF THE CARIBBEAN AND THE HOT EXPANSES OF INDIA. THERE, BRITAIN AND FRANCE CONFRONTED ONE ANOTHER MORE IMMEDIATELY THAN IN EUROPE, AND THERE, BOTH KNEW, LAY THE KEY TO FUTURE WEALTH AND POWER. PITT, AND THOSE WHO THOUGHT AS HE DID, WAS CONVINCED THAT THE DESTINY OF EUROPE WOULD BE DECIDED IN THE LIMITLESS EXPANSES OF THE WORLD BEYOND EUROPE … THE POSSIBILITIES OF A WORLDWIDE THEATRE OF WAR FIRED WILLIAM PITT'S IMAGINATION AND HE BEGAN TO SURROUND HIMSELF WITH THOSE WHO COULD SHARE HIS GLOBAL VISION.

– *Tom Pocock*, Battle for Empire: The Very First World War, 1756–63 *(2001)*

Surat on the Gujarati coast. Jahangir refused after objections were raised by Philip III of Spain. The English king therefore determined to fight the Iberian powers for a share in the expanding trade of the East. And so it was that in 1613 English ships began attacking Portuguese galleons in the Indian Ocean. Military victory impressed Jahangir and many others, and the British were accorded the respect that their fighting prowess warranted. The British entered the trade in pepper and cloth, exchanging cloth in China for tea. Trading posts were opened in Burma in 1619, exporting ivory, timber and tung oil for tanning; three years later a trading agreement took the British to Hormuz, and British interests were soon entrenched in Calcutta and Madras. Through the 1662 Anglo-Portuguese alliance British traders gained access to Portuguese territories and Bombay was presented as a gift to the Crown and leased by Charles II to the East India Company. Bombay grew as a military and banking centre and naval forces based there protected British trading interests, and the East India Company took Cochin from the Dutch. The ground was prepared for the rapid growth of cloth sales to Bengal and along the Coromandel coast, and from 1744 British naval forces were permanently stationed in Asian waters. Wary of the ominous growth of British power, the Mogul Emperor, Aurangzeb (r. 1658–1707), resisted Britain's growing presence and encouraged Louis XIV's ambitions as a counterweight.

Imperial trailblazers

It was East India Company men, such as Stamford Raffles, James Brooke and George Everest, and freebooting adventurers like John Clunies-Ross, who first ran up the flag in diverse outposts such as Borneo, Penang, Singapore and the Cocos (Keeling) Islands. Stamford Raffles (1781–1826) bought a mangrove swamp from the Sultan of Johore and Singapore was born. George Everest (1790–1866) was sent by Raffles to survey Java, later earning fame through the Great Trigonometrical Survey of India and his work in the Himalayas. James Brooke (1803–68) led a band of mercenaries to suppress a civil war in northern Borneo and was rewarded by the Sultan of Brunei with Sarawak, becoming the famous White Rajah whose dynasty ruled until the Japanese invasion of 1941. John Clunies-Ross (1786–1854) took control of the Cocos (Keeling) Islands in the western Indian Ocean, establishing another family fief that endured from 1886 until 1978 when the islands were bought by the Australian government.

The fortunes of empire were kept afloat by the British merchant marine's success in establishing a dominant position as the carrier of the world's trade, a position retained until the Second World War as Britain dictated what was carried, from where and in which vessel throughout most of the world. If the ships of the Merchant Navy did not sail, territories from Britain to India and Australia ceased to be able to function normally, because they were dependent upon global import and export networks developed since the 17th and 18th centuries. This was the *nature* of a trading empire; total interdependence requiring the unfettered movement of goods, people and information.

By force of arms

To protect this great seaborne trading empire Britain fought wars against European foes in the 18th and 19th centuries which determined the balance of world power for generations and decided the fate of empires. From the mid-18th century onwards Britain and France vied for supremacy in India, the West Indies and North America, jostling to corner trade and to occupy the best-positioned trading posts and gain favour with the most useful regional allies. In the wars of commerce and empire of the 18th and early 19th century, the Royal Navy was Britain's instrument of policy, alongside an expeditionary army that could project power ashore almost anywhere in the world. Britain won its imperial spurs through success in the War of the Spanish Succession (1701–13), the War of the Austrian Succession (1740–8), the Seven Years' War (1754–63) and the Revolutionary and Napoleonic Wars (1792–1815).

The Seven Years' War was decisive for British world power as Britain's rivalry with France and its indigenous allies peaked. Victory had been decided almost before the war even started thanks to the power of the East India Company and Robert Clive's victories over Joseph-François Dupleix, governor-general of the French Indies. The British lost Calcutta, an episode notorious for the 'Black Hole' incident; it took six months to recover this key position. With the entry of Spain in the latter stages of the war, the balance of naval power threatened to move decisively against the British. To meet this new threat, East India Company soldiers, transported in a troop convoy protected by a large Royal Navy force, attacked Manila, capital of the Spanish Philippines, besieging it until it surrendered to EIC commander Dawsonne Drake. Thus by 1758 the war had become global, stretching from the Ohio to the Ganges.

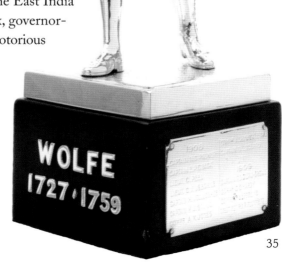

Regimental mess silver statuette of General James Wolfe (1727–59). Wolfe's glorious death at the Battle of the Plains of Abraham, the victory over the French in the Seven Years' War that secured control of Quebec and dominance over Canada, ensured him a permanent place in the pantheon of British imperial heroes.

While there was fighting in Europe itself, the principal *casus belli* was the developing struggle of Britain and France for control of the New World and global trade routes. The war's main battles took place in the Americas, epitomized by General James Wolfe's victory on the Plains of Abraham and the subsequent capture of Quebec, with smaller campaigns in the Caribbean, the East Indies and the Indian Ocean. At the end of the Seven Years' War the 1763 Treaty of Paris left Britain in control of India, Canada and the high seas. In 1765 the East India Company won *diwani* – the right to collect the revenue of Bengal – giving it control of the local opium traffic and a vast income. This set the seal upon Britain's growing presence as a genuine imperial power on the Asian subcontinent during the terminal years of the Mughal Empire. This, in turn, acted as a springboard for Britain's growing power in the Far East, Southeast Asia and the Persian Gulf.

Continuing threats

Even so, British rule in India was still not secure. The next challenge came in the late 18th century during the American War of Independence and the Revolutionary and Napoleonic Wars. Driven out of India and off the high seas by the British, Louis XVI and the people of France were spoiling for revenge. France encouraged the anti-British alliance between Haidar Ali, Nabob of Mysore, the Nizam of Hyderabad and the Marathas of the northwest Deccan. This new challenge led to a period of frenetic military engagement on the subcontinent. In 1781 Haider Ali was defeated at Mysore. In 1798 his son, Tipu Sultan, rose against the British upon hearing news of Napoleon's victory at the Battle of the Pyramids. Arthur Wellesley and Lord Mornington subsequently invaded Mysore, and Tipu's stronghold at Seringapatam was taken. Tipu, implacable enemy of the British and Napoleon's most promising ally, died with sword in hand. The French were driven out of Pondicherry for good, Malabar was annexed and Hyderabad

One of the most famous artefacts of Empire, displayed at the Victoria and Albert Museum in London, is 'Tipu's Tiger'. Made in around 1795 at the behest of Tipu Sultan of Mysore, this gruesome automaton shows an East India Company soldier being mauled to death by a tiger. Separate mechanisms emit noises mimicking the growls of the big cat and the shrieks of its doomed victim.

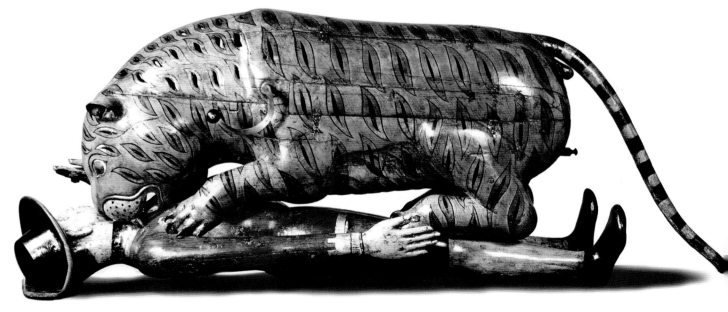

surrounded. In 1803 Mornington occupied Delhi. Now all of India, save for the Punjab, Rajputana and Sind, were under British sway, and the writing was on the wall for those remaining independent regions, which were all subjugated by British arms by the mid-19th century.

The 'Great Game'

Moves by other powers, great and small, prompted many other British actions. Ottoman expansion down the Arabian peninsula caused a British preserve to be more forcefully staked out in the hinterland of Aden. Russian designs in the Persian Gulf were thwarted by British and Indian troops, sloops, diplomats and political agents. East India Company factories, traders, political officers, ships and garrisons made Britain the arbiter of affairs in the Gulf, protected her interests at the Shah's court in Tehran, and influenced the decisions of the Sultan of Zanzibar. Britain's long anti-Russian vigil was the cause of numerous military expeditions. The 1828 Treaty of Turkmanchai, following Russian victory over Persian forces, meant that Russian influence at the Shah's court was in the ascendant. This prompted a British expedition to ensure that Herat, the Gate of India and technically a province of Afghanistan, remained independent of the Shah.

Fear of Russia led Viceroy Lord Curzon to act in another borderland of the Raj in the early 20th century when he sanctioned Sir Francis Younghusband's expedition to Tibet. A strong force crossed the Himalayas, defeated an army of Tibetan warrior-priests, and entered the capital, Lhasa, where the Dalai Lama agreed a treaty curbing Russian influence. Thus Russian threats, real and imagined, were met with determination. Other powers were similarly checked. In the late 19th century German claims in East Africa were ring-fenced by British counter-annexations, London moving with uncharacteristic alacrity to defend its interests as the Scramble for Africa became a serious game of Great Power rivalry.

Victory over European rivals in the wars of the 18th and 19th centuries left Britain the dominant power in the Atlantic and the Mediterranean and the foremost European power in India and the Far East. Through war prizes, new annexations and purchases, the British had gathered to themselves the great maritime gateways – the Malacca Strait, the Suez Canal, Bermuda, Gibraltar and the Cape, along with almost all that lay between – bases that were needed for refuelling and refitting British ships, or that simply could not be left in enemy hands. Asset-stripping opponents empires' was a recognized tactic in this age of global warfare, and the British proved rather good at it. Thus the French were driven out of North America and Asia and the Dutch were evicted from the Cape of Good Hope, Malacca and Ceylon.

The importance of seapower

In establishing imperial authority and power across the seven seas, the Royal Navy was the key instrument of British power. In the East it formed, along with the Indian Army, the 'hammer and anvil' upon which Britain's paramount position

depended. In the words of the naval and empire historian Gerald Graham, 'the Royal Navy was neighbour to every country with a coastline' and it was naval power upon which imperial rule and a global trading economy depended. Seapower not only enabled the Empire to trade, but enabled the British to sustain distant fighting fronts during times of war. Wellington's victories in the Peninsular campaign, for example, depended utterly upon maritime power, while the Boer War demanded the movement of hundreds of thousands of soldiers from all parts of the Empire, and all of their horses and supplies, to then be sustained over a prolonged period. The Royal Navy grew into a global force, with warships and bases across the world bringing a military reach that only sea power could confer, allowing expeditionary land forces to assault places such as Cairo, Colombo, Manila and Peking as the dictates of warfare demanded. The Royal Navy controlled the Atlantic Ocean, the Indian Ocean became a 'British lake' and the Mediterranean's access points through the Dardanelles, Suez and the Straits of Gibraltar were policed by British naval power. European challengers to this British mastery of the seas were defeated and their capacity to contest control of the seas destroyed. Power in Europe became the cornerstone of power in the rest of the world during Britain's century as a global hegemon and the British established an order at sea, based upon the principle of free passage for all lawful traffic. Together they equalled Pax Britannica and gave Britain the power to do whatever it wanted in any part of the world within reach of navigable waters.

Seapower alone, however, was not enough, because imperial authority and Britain's writ often had to be established or confirmed at the point of the bayonet. The 19th century witnessed a breathtaking array of British campaigns against indigenous polities, all of them mounted upon the rock-solid foundation of British seapower and caused by British claims to overlordship wherever British interests were discerned, and the desire of settlers to own land and diminish perceived threats emanating from indigenous societies. These wars shaped the political and national contours of the modern world. As well as wars against European rivals, British forces fought innumerable campaigns against the indigenous inhabitants of territories claimed for Crown or Company, as did settlers dispossessing and quelling the resistance of Aboriginals, Amerindians, Maoris, Zulus and Xhosa.

LEFT 'HMS *Hood*: The Largest British Warship', from the 1924 *Wonder Book of the Navy*. Launched in 1918 at a cost of over £6 million, the 'Mighty Hood' symbolized the importance of seapower to the survival of Britain and the Empire. The flagship of the 'Special Service Squadron' that toured the world in 1923–4, *Hood* was visited by over 750,000 people. Her destruction in 1941 during an engagement with the *Bismarck* came as a great national shock.

BELOW *Our Sailors* (1910) was representative of the huge output of literature celebrating Britain's maritime heritage and the activities of her seamen.

Gunboat diplomacy

In the early years Britain's coastal enclaves in Ceylon struggled to come to terms with the powerful inland kingdom of Kandy and the subsequent British conquest ended 2000 years of Sinhalese independence. Across the Bay of Bengal, British power competed with the Burmese empire, itself an expansionist state intent on controlling its border regions. This brought British soldiers and African and Indian levies into the kingdom of Burma, a hidden land of natural magnificence, teak forests, stunning pagodas and statues of *chintahs* (mythical creatures) guarding the gates of Buddhist temples. To beat back Burmese expansion the British determined in 1823 to attack Rangoon, which would give them access to the Irrawaddy and allow them to project power upriver to the capital, Ava. Steamships provided two essentials of river warfare – power and a shallow draft – as technology was harnessed to expansion. In this endeavour Captain Frederick Marryat, later author of *The Children of the New Forest*, commanded the paddle-steamer *Diana*. The Treaty of Arracan ended a successful British campaign, and Emperor Bagyidaw ceded Arracan, Assam and Tennasserim to Britain. Thus in this and innumerable other colonial campaigns British authority was established all over the world.

In 1867 a large imperial force of over 15,000 servicemen, accompanied by war elephants, steam engines and batteries of Congreve rockets, was transported from Bombay to teach the Abyssinian Emperor Tewodoros (inevitably Anglicized as 'Theodore') a lesson he wouldn't forget for having thumbed his nose at Queen Victoria and taken two of her consuls hostage. British interests came to predominate on the island of Zanzibar as British power expanded into East Africa. In August 1896 the wooden palace of the Sultan of Zanzibar was razed to the ground by HMS *Philomel*, *St George*, *Sparrow* and *Thrush* under the command of Rear Admiral Harry Rawson, Commander-in-Chief Cape and East Africa

A contemporary photograph showing the ruins of the palace of the Sultan of Zanzibar after bombardment by British forces in 1896. In this action, some 500 of the Sultan's forces were killed, while the British suffered only one sailor injured. The short, sharp Anglo-Zanzibar War, at 40 minutes the shortest recorded conflict in history, demonstrated the efficacy of modern firepower.

Station. Sayid Khalid had 'illegally' declared himself Sultan in defiance of the British Resident's wishes upon the death of Sultan Hamed. As *The Times* reported under the headline 'Zanzibar: British Ultimatum', 'British gunboats had taken up positions in the harbour facing the palace ... An ultimatum has been addressed to Sayid Khalid informing him that unless his flag is hauled down and he makes a complete surrender by nine o'clock tomorrow morning, the palace will be bombarded'. When the ultimatum expired the warships began a bombardment that lasted for 40 minutes, firing heavy guns and Maxim machine-guns. *The Times* correspondent reported that 'at so short a range very great damage was done, but the rebels fought with pluck and determination and returned a heavy fire'.

And so the British Empire was established. Two of the most renowned features of British overseas expansion, however, have yet to be encountered; the role of missionaries and explorers in pushing forward the boundaries of European knowledge and of European rule. It is to these themes that the following two chapters turn.

The Congo for Christ

The Story of the Congo Mission

By Rev. J. B. Myers

A Light unto the Gentiles:
Missionaries, Abolitionists
and Humanitarians

SAVING SOULS, LIBERATING SLAVES AND DISPENSING MEDICINE AND EDUCATION in equal measure were powerful motors of British expansion. Just as sportsmen saw the world and wanted to shoot it or climb it, Christian missionaries saw the world and wanted to convert it, or at least make it a better place in which to live.

This, frequently, meant making other people more like themselves, a project that met with an understandably mixed reaction. Proselytizing the world was bound to be controversial, even in Britain itself. The 'live and let live', *laissez-faire* spirit was a characteristic of the Victorian age, though it was outweighed for much of the period by proponents of the 'live like us' school of thought. It was the impulse to humanitarian and religious action within British society that gave missionaries the leverage they required to act so resolutely overseas; the armchair evangelist attending magic lantern lectures and reading the *Christian Intelligencer* and the latest book about the horrors of the slave trade was as important as the missionary toiling at the coal face in some foetid jungle or Eastern slum. The one provided an audience, a source of funds, and a ready-made political and moral lobby that the other could tap into, especially useful when the British government needed to be cajoled into action on behalf of a voiceless tribe threatened by violent neighbours, Muslim slavers or whisky-peddling traders. The spread of Christianity and the work of missionary societies, therefore, are key themes in the expansion of the British Empire and the *manner* in which the British came to understand the new worlds opening up before them and to view themselves as 'civilizers'.

Humanitarian zeal

Missionaries had departed British shores for unknown lands from the earliest days of British expansion. As early as the mid-17th century Protestants such as John Eliot and John Cotton were preaching among the Algonquin Indians in the Massachusetts Bay area, and Quakers soon followed. But it was the 19th century that produced the greatest flowering of Christian endeavour. As the century opened Christians expounding the gospel overseas were looked upon as little more than lunatics, but by the end of the century they were esteemed figures in British

Reverend John Brown Myers of the Baptist Missionary Society wrote *The Congo for Christ* in 1895. It was typical of the literature published by missionary societies advertising and extolling the benefits of their hazardous work uplifting 'heathens', at once garnering support for their cause and reinforcing the popular perception that 'natives' around the world needed the help and enlightenment of the West.

society and part of imperial lore. The evangelical and humanitarian movements that sprang up in the late 18th century, and the resulting desire to save people for Christ and to stamp out 'barbaric' practices, provided the initial spur for action across the globe.

The groundswell of intellectual and popular attention stimulated a new humanitarian concern for the 'noble savage' and a desire to see him as a fellow human being as opposed to an economic raw material that could be bought and sold. Missionaries and humanitarians were motivated by a desire to make restitution for the evils of slavery, in the process turning Africans, Chinese and Tahitians into trouser-wearing Christians. Christianity went hand in hand with the spread of legitimate commerce and civilization. This, of course, fitted happily into the crude logic of the burgeoning workshop of the world; if people formerly enslaved could be turned into producers of raw materials, and consumers of the goods manufactured from them in British mills and factories, then a perfect economic symmetry could emerge. While this process was enriching the nation, so the logic went, benighted foreigners would be Christianized and raised from their state of religious and educational darkness. This naturally appealed to the nation's moral vanity and fuelled its belief in its own exceptional status and destiny.

The growth of missionary societies

All in all, then, the British believed that they were doing God's work while also doing their own. Missionary societies mushroomed from the late 18th century onwards, driven by evangelical zeal and a new sense of duty, that most powerful factor in persuading men of diverse beliefs to minister to the perceived needs of a troubled world. Missionary societies included the Society for the Propagation of Christian Knowledge, the London Missionary Society (founded in 1795), the Church Missionary Society (1799) the China Inland Mission (1865) and the Universities Mission to Central Africa (1857) inspired by the work of David Livingstone. The Oxford Movement too had its global exponents; John Robert Godley of Christ Church founded the city of Canterbury in New Zealand, part of the settlement named Christchurch in his honour. Thereafter, Godley became known as the 'Founder of Canterbury', his name and form commemorated by a series of 1950 postage stamps marking the centenary of his foundation and the construction of the city's cathedral and university college. The Oxford Mission to Calcutta, meanwhile, worked for the conversion of the Raj from the top down.

The missionaries and their worthy metropolitan constituents reached out to the entire world, planting Christian communities in places as diverse as Canton, Fiji, Korea, New Guinea, the Philippines, Samoa, Trinidad and Tobago and

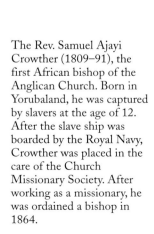

The Rev. Samuel Ajayi Crowther (1809–91), the first African bishop of the Anglican Church. Born in Yorubaland, he was captured by slavers at the age of 12. After the slave ship was boarded by the Royal Navy, Crowther was placed in the care of the Church Missionary Society. After working as a missionary, he was ordained a bishop in 1864.

THE UNIVERSITIES' MISSION TO CENTRAL AFRICA

The creation of the UMCA demonstrated the missionary fervour that characterized mid-Victorian confidence in Britain's ability to act upon the world for its own good. It was Livingstone's return from Africa in 1857, and the dissemination of his opinions and discoveries in books and public lectures, that provided the spur.

In particular, the great missionary-explorer issued a challenge during a series of lectures he delivered at Oxford and Cambridge. The universities rose to it, and prepared to send a mission to Central Africa to carry on Livingstone's work. The mission was led by a bishop, Charles Mackenzie, consecrated in 1860. In 1861 the mission sailed up the Zambezi and Shire rivers and established stations. Malaria forced the mission to retreat to Zanzibar in 1864, though by the 1880s mainland stations had been established in Tanganyika and on Lake Nyasa. The mission's aim was to establish the church in Central Africa and to oppose the evils of the slave trade, the heart of Livingstone's challenge. European men and women and African converts worked together providing pastoral and medical care, as well as evangelizing the peoples among whom they lived and worked. In particular, the mission made a major contribution to the fight against leprosy.

In the 20th century, the UMCA missionary the Right Reverend Trevor Huddleston (1913–98) gained fame as an anti-apartheid campaigner. Sent to South Africa in 1943, his career illustrates the global dimensions of British missionary endeavour and the spread of the Anglican Church and its fusion with humanitarian causes. Huddleston variously served as Bishop of Masasi in Tanganyika/Tanzania, as Bishop Suffragan of Stepney in London, as Bishop of Mauritius and as Archbishop of the Indian Ocean. He also served as President of the Anti-Apartheid Movement, and was made a Knight Commander of the Order of St Michael and St George in recognition of his work. Huddleston also fostered the career of the legendary South African jazz trumpeter Hugh Masekela, by giving him his first instrument in 1954.

The UMCA celebrated its centenary in 1957 in the context of decolonization and a falling off of British interest in missionary endeavour overseas, and in 1965 it merged with the Society for the Propagation of the Gospel.

Uganda. While they won some converts, their presence often had entirely unintended consequences; the Indian Mutiny of 1857 was to a large extent caused by the fear that the British intended to forcibly convert sepoys (as native Indian troops were known); Hong Xiuquan, leader of the long-running Taiping Rebellion against the Qing government (1850–64), believed himself to be the Son of God, and spent time correcting his copy of the Bible in vermillion ink, a result of his brush with Protestant missionaries in Canton; and in Kenya in the 1920s missionary opposition to female circumcision among the Kikuyu was a spur to early nationalism, to the chagrin of the colonial government. Perhaps most ironic of all, it was missionaries who taught Africans and Asians to philosophize and write in Western ways and to communicate in the English language, powerful intellectual tools that allowed them to confront the white man on his own textual turf. This meant that missionaries taught many of the most famous nationalists and first-generation presidents of independent nations to read and write, allowing them to quote

Two major figures of postcolonial Africa – Archbishop Desmond Tutu of Cape Town and former President Kenneth Kaunda of Zambia – attending an AIDS conference in 2004. Like many other prominent African politicians and religious leaders, Tutu and Kaunda are both products of the missionary school system.

apposite passages from Shakespeare, Locke and the Bible as they locked horns with their colonial overlords. As well as education, missionaries were for long the main source of Western medicine available to indigenous populations, running dispensaries and founding homes for lepers and blind children.

Martyrs to the cause

Missionaries did not act in the wider world with the official blessing of the British state (and were often, in fact, considered a darned nuisance by colonial governments). There was no congruence of sacred and secular interests such as that which existed between the conquistadors and the Catholic Church in the Spanish conquest of the Americas. Missionaries were usually present in distant lands long before their formal accession to the Empire. They were, therefore, dangerously exposed and unprotected. The missionary's calling could lead to ill health through tropical disease, to a cannibal's cooking-pot in the Pacific, and to life-after-death in stained-glass memorials following an unpleasant end in darkest Africa. This fate befell Bishop James Hannington. Hearing of the murder of two missionaries on the banks of Lake Victoria, he offered his services to the Church Missionary Society. Ordained as Bishop of Equatorial Africa, he made his way inland from Mombasa along the Uganda road. This was a region in which British power had yet to be fully extended, and one, therefore, in which African chiefs and kings still ruled the roost. Captured by King Mwanga II, Kabaka of Buganda, his party was put to death, Hannington himself dying on 29 October 1885, speared in both sides of his body. A Uganda-based Roman Catholic priest sportingly complained to Mwanga, and was swiftly beheaded.

The situation in Uganda revealed a number of things. It illustrated the dilemmas facing indigenous leaders as they came to terms with incessant Western encroachment; the manner in which missionary activity could become intertwined with other strands of imperial endeavour; and the connection between the actors on the ground and their audience back in Britain. Unlike his father Mutesa, who had sought to play Roman Catholics off against Anglicans for his own benefit, Mwanga had decided that Christian missionaries were the greatest threat to his kingdom's independence. Foreigners, therefore, had to be killed and African converts coerced into abandoning their faith, the alternative being the sharp end of a spear. But such a bloody reception to the Gospel and its ministers did little to aid

African leaders hoping to stem the tide of European encroachment. In fact, the reverse was the case. In Britain, Hannington immediately became a posthumous celebrity, and joined a fast-growing band of Martyrs of Uganda, his death fanning the flames of righteous indignation that could only lead to one thing – more missionaries and intense pressure on the British government to 'do something'. As happened in other parts of the non-European world, though missionaries and colonial administrations were not formally linked, the tougher the going got on the ground, the more likely missionaries were to lobby for protection, and that meant annexation. Mwanga's actions, therefore, pushed the missionaries more and more into league with the Imperial British East Africa Company, which was permitted by the British government to arm itself and defend British interests against the Kabaka. Thus Christianity and the chartered company combined, and there could only be one result in the frenetic years of the Scramble for Africa.

Britain's powerful missionary lobby was quick to react to Hannington's sad end and the press afforded the episode extensive coverage. Hannington's diary survived and was published a year after his death, adding to the clamour for action and resolve in sorting out this apparently benighted and bloodthirsty land. In an age that adored hagiographical biographies, it was not long before a Life of Hannington appeared, serving to further increase British interest in this part of the

A 19th-century lithograph showing Mutesa I, Kabaka (king) of Buganda (r. 1856–84) and his vassal rulers. Mutesa resisted the spread of Christianity in his kingdom, since it banned polygamy, but shrewdly refrained from persecuting missionaries. His son Mwanga took a more militant approach, which led the British to destabilize and topple him.

world and its inhabitants. The Church of England dedicated a Feast Day in Hannington's name, and later a Bishop Hannington Memorial Church was consecrated in Hove, Sussex. In the Hannington Hall of St Peter's College, Oxford, above High Table, Hannington is depicted in a huge stained-glass window. His halo is supported by a rhinoceros, a lion and an elephant; the spears which killed him are by his side and the martyr's palm and crown at his feet.

Missionaries were in an extremely exposed position, particularly in the early phase of expansion when they acted in foreign lands at the mercy of the local people. Wielding cosmological and often political power that at once fascinated and threatened indigenous leaders, they were only a hair's breadth away from an unpleasant end. Hannington's demise was mirrored by that of another Oxford man, John Coleridge Patteson. Like Hannington, he was appointed to a rather dubious, though admittedly very large, see, in his case styled Bishop of Melanesia. A product of Eton and Balliol, he spoke 23 languages and prepared grammar in 17, expertise that illustrated one of the lasting legacies of missionary endeavour – a pioneering contribution to Western knowledge of the non-European world through their recorded observations, anthropological treatises and the part they played in the transformation of pre-literate into literate societies. From his Norfolk Island headquarters, Patteson campaigned for the better treatment of the indigenous inhabitants of New Zealand and Tasmania, among whom he worked in the 1850s. However, this was an age in which 'blackbirders' preyed on those very populations for slave labour to be shipped to Queensland and other nascent European settlements. Like other missionaries, Patteson was part of the whole process of European expansion that so destabilized these communities. Lines of distinction between the various strands of imperial expansion were not always evident to indigenous people, and holy men could be implicated in the depravations wrought by the profane, in this case the traffickers in stolen humans. Patteson died because of this, stabbed to death on a visit to Nakupu in the Solomon Islands in 1871 in revenge for the kidnap of some islanders. Some good emerged from Patteson's work and his tragic end in the form of an Act of Parliament banning blackbirding, and Patteson's memory lives on in a memorial in the Chapel of Merton College, Oxford.

The slowness of conversion

Missionaries such as Hannington, Livingstone and Patteson typified the great age of the Victorian missionary, an age in which there was no shortage of men and women (for these men were usually married before being dispatched to foreign lands, in order to provide support and fend off temptation) eager to travel for thousands of miles to take the Gospel into dangerous and unknown lands. Perhaps even more remarkable was the fact that they still went despite the signal failure of most missions, particularly Protestant ones, to win significant numbers of converts (Catholicism was more attractive because of its incense, iconography, tinkling bells and more relaxed attitude towards baptism). It was common to find that when a

IT IS YOUR CUSTOM TO BURN WIDOWS. VERY WELL. WE ALSO HAVE A CUSTOM: WHEN MEN BURN WOMEN ALIVE, WE TIE A ROPE AROUND THEIR NECKS AND HANG THEM. BUILD YOUR FUNERAL PYRE AND BESIDE IT MY CARPENTERS WILL BUILD A GALLOWS. YOU MAY FOLLOW YOUR NATIONAL CUSTOM, AND WE SHALL FOLLOW OURS.

– *General Sir Charles Napier, addressing an Indian delegation protesting against British suppression of* suttee

The practice of *suttee* – in which Hindu widows were expected to immolate themselves on their husbands' funeral pyres – was long tolerated by the British in India, but was abhorrent to later evangelical missionaries who campaigned successfully to have it outlawed. This engraving is by the Italian artist Gaetano Zancon (1771–1816).

missionary retired (if he lived that long) and wrote the inevitable memoir, with a title along the lines of *Ten Years North of the Orange River* or *In Dwarf Land and Cannibal Country*, there had been few converts.* Even those who had allegedly converted, it would transpire, were 'backsliders', retaining an attachment to drink or some banned facet of indigenous culture such as polygamy or the collection of human skulls.

Apart from attempting to convert heathens, the missionaries' main role was to eradicate practices and customs deemed uncivilized by Europeans. It was widely believed that the non-European world was full of barbaric practices that had to be removed, and missionaries variously campaigned against things such as human sacrifice, slave raiding, *thuggee*, *suttee*, foot-binding, witchcraft, the burial of slaves as a retinue for the dead, trial by poison and cannibalism. Many people had no doubt that only European tutelage could guide backward Pacific islands or the Dark Continent itself along the path of progress, helping to regenerate their people through Christianity, commerce and civilization. This global mission, of course, found ready support among a British public obsessed with progress.

The manner in which missionary work was often intertwined with official policy, and Christian duty fused with humanitarian sentiment, is well captured in the career of Sir Thomas Fowell Buxton and his grandson of the same name. Buxton took over the leadership of the Anti-Slavery Society in the declining years of its celebrated founder, William Wilberforce, who was himself a keen advocate of the missionary societies. As a member of parliament, Buxton became the anti-slavery campaign's chief spokesman. His grandson, the third baronet, was an Evangelical Anglican, heavily involved with the Church Mission and British and Foreign Bible Societies, Vice President of the British and Foreign Aborigines Protection Society and on the Committee of the British and Foreign Anti-Slavery Society. Buxton was also a keen supporter of the Imperial Federation League and an imperial proconsul, serving as Governor of South Australia. Later in life he served not only as a Director of the Imperial British East Africa Company but also as Treasurer of the Church Mission Society, a telling blend of Christ and the chartered company, arguably the most powerful private interests involved in opening up the African continent to European eyes and European rule.

Missionaries and Christians at home

As well as causing missionaries to interfere and evangelize overseas, Christianity fuelled empire in other ways. Religion was important to large sections of Britain's increasingly literate and enfranchised population. Muscular Christianity, and the growing popularity of organizations such as the Boy Scouts and the Church Lads Brigade, put down deep roots in British society, and were widely associated with

---

* A.B. Lloyd, *In Dwarf Land and Cannibal Country: A Record of Travel and Discovery in Central Africa* (1899). John MacKenzie, *Ten Years North of the Orange River: A Story of Everyday Life among the South African Tribes* (1871).

'THE WHITE MAN'S BURDEN'

There was genuine enthusiasm for the work of missionaries and belief in the good they could do, as religious upliftment was conflated with woolly notions of 'progress' and Britain's role as the world's chief 'civilizer'. 19th-century Europe was encountering other cultures on a greater scale than ever before, sometimes, as in Africa and the Pacific, coming face to face with peoples they hadn't known existed. It was the great age of Victorian self-confidence, and it bred men secure in the knowledge that it was their Christian duty to try and uplift those in other parts of the world, to show them civilization and the works of the Lord even if they spurned Him. This was the spirit struck in Rudyard Kipling's poem 'The White Man's Burden', succinctly capturing the connection that the Victorians forged between overseas action and God-ordained duty. Dedicated to America on its assumption of widespread colonial responsibilities following its victory over the Spanish Empire in the 1890s, it addressed the USA as a young land now entering adulthood and fit, therefore, for the challenge of ruling 'lesser' breeds (the subtitle was 'The United States and the Philippine Islands', though the poem had initially been written for Victoria's Golden Jubilee in 1897). It exhorted America to 'send forth the best ye breed' in order to rule and enlighten 'your new-caught sullen peoples/Half-devil and half-child'.

> *Take up the White Man's Burden,*
> *The savage wars of peace*
> *Fill full the mouth of Famine*
> *And bid the sickness cease.*

The image of the white man's burden became a common one, and was even used to advertise soap, eliding its cleansing properties with the work of Europeans in spreading light and purity in the world. One Pears' soap advert showed an upright gentleman in white tropical uniform contemplating the washstand, the corners of the picture showing cases of soap transported across the oceans, deposited in foreign ports and then offered to natives. 'The first step to lightening the White Man's Burden is through teaching the virtues of cleanliness. PEARS' SOAP is a potent factor in brightening the dark corners of the earth as civilization advances.'

In this 1899 cartoon, ironically entitled 'The White Man's Burden,' all Western nations, including the United States (which the year before had seized Cuba and the Philippines) are castigated for imposing their intolerable colonial weight on the indigenous peoples under their control. Behind Uncle Sam, John Bull is carried by a struggling Indian, while bringing up the rear are Germany and France.

IT IS AN INSPIRING THOUGHT THAT THROUGHOUT THIS VAST REGION THE PAX BRITANNICA NOW
PREVAILS, AND THAT OUR EMPIRE'S POWER IS FELT ALONG THE WHOLE COURSE OF THE NILE,
FROM THE GREAT LAKES IN WHICH IT TAKES ITS RISE, TO THE DELTA AND THE MEDITERRANEAN.
GOD HAS COMMITTED TO OUR CARE THE MILLIONS, OF MANY DIVERSE RACES AND TRIBES, WHO
DEPEND UPON THIS MIGHTY RIVER; AND WE MAY BE PROUD OF THE CIVILISING WORK WHICH IS
STEADILY BEING CARRIED OUT BY OUR ADMINISTRATORS. BUT THERE ARE LIMITS TO THE GOOD
THAT MAY BE ACCOMPLISHED BY GOVERNMENT; AND IT IS SURELY NOT FOR MATERIAL BLESSINGS
ALONE THAT THESE PEOPLE HAVE COME UNDER OUR INFLUENCE. MANY YEARS AGO THAT
BRILLIANT ADMINISTRATOR, SIR HERBERT EDWARDES, ASKED WITH REFERENCE TO ANOTHER
PART OF OUR EMPIRE: 'WHY HAS GOD GIVEN INDIA TO ENGLAND? WAS IT FOR NO HIGHER
OBJECT THAN THE SPREAD OF EDUCATION, THE REDUCTION OF TAXES, THE BUILDING OF BRIDGES,
THE INCREASE OF COMMERCE … ALL HIS PURPOSES LOOK THROUGH TIME INTO ETERNITY, AND
WE MAY REST ASSURED THAT THE EAST HAS BEEN GIVEN TO OUR COUNTRY FOR A MISSION, NOT
MERELY TO THE MINDS OR BODIES, BUT TO THE SOULS OF MEN'.

– Foreword by Victor Buxton to Reverend A.B. Lloyd's Uganda to Khartoum *(1906)*

Despite being subtitled 'Life and Adventure on the Upper Nile', Lloyd's *Uganda to Khartoum*
was chiefly about the triumphant spread of Christianity in darkest Africa

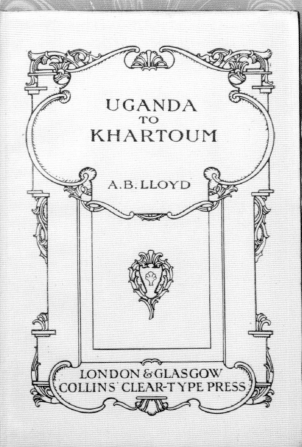
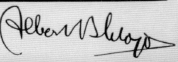

imperialism and British national efficiency. The public schools masterfully conflated God and Empire (forming a quasi-spiritual quorum along with team games and faith in the Royal Navy). The cover of *The Golden Book of Children's Hymns* (1952) showed St George in shining armour upon his charger, lance in one hand, a shield with the Cross of St George in the other. It was a common image of national purpose, of chivalric legend embodying England and of quasi-religious sentiment. The book contained popular hymns such as 'Fight the Good Fight' (illustrated by an English crusader leading women and children to safety); 'Stand Up For Jesus' (a knight offering his sword to the flag of Christ); and 'Onward Christian Soldiers' (showing Boy Scouts marching behind a pageboy bearing a cross).

Conveying the Christian message

Britain's busy religious publishing houses found inspiration and religious homilies in imperial exploits. In 1870 the Religious Tract Society, for example, published *Captain Cook: His Life, Voyages and Discoveries*. Edwin Gomes, author of the splendidly-titled *Seventeen Years among the Sea Dyaks of Borneo*, wrote *Children of Borneo* for the Children's Missionary Series. Books for adults and children aimed to wrap a religious message in attractive packaging that tapped into the great adventure and hero traditions of the time. Thus Ernest Baker's book *Arnot: A Knight of Africa* (1932) had the longwinded subtitle 'A Stirring Account of the Life of an Intrepid Explorer, a Zealous Missionary and a Knight-Errant in the Best Sense of the Term, Re-Told for Young People'. As well as Christianity, the book told of adventures in Angola and the Zambezi region, encounters with Chief Lewanika of the Barotse, of troubles with carriers, slaves and drummers, and of wild beasts. Chapters bore titles such as 'Some African Horrors and Some Great Deliverances'. The purpose was to fascinate the reader with the subject (hence adventure and wild animals) whilst also appalling him with the barbarity and backwardness of native life, thereby stimulating sympathy for the mission's cause.

Another form of literature in which religion and empire frequently meshed was the hero-and-martyr tradition so common in popular writing. Hagiographies of great imperial heroes or, even better, great imperial martyrs, were much in evidence. The flames of martyrdom burnt longest and brightest around the figure of General Gordon, and he was held up as a model to generations of schoolchildren. Seton Churchill's ever-so-slightly partisan account, *General Gordon: A Christian Hero*, began with the dedication: 'Dedicated to the Young Men of England with the earnest desire that some of the noble godlike characteristics of this CHRISTIAN SOLDIER AND HERO may be reproduced in future generations'. Municipal worthies around the empire rushed to pay homage: suburbs such as Sydney's Gordon and Brisbane's Gordon Park were named after

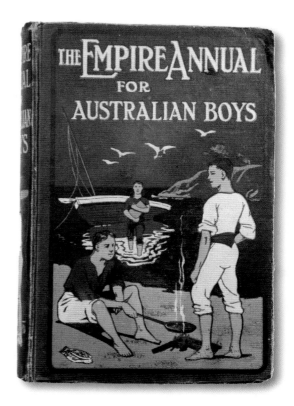

The Empire Annual for Australian Boys, published in 1917 by the Religious Tract Society, illustrates the considerable influence of Christian publishing houses in purveying tales of derring-do to children. Stories included 'An Act of Heroism', 'How to Make a Century' and 'In the Great Australian Desert'.

the general. At home, 'Gordon Road's sprang up throughout British cities; in Southampton, the late-Victorian suburb of Highfield boasts, in close proximity, Khartoum Road, Omdurman Road, and Gordon Avenue. Between the 1870s and the 1950s over 70 Gordon biographies appeared, and over 100 on the life and death of David Livingstone.

The indomitable King Khama of Bechuanaland

Heroes were occasionally non-Europeans, or 'natives' in the accepted parlance of the time. Just as 'bad' natives were painted as 'baddies', 'good', especially 'good' and 'loyal' natives, were cast in a favourable light, showing the public that it *was* possible to raise the heathen towards Western standards of civilization. Arthur Southon wrote *Khama, the Conqueror: A Historical Novel* glorifying the life and work of King Khama of the Bangwato in Bechuanaland.* Khama was a favourite of the British public because he was the model of a Westernized African, a devout Christian who looked dignified in frock coat and top hat. But Khama cleverly used Christianity for his own ends, playing up to the missionary audience and accepting their adulation, whilst keeping his eyes fixed firmly on the secular needs of his own people. He was, in fact, more a consummate statesman than a household god. Khama was baptized in 1860 and had allowed the London Missionary Society to establish a station in his territory. He thus garnered missionary support when he overthrew his father, citing his non-Christian ways as justification for his action. His stock rose even higher when he abolished 'un-Christian' practices such as bride-wealth, circumcision and rain-making.

Khama welcomed Sir Charles Warren when he arrived at the head of over 4000 troops in 1885 to declare Bechuanaland a British protectorate, seeing in the British presence a guarantee against Boer land grabs. In 1890 Khama aided Cecil Rhodes' Pioneer Column as it entered what was to become Southern Rhodesia, calculating that the would-be settlers were likely to give his warlike neighbours, the Ndebele, an almighty walloping. Rhodes, however, became Khama's foe five years later when he tried to take over his territory, seeking to replace Crown rule with British South Africa Company rule. In the intervening five years Khama had had a grandstand view of what Company rule had done for the Ndebele, and was not impressed. He was received by the Queen when he visited Britain in 1895 as he campaigned to prevent his land being handed over to Rhodes. As Rhodes fumed at being beaten by 'this canting nigger', Queen Victoria presented the triumphant Khama with a Bible, in which she inscribed the words 'The secret of Khama's greatness'.

* Southon also wrote *Drums of Fate: A Romance of West Africa* and *Jackson's Ju-Ju: A Tale Reproducing the Atmosphere of the Bush*, classic titles in an age of heroic white bravery in untamed lands beyond the seas.

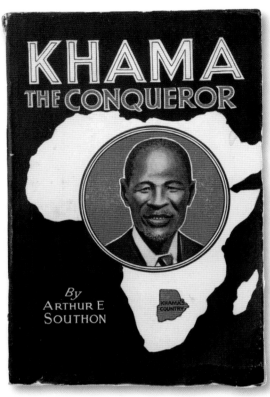

ABOVE *Khama the Conqueror: A Historical Novel* (1930) dramatized the life and work of Khama III, ruler of the Bangwato tribe in what became the Bechuanaland Protectorate in 1884. Its author, Arthur Eustace Southon, wrote other adventures with a Christian twist, including *Gold Coast Methodism*, *The Whispering Bush* and *The God of Gold: A Tale of the West African Coast.*

LEFT The Irish artist George William Joy's famous canvas *General Gordon's Last Stand*, painted in 1885, the year of the governor of Sudan's violent death, helped promote the romantic legend of the stoic martyr slaughtered by savages. An instant outpouring of grief at the death of this Christian evangelist soldier saw the erection by public subscription of numerous memorials throughout the Empire.

'Mr and Mrs Holman Bentley and their Congo assistants': a plate from *The Congo for Christ*. Bentley, who was 'philologist and translator' to the Congo Baptist Mission, was responsible for capturing native languages in written form. The help of indigenous people was central to the work of missionaries.

Khama's victory over Rhodes illustrated the power of the missionary lobby, for he had been aided by the diplomatic skills and lobbying of the London Missionary Society, and it had been that organization that had choreographed his 1895 visit to Britain. This saw Khama and two fellow chiefs fêted in town squares and temperance halls up and down the land, lauded for their opposition to drink and adherence to the Bible's teachings. The LMS had been actively lobbying for British annexation of Bechuanaland, and cleverly developed the slogan of the 'road to the north', encapsulating the idea that, if the British government did not act, German expansion from the west and east of Africa, and anti-British Boer expansion from the Transvaal, would cut the British off from Central Africa, killing the dream of the Cape to Cairo route forever. The LMS and its supporters formed the South Africa Committee to lobby for annexation, neatly bringing together humanitarian, missionary and trader interests, all arguing (naturally) that the 'protection' of the Tswana people was necessary, and that only benign British rule could effect it. The missionaries were particularly concerned about the threat of Boer land grabs against Tswana kingdoms. They had other motives, not so widely touted, for urging British rule. The LMS's main representative on the ground in Bechuanaland, John Mackenzie, had concluded that formal British rule would help dissolve societal resistance to Christianity. Like so many other missionaries, after years of endeavour Mackenzie and his organization were finding Africa bafflingly impervious to their spiritual message. Mackenzie subsequently took the link between missionaries and imperial expansion to an extreme when he served as Deputy Commissioner of the newly established Bechuanaland Protectorate.

A bulwark against slavery

As 'messengers of grace', but also as harbingers of imperial rule, missionaries had a paradoxical and complex relationship with indigenous societies, though in British literature they were nearly always presented as saviours and educators. There is no denying that in some instances they helped to soften the worst abuses of imperialism, often acting as whistleblowers attracting international attention and government notice to wicked acts in distant lands. Thus, with the Royal Navy intercepting precious few slave-laden dhows in the Indian Ocean, missionaries drew public attention to the *internal* slave trade that was flourishing further inland and that was, in fact, the major cause of slave-raiding. Livingstone campaigned tirelessly against the evils of slavery long after Britain had given up the nefarious trade. Much of what became British Central and Southern Africa owed a great deal to his high profile work, as well as that of the LMS and the Church of Scotland missions. In Barotseland, in what became Northern Rhodesia, the Paris Evangelical Society campaigned for British rule in order to end Ndebele raids and stave off possible German or Portuguese rule. In Northern Rhodesia's northeast, the LMS was fervently imperialist and tried to further the aims of both the British South Africa Company and the Foreign Office. Church of Scotland missions mobilized to 'save' Nyasaland from the evils of Arab slaving, and their *cri de coeur* – along with the willingness of Cecil Rhodes to invest in the region – became the pretext and justification for British annexation. In the Congo, US and British Baptist missionaries were instrumental in exposing the barbarous regime in King Leopold's vast fiefdom. So effective was the pressure surrounding the 'red rubber' scandal that Leopold was forced to give up his demesne, which was taken over by the Belgian government in 1909.

Vitally, missionaries showed the British public the ways in which the world could be 'improved', and helped define Britain's image of itself and its role in the world. Yet no matter how hard they tried to distance themselves from temporal affairs, missionaries were intimately bound up in patterns of annexation. They gathered knowledge and purveyed Western ways, and the result of their activities was often indistinguishable from that other classic 19th-century skein of British expansion – exploration. The two converged most famously in the career of David Livingstone, and it is to exploration that the next chapter turns.

Another major missionary theme used to capture the attention of the reading public related to the nature of the evils from which Africans had to be saved. As well as the stereotypical evil African king, awash with booze and barbarous practices, a favourite bogeyman was the Muslim slave trader. Alfred Horn's *Trader Horn in Madagascar* (1928) offered 'a true record of a wild past in Madagascar … a serious indictment of Mohomedan Slave Trade … [and a] narration of the sinister happenings in Madagascar and the East Coast of Africa'.

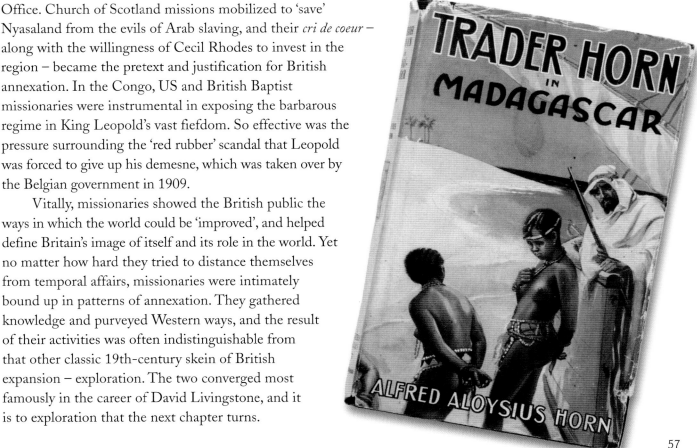

The Source of the Nile: Exploration and Knowledge

THRILLING ADVENTURE SET AGAINST EXOTIC BACKDROPS was one of the British Empire's most alluring features, as new worlds and strange lands were revealed for the first time to a fascinated European public.

Portrait of the British Indian Army officer and African explorer John Hanning Speke (1827–64) by the painter James Watney Wilson. The early posed studio photograph from which this picture was painted was taken in September 1864. Shortly afterwards Speke, who was due to take part in a public debate with Richard Burton (who disputed his claim to have found the source of the Nile) was found dead from self-inflicted gunshot wounds.

In the minds of millions of armchair travellers, empire became a byword for epic journeys in search of legendary cities, scientific truth, the source of the world's great rivers, lost legions and lost souls. It was a lasting fascination and the feats of imperial adventurers – over mountains, through jungles and across Arctic tundra – enraptured the British public in the 1950s just as they had done a century before. Exploration and the quest for knowledge were integral aspects of imperial expansion and the imagination and self-regard of Britons as they scanned the far horizons and considered their place in the world.

Exploration had been a driving force since the earliest days of British expansion. In 1496 John Cabot, an Italian living in England and in the employ of Henry VII, set out from Bristol aboard the *Matthew* to find a direct route to the spice-rich lands of Asia, and ended up discovering Newfoundland and bringing home news of the extent of the American continent and the Grand Bank fishing grounds. From the 13th to the 16th centuries men searched for the mythical Christian king known as Prester John in Central Asia, China and Abyssinia, and his legend remained strong into the 20th century, kept alive in popular novels. Henry Hudson, who gave his name to Hudson Bay and a famous chartered company, began by establishing a fur-trading post at Manhattan in the service of the Dutch East India Company. Captain James Cook, meanwhile, voyaged to the Pacific to observe the passage of Venus across the sun and to settle once and for all the question of whether or not a Great Southern Continent – *Terra Australis Incognita* – existed.

In the 19th century the fringes of empire became an imaginative destination for children and adults enthralled by accounts of hunters, missionaries and explorers fighting against the odds in dangerous and unknown lands. Whilst the exploits of famous men such as Sir Charles Darwin, gathering knowledge of new worlds from South America and the Pacific before bringing it home aboard the *Beagle*, captivated intellectual circles, newspapers, museums and publishers processed this material and packaged it for public consumption. Thus newspapers reported the findings of British explorers, collectors and scientists, and publishers

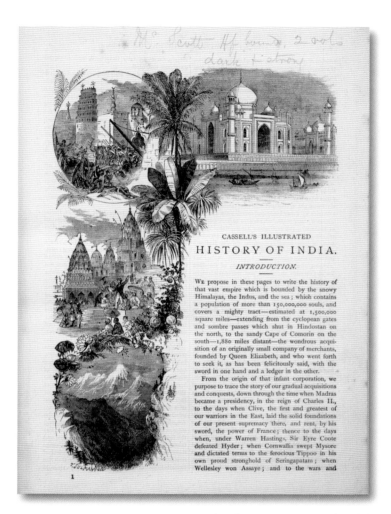

CASSELL'S ILLUSTRATED

HISTORY OF INDIA.

INTRODUCTION.

We propose in these pages to write the history of that vast empire which is bounded by the snowy Himalayas, the Indus, and the sea ; which contains a population of more than 150,000,000 souls, and covers a mighty tract—estimated at 1,500,000 square miles—extending from the cyclopean gates and sombre passes which shut in Hindostan on the north, to the sandy Cape of Comorin on the south—1,880 miles distant—the wondrous acquisition of an originally small company of merchants, founded by Queen Elizabeth, and who went forth to seek it, as has been felicitously said, with the sword in one hand and a ledger in the other.

From the origin of that infant corporation, we purpose to trace the story of our gradual acquisitions and conquests, down through the time when Madras became a presidency, in the reign of Charles II., to the days when Clive, the first and greatest of our warriors in the East, laid the solid foundations of our present supremacy there, and rent, by his sword, the power of France ; thence to the days when, under Warren Hastings, Sir Eyre Coote defeated Hyder ; when Cornwallis swept Mysore and dictated terms to the ferocious Tippoo in his own proud stronghold of Seringapatam ; when Wellesley won Assaye ; and to the wars and

A major work of scholarship: with over 1100 pages and hundreds of illustrations, James Grant's *Cassell's Illustrated History of India* (c.1880) signalled the appropriation of knowledge by Britain as it became the custodian of other cultures' secrets and lore. It presented a view of history that conveyed the justness of British expansion and the beneficence of British rule.

launched densely detailed, beautifully illustrated volumes such as *Cassell's Illustrated History of India* as the British became the guardians and purveyors of other peoples' cultures.

Catalysts for exploration

Western wanderlust was fired by the desire to chart the course of the Nile, the Niger or the Irrawaddy and to cross deserts to discover a great inland lake in the Australian interior or a fabled city of gold in the Sahara. The snow-capped peaks of Mount Kilimanjaro and Mount Kenya acted as magnets to adventurers, just as uncharted rivers and unknown peoples captured the imagination of Europeans dreaming of diamonds and abundant produce. In addition to the inspiration provided by science, religion, cartography and national rivalry, the best motivation of all was the simple desire to do something because it was there to be done, be it to paddle up a river to its source, reach a mountain summit lost in the heavens, or cross a desert from one side to the other. Henry Morton Stanley simply decided as a young man to cross the planet from one side to the other; the 16th-century Spanish explorer Juan Ponce de León set out for the Americas in search of the Fountain of Youth; and the great Portuguese navigators sought to prove, by circumnavigating entire continents, that lands and seaways existed. When asked why he wanted to climb Everest, George Mallory answered, 'because it's there'. In the 20th century the race to conquer Everest, or to be the first to fly non-stop to the furthermost part of the globe in aircraft made of little more than sticks and tarpaulin, replaced the excitement of the 19th century's clipper races from the Far East to Britain and the hunt for the source of the Nile. But the quest for knowledge and achievement remained the same, and the audience just as receptive.

Overseas exploration was financed by private institutions, government and the military, and expeditions were often led by officers of the British and Indian armies. Famous 19th-century explorers included Sir Richard Burton, John Hanning Speke, Sir Samuel Baker, Sir Roderick Impey Murchison, James Augustus Grant and Verney Lovett Cameron. They found their 20th-century successors in men such as Sir Vivian Fuchs, Sir Edmund Hillary, Captain Robert Scott and Sir Wilfred Thesiger. It was their job to build Western knowledge as they withstood the ravages of unfriendly climes, impossible terrain and hostile locals. Their discoveries informed contemporaries about the state of the world while reinforcing a prevalent image of white superiority over other races. They became vicarious vectors for stay-at-homes longing for a freer way of life, escaping rules and constraints increasingly common in industrial Britain. Explorers were part of the romance of the Western imagination, and in David Cannadine's words 'rivers, towns and mountains could only be said to exist once they had been "discovered" and named by Europeans'.

Exploration was not a calling for the fainthearted, however, and the hazards associated with exploration were integral to its allure. Cook was murdered; Livingstone died in the heart of Africa; Speke died suspiciously, probably by his own hand, after a public row with Burton. One of Burton and Speke's expeditions was ambushed by Somalis while returning to Aden from the interior. An Indian navy lieutenant, William Stroyan, was killed, Speke suffered 11 wounds and Burton was speared through the face. Scott and his expedition starved and froze to death in the unimaginable loneliness of the Antarctic. George Leigh Mallory fell to his death on Mount Everest in 1924 while making – or possibly returning from – an attempt on the summit. His betweeded body, dressed for fell-walking rather than climbing 27,000-ft high mountains, lay undiscovered for 75 years.

Public knowledge and the great age of museums

The breathless excitement that accompanied the journeys, dispatches and triumphant homecomings of adventurers and explorers was sparked by a feverish and expanding popular press and the public's thirst for knowledge and discovery, an enduring characteristic of the Victorian era which survived long into the 20th century. Their journeys swelled the collections of Britain's great houses and burgeoning museums during an age in which it was widely believed that everything could be known, classified, named in Latin, bottled and labelled, from

Colour engraving from a sketch entitled 'Our Desert Camp' by the 19th-century explorer and Orientalist Sir Richard Burton. Burton was an extraordinary polymath who mastered over 30 European, Asian and African laguages and who steeped himself in alien cultures so thoroughly that he could pass as a native. Most famously, he undertook the *hajj* to Mecca disguised as a Muslim pilgrim in 1853.

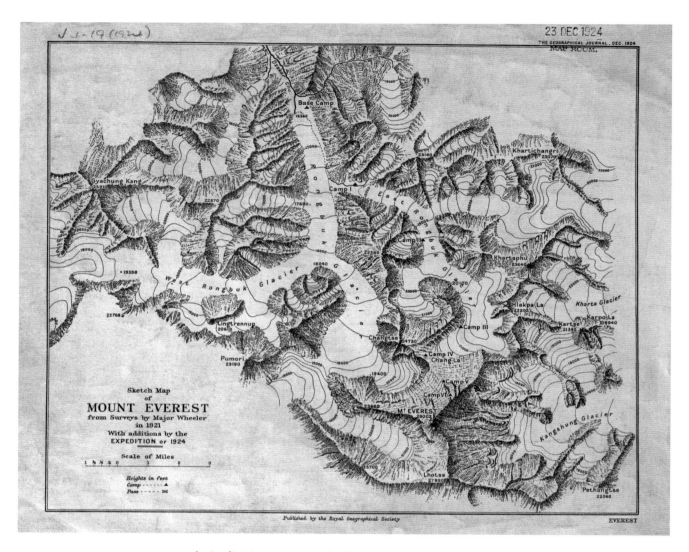

A sketched relief map of Mount Everest from surveys undertaken by Major Wheeler in 1921. This map, published in *The Geographical Journal* in December 1924, also contains additions gleaned from the British expedition earlier that year, on which George Mallory and his climbing partner Andrew Irvine met their deaths.

ethnic divisions among the Pygmies to the size of Bushmen's brains, the species of mountain flowers growing in the Himalayas and the traditional weaponry of native Americans. Sir Robert Brownrigg, Governor of Ceylon in the early 19th century, brought home with him an ancient Buddhist statue, now one of the jewels of the British Museum's collection. Upon the conquest of the Kingdom of Kandy in 1815, the King's ceremonial throne and footstool were sent as a gift to the Prince Regent at Windsor Castle, where they remained for over a hundred years. The throne, covered in gold and studded with precious stones, its arms in the form of lions couchant with amethyst eyes bigger than musket balls, was used for the investiture of knights of the Garter. The Pitt Rivers Museum in Oxford was a classic Victorian creation, a collection of artefacts and curios massed from all over the world. General Augustus Lane Fox Pitt Rivers (1827–1900) left a collection of over 14,000 items, including those of Reinhold Forster, a naturalist who had accompanied Captain Cook to the Pacific. What made the collection unique was Pitt Rivers' penchant for collecting everyday objects, and the manner in which the collection was displayed, diverse and curious items paraded in jumbled disorder.

Thus to this day masks, jewellery, totem poles, kayaks, knives and axes are displayed in crowded proximity to mummified babies and shrunken heads. This was the Age of Curiosity, supercharged by a healthy dollop of national rivalry, prestige and male testosterone thrown in.

A thirst for adventure

Explorers were moved by the desire to map mountain ranges and discover new flora, fauna and civilizations, fuelled by a public hungry for romanticized tales of fabulous cities, resplendent kings and the struggle against nature. Whether it was the bitterly contested race to discover the source of the Nile, the dramatic Emin Pasha Relief Expedition dispatched to the Equatorial province of the Sudan to look for Gordon's 'lost' legion, or H.M. Stanley's famous search for Livingstone, public attention was guaranteed (indeed, Stanley's expedition was sponsored by the *New York Herald* expressly to increase circulation). The groundswell of public interest was fanned by explorers and missionaries' accounts of their exploits and

'The Conquest of Africa', a board game based on the travels of Henry Morton Stanley and David Livingstone. Livingstone's extensive travels around southern Africa to combat the slave trade, and Stanley's self-publicizing expedition to locate him, created a huge surge of public interest in the West in 'civilizing' the 'Dark Continent'.

the novelists, poets and lyricists whom they inspired. All of this reflected European confidence concerning their place in the world and the widespread sense that non-European lands represented a vast adventure playground in which men could test their mettle while discovering new things and scoring patriotic points. For generations of young Britons the world was their oyster, be they the sons and daughters of the poor, seeking new life and new prosperity through emigration, or the scions of the idle rich, seeking new diversions, new careers, new business opportunities and new wealth in the colonies.

British history was heavily marked by the exploits of famous explorers and their epic voyages of discovery. The prototype of the inquiring, intrepid hero-adventurer was Captain James Cook (1728–79), whose three voyages to the Pacific entirely transformed Europe's knowledge of that vast region. From Antarctica to the Bering Strait, through Cook's voyages 'the Grand Bounds of the four Quarters of the Globe are known', as one of his officers expressed it. The son of a farm labourer, Cook joined the Royal Navy and came to prominence while charting the St Lawrence River, in the process helping to facilitate Britain's victory at Quebec in the Seven Years' War. He was then employed by the Governor of Newfoundland to survey the coastlines of Newfoundland and Nova Scotia. While at large in

An unsigned print of *c*.1790–1810 shows Captain James Cook visiting Easter Island in 1774, during his second voyage, and examining one of the *moai* statues there. Cook's three voyages to the South Seas, culminating in his heroic death on Hawaii, set the benchmark for later explorers.

Britain's newly-acquired North American domains Cook observed a solar eclipse. On the basis of this work, and his renowned navigation skills, he was selected in 1766 to lead a joint Royal Society and Royal Navy expedition to the Pacific. His mission was to observe the transit of Venus across the sun, which would enable mathematicians to better calculate the distance between sun and earth. A second task was to investigate the ancient belief that there existed a Great Southern Continent. In 1768, Cook left on the first of three voyages to the Pacific, bound for the recently discovered island of Tahiti.

Cook returned from his first voyage in 1771. He had successfully observed the transit of Venus across the sun from Tahiti, and charted both islands of New Zealand and the eastern coast of Australia, returning with a treasure trove of new botanical and zoological specimens. During his second voyage (1772–5) he established once and for all that there was no great inhabitable continent to the south of Australia, and, sailing into the dense pack-ice of Antarctica, ventured further south than anyone had ever done before. On this voyage new lands such as Tonga and South Georgia were charted. Cook's third and final voyage began in 1776, dedicated to the northern Pacific and the discovery of the Northwest Passage. Although he failed in this he made the first detailed survey of northwest America and discovered the Hawaiian islands. In February 1779 the *Resolution* anchored in Kealakekua Bay in Hawaii and was treated to a rapturous welcome. The deck groaned beneath the weight of hogs, breadfruit and plantains brought as gifts, and Cook was treated in a manner 'which more resembled that due to a deity than a human being'. The ship was forced to return to the island soon after departing, and this time the mood was far less welcoming. An altercation with the island's inhabitants over the theft of *Resolution*'s cutter soon developed, during which Cook was killed. This was an heroic martyrdom in the name of science that earned him enduring fame and, rather than warning off potential emulators, only recruited them in large numbers. As Cook's exploits in the Pacific came to an end, other regions opened up to British explorers and became familiar to the public as a result. These included the Amazon rainforests of South America, where British scientists and explorers were active, and the African interior, the classic arena of 19th-century British exploration.

Probing the 'Dark Continent'
The African continent remains indelibly associated with the deeds of the great explorers of the 19th century. Here the thirst for knowledge and the imperatives of scientific enquiry and geographical curiosity meshed with national rivalry and religious and economic impulses. At the beginning of the 19th century the African interior was *terra incognita* and a fertile canvas, therefore, for rumours concerning headless monsters, creatures half-man-half-beast, cannibalism and witchcraft. Explorers probed the continent, and purveyed their findings to a fascinated public. In 1788 the African Association was founded as a private members' club by Sir Joseph Banks, a botanist who had accompanied Captain Cook and drawn exquisite

Continued on page 68

AFRICAN EXPLORATION

'An Exciting Moment', the cover of Darton's *Heroes in Africa*, *c.*1890, a lavishly illustrated pamphlet about the 'opening up' of Africa. It begins with these words: 'Twenty years ago the map of Africa was very different from what it is now. All the centre was marked "unexplored". Now it is almost covered with the names of tribes, towns, mountains, and rivers. It is no longer the "Dark Continent". It has been opened up by Livingstone, Stanley, Baker, and many others'.

Samuel Baker and his wife discovered Lake Albert and the Murchison Falls, named after the then president of the Royal Geographical Society. Baker had bought a farm in Ceylon while still in his mid-twenties. At a time when British colonists were moving regularly to Australia, Canada and New Zealand, Ceylon became known as a colony in which white settlement was both practicable and desirable. Baker made a home there in 1845 when he established a farm in the idyllic settlement of Nuwara Eliya, importing English agricultural techniques and vegetables into the central highlands, producing gardens of leeks and carrots that flourish to this day. Later the rumbustious Baker, who shot elephants with gay abandon, set out to explore the Nile and locate its origin in the company of his Hungarian wife, Florence, whom he had rescued from white slavers. Arriving in Cairo in 1861 to search for the source of the great river, Baker met John Hanning Speke and James Augustus Grant at Juba on the Nile in the following year.

Speke's search for the source of the Nile

Speke, after an earlier expedition with Burton, had claimed Lake Victoria as the source of the Nile, leading to a celebrated and very public row between the two men (it was just before a scheduled public debate in 1864 that Speke died of gunshot wounds). The great river's source, however, had not been conclusively proven, and there remained more exploring to be done. In 1863, following a request from the Royal Geographical Society, Baker was sent by the British consul in Khartoum to look for two lost explorers. In the following year he became the first European to set eyes upon the African inland sea that he named Lake Albert Nyanza (after Victoria's consort, Prince Albert), which was fed by the waters of Lake Victoria and in turn the Nile, a complex ecosystem originating with rainfall in the Mountains of the Moon. Baker was subsequently knighted and attended on the Prince of Wales at the opening of the Suez Canal in 1869. In the same year he was appointed by Ismail, King of Egypt, to connect the Nile with the Great Lakes by steamer and rail and to suppress slavery, commanding a handsome salary of £10,000 per annum. Ismail also appointed Baker governor of the Equatorial Province of the Sudan.

An inspiring missionary-explorer

Further south, David Livingstone's early career took him from the Cape to the Kalahari Desert. He mapped a route from Angola to the mouth of the Zambezi in Mozambique while at the same time carrying out the godly work of the London Missionary Society. Livingstone has been described as a medical missionary, an ambassador of civilization and an explorer. He took with him a sextant, a thermometer, a compass, a telescope and a magic lantern with which to show scenes from the Holy

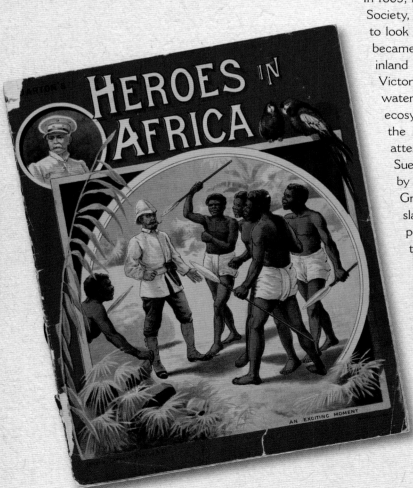

DARTON'S HEROES IN AFRICA

AN EXCITING MOMENT

Bible to African villagers. His 1857 book *Missionary Travels and Researches in South Africa* was an instant best-seller, shifting over 70,000 copies. In Alice Hugon's words, it appealed to 'armchair travellers eager for tales of adventure, geographers wishing to fill gaps in their knowledge of the Dark Continent, missionaries drawn by pagan lands, businessmen dreaming of new markets and humanists horrified by the pages devoted to the traffic in slaves'. Livingstone's celebrity led to his appointment by the Foreign Office as a consul, entrusted with tasks such as the foundation of a government station on the Zambezi.

'Dr Livingstone, I presume'

In the late 1860s the Scottish doctor was investigating the source of the Nile, though went missing in 1871. Search parties were dispatched, most famously that led by Henry Morton Stanley, sponsored by the *New York Herald*, and the two men encountered each other at Ujiji, where Stanley delivered his immortal words, 'Dr Livingstone, I presume'. Livingstone remained in Africa, where he died on 1 May 1873 in the Ulala district, discovered kneeling at the foot of his bed by his servants. They embalmed his body in salt and alcohol, and carried it to Zanzibar before accompanying it by sea to England. Nearly a year later he was buried in Westminster Abbey. Finding Livingstone was only the start of Stanley's fame and he became a highly visible explorer in his own right. Born in Wales, he had gone to America aged 18. His expeditions were renowned for their size and sometimes for their violence. On a mission to the Congo in 1874 he took 999 followers, 242 of whom died. He then served the Belgian king, Leopold II, during the Scramble for Africa.

The Stanley and African Exhibition, held at London's Victoria Gallery in 1890, was a classic blend of contemporary scholarship and European clichés regarding Africa, bringing together science, African art, anthropology and mass entertainment under one roof.

pictures of the flora found on the Pacific islands. The Association's purpose was simply to discover more about Africa, the 'Dark Continent' still little known to the Western eye though fabled in the Western imagination. It sent out a series of expeditions, such as the one commissioned in 1795 and led by the young Scottish doctor Mungo Park, who died on an expedition to chart the course of the Niger River and visit the golden city of Timbuktu. In 1830 John and Richard Lander from Cornwall navigated the Niger, opening up West Africa as a region ripe for commercial and humanitarian exploitation. In the 19th century the African Association evolved into the Royal Geographical Society, a byword for high-profile ventures into the unknown.

Other motors of 19th-century imperial expansion contributed to this epic age of exploration, such as the Anti-Slavery Society and the intrepid characters it sponsored. These included Heinrich Barth, who travelled over 10,000 miles as he crossed the Sahara from Tripoli to Lake Chad and then down the Niger River, providing a detailed account of the geography of this diverse region stretching from the Mediterranean to the Gulf of Guinea. The British could claim many famous explorers as their own, including celebrities of their day such as Richard Burton and John Hanning Speke, who reached Lake Tanganyika together in 1858. Sent in the 1850s by the Foreign Office and the Royal Geographical Society to find the source of the Nile, the two men moved inland from Zanzibar. They were

Such was the popularity of African exploration in the 19th century that commercial enterprises lost no time in associating their products with famous adventurers. This trade card for a Belgian meat extract recalls Heinrich Barth's Trans-Saharan journey of 1850–5.

the archetypal Victorian explorers: Speke, a big-game hunter, trained botanist and geologist, had already travelled in the Himalayas and Tibet. Burton, with his dramatic good looks and long moustaches, was irresistibly drawn to the exotic Orient, and had travelled to Mecca disguised as an Afghan pilgrim and penetrated the forbidden city of Harar on the Horn of Africa. He spoke over 30 languages and had translated erotic Indian texts and the *Arabian Nights* into English.

Africa: the dream-canvas

Like their counterparts in the Pacific in the 18th century and their camera-wielding 20th century successors, 19th-century explorers were there to record what they saw in images as well as the words entered in their densely-packed journals. Their pictures ranged from crude pencil sketches and child-like maps to the most detailed and breathtaking canvases. Along with their journals, visual representations were turned into illustrated books and news articles for mass consumption. Depictions of plunging valleys and torrents of water, herds of wild animals roaming free, giant trees and colourful flowers adorned the watercolours produced by the explorers themselves or by the professional artists that accompanied them. James Bruce produced beautiful engravings of birds and beasts encountered in Abyssinia. Thomas Baines' glorious aquatints of the Zambezi River and the environs of the Victoria Falls revealed secret places, like a view from Conan Doyle's *Lost World*, in which one almost expected to see dinosaurs browsing among

The artist Thomas Baines (1820–75) was invited to accompany Livingstone on an expedition in 1858–9 to investigate the navigability of the Zambezi River. They embarked on the paddle steamer *Ma Roberts* (a vessel so slow that Livingstone complained its engines might be more suitable for grinding coffee). Baines fell out with Livingstone and was sent home, but one iconic canvas to result from this trip was *The* Ma Roberts *and Elephant in the Shallows.*

IMPERIAL ANIMALS

In some parts of the world native peoples believed that the peculiar Europeans that came amongst them as explorers must have been sent as penance for appalling sins. Why else, they reasoned, would they countenance such discomfort, why would they so readily court death? Of course, these men, impressive though they were, never travelled alone. Wherever they ventured they were accompanied by animals as well as human porters and guides, without whom their missions would have had no chance of success. Animals were pressed into the service of itinerant Britons intent upon conquering new horizons. They served as beasts of burden, as pets, and as mobile food. John Rae, an Arctic explorer, was taught to use dog sleds by the Eskimos. Captain Cook's goat provided milk for the wardroom coffee. Oxen, elephants, camels, mules and yaks were load carriers; in wartime, as Trevor Fishlock puts it, 'donkeys brought the bullets and pigeons the news'. During the Second World War muleteers from Basutoland were recruited, along with their

Tom Crean, second officer on Ernest Shackleton's Imperial Trans-Antarctic Expedition of 1914–16 holding the husky sled-dog puppies Roger, Nell, Toby and Nelson.

four-legged companions, to serve with the British Army in the Italian mountains, transporting ammunition and supplies to the front-line and evacuating the wounded on the return journey.

Ships' cats and pet dogs were often the last animals into the pot when food became scarce. The sea cat 'Trim' sailed from 1801 to 1803 with Matthew Flinders, the circumnavigator who named Australia. Trim survived shipwreck and imprisonment in the process. 'Kandahar' was an Indian Army mule that saw service in seven campaigns and wore five medal ribbons on his headband, including those for good conduct and long service (joined 1879, died 1912). Camels were essential in taming the Australian outback, crossing terrain that horses could not handle. Along with their drivers from Afghanistan, Baluchistan, Iran, Kashmir and the Punjab, camels built the Overland Telegraph from Adelaide to Darwin in 1870–2 and carried mining machinery, dingo fencing, iron, timber, whisky, wool, mail and policemen. Livingstone rode an ox called Sinbad and was accompanied by his poodle, Chitane.

THE NATIVE SHEEP IS A HAIRY ANIMAL, LOOKING TO THE UNPRACTISED EYE MORE LIKE A GOAT THAN A SHEEP. CROSSED WITH SUSSEX OR AUSTRALIAN BLOOD, HIS DESCENDANT IS TRANSFORMED INTO A WOOLLED BEAST OF FAMILIAR ASPECT. AT THE NEXT CROSS THE PROGENY IS ALMOST INDISTINGUISHABLE FROM THE PURE-BRED ENGLISH IN APPEARANCE, BUT BETTER ADAPTED TO THE AFRICAN SUN AND CLIMATE. IT IS THE SAME WITH CATTLE. IN THE FIRST GENERATION THE HUMP OF THE AFRICAN OX VANISHES. IN THE SECOND HE EMERGES A RESPECTABLE BRITISH SHORTHORN.

– *Winston Churchill on a visit to a government stock farm, Naivasha, Kenya, 1908*

the bushes and pterodactyls circling overhead. Mangrove swamps and lone baobabs, strange birds, charging elephants, grass-roofed huts and elegant, imperious, sometimes naked people – these were the images against which Europeans were painted as they punted up uncharted rivers and beheld new lakes and new species, and which intoxicated the public back at home.

Polar and maritime exploration

As well as conquering continents, the British Empire fostered adventurous individuals who charted new seas and struck out across blizzard-bound horizons of snowy flatness at forty below freezing, intent upon determining the true position of the Pole. Polar exploration in turn fostered mountain exploration, the Royal Geographical Society, for example, linking hands with the Alpine Club in the inter-war years for an assault on Everest. Many of the men involved in polar exploration were serving officers of the Royal Navy, the undisputed leader in polar exploration for three centuries. In 1845 the Admiralty dispatched HMS *Erebus* and HMS *Terror* across the Atlantic, continuing a 200-year search for a North-West Passage linking the Atlantic and the Pacific via North America. Sir John Franklin's mission met with disaster, however, and despite over 40 relief expeditions none of the men were ever seen again. It was not until much later that reports from the Inuit people and the recovery of some relics shed light upon the disappearance of Franklin and his 137 men.

Deep-sea exploration and coastal mapping produced the charts that mariners of the world rely on to this day. In the 1870s Sir George Strong Nares, an officer

The *Erebus* and *Terror* caught fast in the pack-ice during a voyage to the Arctic in 1842. On Franklin's ill-fated expedition three years later, these two ships and their combined complement of 133 men vanished almost without trace, victims of an unknown fate. On embarking on the voyage, with typical Victorian gusto, one of *Erebus'* crew wrote: 'You have no idea how happy we all feel – how determined we all are to be frozen and how anxious to be among the ice. I never left England with less regret.'

in the Royal Navy, led two great oceanographic surveys, the first beginning when he set sail in HMS *Challenger* on a voyage that was to cover all of the world's oceans bar the Arctic. *Challenger* covered nearly 70,000 miles and made around 500 soundings. The wealth of data relating to marine life and the geography of sea beds and coastlines were collated and subsequently published in over fifty volumes. Among other things, the voyage established the existence of the underwater mountains now known as the Mid-Atlantic Range. Nares embarked on his second voyage of exploration in 1875 in command of the sloop HMS *Alert* and the whaler *Discovery*, which he led to the Arctic Sea. Here he charted the strait that was to bear his name and established a station on Ellesmere Island, the northernmost point ever reached by ship. He then sent sledge teams on foot to the northernmost point ever reached by man, an essay in determination and endurance in the face of scurvy, snow-blindness and crude technology. Once again, significant geological and natural history data was recorded and returned to Britain. As in so many other episodes of exploration, the quest for knowledge and discovery had its imperial and strategic repercussions – Nares' voyage established a British and hence a Canadian claim to Ellesmere Island. As well as the Nares Strait, Nares, who ended his career as a vice-admiral, also gave his name to the Nares Basin in the Sargasso Sea and Nares Land in northwest Greenland.

SCOTT OF THE ANTARCTIC

Probably the most famous snowbound expedition was that led by Captain Robert Falcon Scott, an officer in the Royal Navy appointed leader of the British National Antarctic Expedition in 1900 after being plucked from the West Indies Training Squadron. His first trip, aboard the purpose-built icebreaker *Discovery*, took place in 1902–03, sponsored by the Royal Geographical Society and the Royal Society. Sailing via New Zealand, the party landed at Cape Adare in January 1902 and gathered a wealth of scientific data during incursions inland, including a 200 mile crossing of the Ross Ice Shelf towards the South Pole, the furthest point south ever reached by man. Problems with the dog teams and an outbreak of scurvy, however, brought a premature end to this venture.

The epic climax to this phase of polar exploration came in 1910 when Scott left Britain aboard the *Terra Nova*. En route he received news of a similar attempt on the Pole being mounted by the Norwegian explorer Roald Amundsen, which led to a race that put undue pressure on the British expedition to get underway as quickly as possible. Even so, a year was spent preparing for the attempt on the Pole, including the laying of a chain of food supplies across the ice shelf. The party finally set out on 1 November 1911. The trek was dogged by problems, the ponies becoming so weak that they had to be destroyed, the dogs being returned to the base camp. This meant that the final stages of the trip saw Scott and his team hauling their own sleds. They reached the South Pole on 16 January 1912 to find the Norwegian flag and Amundsen's tent already in occupation. Amundsen had won by 33 days. The tragic return journey saw one member of the party die in a fall and Captain Oates make his famous sacrifice, wandering off into the snow in the hope that his death would enable the others to survive. But it was not to be. The remainder of the party, including Scott, died of exposure and starvation. The tent in which they died, and the important scientific information that it contained, was not discovered for a further eight months.

Another famous Arctic explorer of this period was the Irishman Ernest Shackleton (1874–1922). He had set out to try and reach the South Pole as leader of the Nimrod expedition of 1907–09, coming within 100 miles (160 km) of the pole, and during his famous 1914–16 expedition his ship, *Endurance*, was slowly crushed by pack ice and eventually sunk. The crew then floated in an open boat for five months, before landing on Elephant Island. A small party went on, rowing 1000 miles to South Georgia. Here, led by Shackleton, they made the first crossing of the mountainous island in order to summon help from the whaling station on its northern shore.

These episodes were by no means the end of British polar exploration. During the 1950s Sir Vivian Fuchs led the Commonwealth Trans-Antarctic Expedition. This made the first crossing of the continent, 2158 miles (3453 km) from the Weddell Sea to the Ross Sea. Fuchs had previously been a member of the 1929 Cambridge East Greenland Expedition and had spent the 1930s surveying in East Africa. Between 1979 and 1982 Ranulph Fiennes and Charles Burton's Transglobe Expedition traversed both poles. Today permanent research stations exist in British Antarctic Territory, and the Royal Navy maintains the regular deployment of HMS *Endurance* to the oceans around the icy continent.

A 1953 halfpenny stamp from the Falkland Island Dependencies depicts the British Antarctic Survey vessel RRS *John Biscoe*. This ship was named after Captain John Biscoe of the Royal Navy, who made the first undisputed sighting of the Antarctic mainland in 1831.

Desert exploration

Exploration took forms other than the classic sledge towards the pole or the pith-helmeted column snaking its way into the African interior. Desert exploration was another distinct form of activity. Charles Sturt and John Stuart moved inland from Australia's fledgling coastal settlements, Stuart twice almost crossing the continent from Adelaide to the Northern Territories in the 1860s. He finally succeeded in 1862, using camels and horses to make the 2200-mile (3520-km) journey. Often guided by Aboriginals, the continent was gradually mapped; Ernest Giles was the first European to behold Ayers Rock (Uluru) in 1872, and Gibson and Simpson mapped the deserts that were named after them.

During the inter-war years the Western Desert of Egypt and Libya was probed and information gleaned on passable routes and water sources. The Hungarian aristocrat and desert explorer Count László Almásy (subject of Michael Ondaatje's 1992 novel and Anthony Minghella's 1996 film *The English Patient*) organized hunting expeditions in the Egyptian desert in this period. In 1926 he drove from Egypt to the Sudan along the Nile and, while working for the Austrian automobile manufacturer Steyr, demonstrated the capabilities of their vehicles in desert conditions. In 1932 he joined an expedition searching for the legendary oasis of Zerzura, the 'Oasis of the Birds', in the company of three British explorers. The expedition employed cars and aeroplanes. In 1934 Almásy published *The Unknown Sahara*, and during the Second World War worked for General Rommel smuggling German spies into Cairo. Information gained from Almásy's earlier expeditions also proved invaluable to the British when war came to the Western Desert in 1940.

Sir Wilfred Thesiger (1910–2003) became a renowned desert explorer. Born in Addis Ababa and educated at Eton and Magdalen College, Oxford, he returned to Abyssinia in 1934 to cross the Danakil Desert in search of the source of the Awash River, one of Africa's last mysteries. His mission was successful and he found the river's mouth. Thesiger then became a district commissioner in the Sudan Political Service. During the war he served in the SAS, putting to good use his desert and survival skills. Following the war Thesiger spent five years in the Empty Quarter of Arabia living among the Bedu people. This was followed by seven years among the Marsh Arabs in Iraq, and many more years living in Kenya's Northern Frontier District. In all of his explorative and anthropological incarnations, Thesiger recorded and published his experiences to cement his reputation as one of the last great explorers. This was because, by the time he died in 2003 at the age of 93, pretty much everything in the world had been explored, and hot air balloons and rich men's fancies were all that was left.

Naturalists and botanical gardens

A distinct subset of Britain's history of overseas exploration and research was the gathering of information about the natural environment, and the transplantation of species from one part of the world to another. All sorts of species were introduced into foreign climes or brought home to botanical and private gardens. Breadfruit was transplanted from the Pacific to the West Indies as a cheap source of food for slaves. Tea and coffee were introduced into lands such as India and Ceylon, tobacco into Southern Rhodesia. Botanical gardens were established around the world, such as the Perediniya Botanical Gardens near Kandy in Ceylon, Pample-mousse Botanical Garden in Mauritius, the Royal Botanical Garden of Tasmania and, in Britain, the Oxford Botanic Garden and the Royal Botanic Garden at Kew, where special wheat for the Canadian prairies was developed as well as the best kind of rubber trees for Malaya. As the British image of 'tropical jungle' developed, encouraged by the idea that tropical lands were much more fecund and lush than their own, the well-to-do imported all sorts of exotic plants in order to show off their gardens, and huge glasshouses at places such as Kew Gardens enabled the public to share this vision of an overripe East.

Robert Fortune (1812–80) was a Scottish botanist who made botanical history and changed the face of global commodity production as well as the English garden. In 1848 he was commissioned by the East India Company to investigate tea-growing in China and the possibility of its extension to India, thereby breaking the Chinese dynasty's monopoly on this most desirable product.

Lithograph ('Tea Plantations in the Green Tea District') from botanist Robert Fortune's *A Journey to the Tea Countries of China* (1852), which describes his second journey to that country. Fortune made a total of four journeys to China, and was repsonsible for the introduction of over 120 plant species from the East to Western gardens.

WHEN THEY FOUND THAT, NOTWITHSTANDING ALL THEIR DESCRIPTIONS OF THE FIERCE AND HOSTILE DISPOSITION OF THE PEOPLE, I WAS STILL DETERMINED TO GO, THEY DECLARED THAT NO TEA WAS GROWN IN THIS DISTRICT; BEING FULLY PERSUADED THAT AN ENGLISHMAN COULD HAVE NO OTHER OBJECT IN EXPLORING THE COUNTRY THAN TO SEE THE CULTIVATION OF HIS FAVOURITE BEVERAGE. INDEED, EVERY CHINAMAN FIRMLY BELIEVES WE COULD NOT EXIST AS A NATION WERE IT NOT FOR THE PRODUCTIONS OF THE CELESTIAL EMPIRE. IT HAS BEEN STATED THAT HIS CELESTIAL MAJESTY, THE EMPEROR HIMSELF, DURING THE [FIRST OPIUM] WAR, RECOMMENDED HIS SUBJECTS TO USE EVERY MEANS IN THEIR POWER TO PREVENT THE ENGLISH FROM GETTING TEA AND RHUBARB — THE ONE BEING WHAT THEY LIVED UPON, AND THE OTHER THEIR MEDICINE, WITHOUT WHICH, HIS MAJESTY SAID, THEY COULD NOT CONTINUE TO EXIST FOR ANY LENGTH OF TIME; AND CONSEQUENTLY WOULD BE MORE EASILY CONQUERED IN THIS WAY THAN BY THE SWORD.

— *Robert Fortune,* Three Years' Wanderings in the Northern Provinces of China, A Visit to the Tea, Silk and Cotton Countries *(1847)*

Subsequently Fortune introduced 20,000 tea plants into Darjeeling and began the lucrative tea industries of India and Ceylon. He was also responsible for introducing many fruits and beautiful flowers from China and Japan into European gardens, including the kumquat, the climbing double yellow rose, peonies, azaleas and chrysanthemums.

Naturalists and scientists probed the fringes of empire and developed knowledge of the world that remains the foundation of scholarship, national museums and national histories. Charles Hose, an official working for James Brooke, the White Rajah of Sarawak, studied that country's flora and fauna for 23 years. From this experience, this humane and modest man wrote the classic *The Field-Book of a Jungle-Wallah: Shore, River, and Forest Life in Sarawak,* as well as *Pagan Tribes of Borneo.*

I awoke with the dawn and, for a moment, wondered where I was; for the early morning in the tropics has a romantic element, bringing recognition and arousing mystery. Here was I, in my own familiar corner of the world — anchored in a small sailing vessel at the mouth of a minor river on the Bornean coast … Looking through my mosquito-curtains and waiting for the coffee which my servant, with Chinese precision, was preparing, I watched the opening of the day. On the shore the mist was lifting from the woods and the dew stood out clear and bold on the undergrowth. Around me I heard the cry of awakening beasts, the whistles and calls of many birds, the high treble of insects, many varying voices; beneath them all the ground-bass of the infinite Sea.

The continuing lure of exploration in the 20th century

While the Victorians built the museums and set the trends, their successors continued the tradition of exploration, enjoying their own 'Eureka!' moments such as Sir Edmund Hillary's conquest of Everest in 1953 or Sir Vivian Fuchs' crossing of Antarctica five years later, the first land crossing of the continent. Capturing the full flavour of exploration and the quest for knowledge was Sir Howard Carter's 1922 discovery of the tomb of Tutankhamun in the Valley of the Kings. The boy king's body, his stunning funeral mask and a host of riches had lain undisturbed since the 14th century bc. Carter had served in the Egyptian government's Archaeological Survey and later in the Department of Antiquities, as the British became the caretakers of Egypt's ancient civilization, just as they dominated that country's military and foreign policy.

The exotic world, in which Britons appeared to move so effortlessly as masters, was one in which British rule was a reality manifest through district commissioners, governors and subordinate indigenous chiefs and kings. The system of rule and dispensation of authority that provided empire with meaning and London with control was an essential feature of the British Empire. Governing the world's largest empire involved the figure and authority of the British sovereign, who sat at the epicentre of an imperialized monarchy that became a defining feature of British rule. It is the subject of the following chapter.

The Wide World magazine, which was aimed at an adult male readership, ran from 1898 until 1965 and served up 'true' stories of exploration and adventure overseas.

"VICTORIA,"
QUEEN OF THE BRITISH EMPIRE.

Crown Imperial:
The Imperial Monarchy
and its Native Allies

IT ALWAYS BEGAN WITH THE IMPERIAL MONARCH. History books and children's annuals, Gaumont newsreels and cinema films, national holidays, commemorations, exhibitions and even the FA Cup Final – the monarchy was everywhere, and what passed in Britain as 'imperial' was often just royalty writ large.

LEFT Queen Victoria's Diamond Jubilee in 1897 was celebrated by a welter of commemorative goods readily available to the public. Bookmarks, hagiographical books, pamphlets and posters appeared in their hundreds of thousands. One poster entitled 'Queen Victoria: Empress' showed the monarch's familiar, dour face, surrounded by artist's impressions of life in Australia, Canada, India and South Africa.

RIGHT A Union Jack lapel pin, produced to celebrate the coronation of George VI in May 1937.

Empire was underpinned by the cult of monarchy, an integral part of the ruling architecture and trans-oceanic myths of the British Empire, the central symbol of a global political and imaginative community. King and Empire were at the heart of what it meant to be British, and a matter of supreme importance to nearly five hundred million people spread across the world, a world in which scores of places were named for the British king or queen, symbolizing British possession and power as well as veneration of the Crown. The monarchy and the manner in which it became associated with British rule is the subject of this chapter.

Pomp, circumstance and a public monarchy

Royal rituals and pageantry connected the residents of Buckingham Palace to haughty nawabs and nizams, Muslim emirs and humble chiefs in dusty African kraals. The Victorians crystallized this pageantry in the form of the royal jubilee, and their successors brought its splendour to coronations and durbars. The monarch's head appeared on coins from Vancouver to Tasmania as well as on the Empire's stylish postage stamps. A British vision of tradition and hierarchy was grafted onto the world as indigenous rulers and aristocracies were enlisted in the creation of a world order centred upon kingship and a romantic view of the social order, at once

'I FELT THIS MORNING THAT THE WHOLE EMPIRE WAS IN VERY TRUTH GATHERED WITHIN THE WALLS OF WESTMINSTER ABBEY'.

– George VI after his coronation, 1937

In 1914, King George V became the first reigning monarch to watch the FA Cup Final, when he visited Crystal Palace to see Burnley defeat Liverpool 1–0. His attendance set the tone for an increasingly public monarchy in the 20th century. Members of the royal family have presented the trophies at Cup finals and other major sporting occasions ever since.

conservative, feudal and neo-traditional. From the Victorian era the monarchy assumed great prominence in the affairs of the British nation and the British Empire, and stimulated fascination around the world, interest that only grew as the monarchies of Europe fell as a result of wars and revolutions.

The monarchy was the epicentre of the British Empire's pomp and ceremony, its ritualistic displays and spectaculars. Churchill, along with many others, loved the Empire for 'its glitter, pomp and iced champagne, its high-sounding titles, its tradition, form and ceremony', and devoted his political life 'to two public causes which I think stand supreme – the maintenance of the enduring greatness of Britain and her Empire, and the historical continuity of our island life'. Royal events such as state visits, weddings, jubilees, anniversaries and coronations were carefully choreographed and marketed occasions, and from the 1930s wireless took the voice of the monarch into homes and public meeting places all over the world. The BBC broadcast the wedding of the Duke of York in 1923 and from then on, as Robert Giddings writes, covered all such national events:

With well positioned microphones to pick up the sound of bells, carriages, horses, shouts of command and bands. The whole confection comes packaged with a genuflecting commentary which invariably emphasizes the purported archaeology of the ritual … Broadcasting, film, gramophone recordings, newspaper publicity and mass-produced ephemera – such as cigarette cards, coronation mugs, presentation volumes for children and so on – all served to give the event a place in the popular imagination.

Schooled in imperial values

The habit of ceremonial prize-giving was a quintessentially British trait, teaching children the benefits of self-discipline and scholarly or religious endeavour and linking these efforts to wider responsibilities to school, church, King and Empire. On 26 June 1902 schoolboy C.H. Deavin was presented by Archdeacon Hayward with an attractive book entitled *King Edward's Realm: Story of the Making of the Empire*, published to commemorate the Coronation of Edward VII (see page 14). Its opening page bore a photograph of the new king, his signature beneath it. Almost 35 years later, on 12 May 1937 Arthur Townshend and his schoolmates each received a framed picture of their school, Queen Elizabeth Hospital, from 'the Corporation of the City of Bristol, to commemorate The Coronation of Their Majesties King George VI and Queen Elizabeth'. On the same day, 200 miles north, Jean Roderick and the boys and girls of Frodingham School were presented with a book by the Councillors of the Borough of Scunthorpe. It was called *George VI: King and Emperor*, and commemorated 'the Coronation of Their Majesties King George VI and Queen Elizabeth'.

Jean Roderick and her fellow pupils – indeed, all of the children of Britain – knew about the imperial monarchy through official portraits and history lessons, imperial exhibitions, jubilee and coronation mugs, souvenir bookmarks, letter boxes sporting the royal cypher, statues, postage stamps and cigarette cards. Empire Day, inaugurated in 1904 and falling each year on Queen Victoria's birthday (24 May), regularly featured school pageants and civic commemorations. Royal scenes and

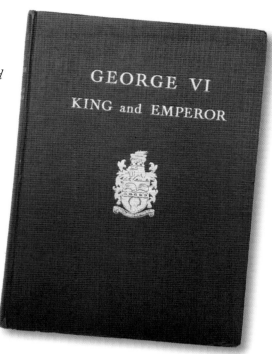

Cover of the 1937 royal commemorative volume *George VI: King and Emperor*. Its first page was emblazoned with a photograph of the new king – an example of the formal royal portrait, in uniform or royal regalia, that was to be found at the beginning of so many books about Britain or her imperial holdings, from Empire and Commonwealth annuals to popular collections of photographs depicting the year's news.

As a symbol of that unity we have one king, one flag. The king, indeed, is more than a symbol of unity, he is a link, a living link, that actually binds the parts together. Every true Briton throughout the Empire looks to the sovereign as the head and centre of national life, from whom all who administer the laws, exercise command in the army or navy, derive their authority.

– Reverend C.S. Dawe, King Edward's Realm: Story of the Making of the Empire *(1902)*

THE POWERFUL AND WIDESPREAD SENSE OF THE MONARCH THROUGHOUT THE EMPIRE WAS NOT JUST CARTOGRAPHICAL, SCULPTURAL, ARCHITECTURAL OR CADASTRAL. THE SOVEREIGN ALSO INTRUDED HIMSELF IN OTHER WAYS; AS HEAD OF THE ARMED FORCES, AND AS KEEPER OF THE SUPREME REWARD FOR VALOUR, THE VICTORIA CROSS. COINS, STAMPS AND LETTERBOXES BORE THEIR IMAGE OR CYPHER THROUGHOUT THE WORLD; POST TRAVELLED IN THE ROYAL MAIL, OFFICIAL CORRESPONDENCE UNDER THE BANNER "ON HER MAJESTY'S SERVICE".

– David Cannadine, Ornamentalism: How the British Saw Their Empire *(2001)*

settings were simply part of the furniture of the visual world. The *Country Life Picture Book of Britain* (1937) featured photographs of royal residences and buildings with royal connections such as Buckingham Palace, Glamis Castle, Hampton Court, the Palace of Holyroodhouse, Sandringham, St James's Palace, the Tower of London and Westminster Abbey. Even the pennies in the pockets of youngsters such as Jean Roderick and Arthur Townshend proclaimed the majesty of their sovereign: around a raised image of the King's head appeared the words 'BRITT: OMN: REX ... IND: IMP' – King of All the Britains ... Emperor of India'.

The imperial jewels at the centre of the British monarch's crown were frequently used to analogize the relationship between Britain and its Empire. As it was put by the Mayor and Aldermen of Scunthorpe in the foreword to *George VI: King and Emperor*, the King was monarch of '"All the Britains" – all the British Dominions beyond the seas, stretching round the globe circlewise, like the Imperial Crown itself, set with great jewels like Canada, Australia, India, New Zealand, South Africa and with lesser gems, though no less bright, like Ceylon, the West Indies, Rhodesia, Newfoundland, Malta and Gibraltar'. From 1876 sovereigns were empresses or emperors of India as well as queens or kings of the United Kingdom and Ireland, and from Edward VII's day were styled ruler of 'the

Published by the *Daily Express* and Purnell to commemorate the coronation of Elizabeth II, the 'Stand Up Model of the Royal State Coach' also contained pictures and information on coronation regalia and robes.

Continued on page 87

IMPERIAL CORONATIONS

This was majesty: the splendour of a line of monarchs stretching back to the days of legend and taken onto a global stage by the growth of the British Empire. No other monarch in the world could match it. Coronations featured ancient regalia, including a Coronation Chair first used in 1300. It was for these moments of high drama that the great palaces, halls and cathedrals of London were built, and for which leading musicians composed anthems: George Frideric Handel was commissioned to write 'Zadok the Priest' for the coronation of George II in 1727; Hubert Parry's 'I Was Glad' was written for the coronation of Edward VII; William Walton's 'Crown Imperial' was commissioned for the Coronation of George VI; and Walton's 'Orb and Sceptre', a more jaunty piece, celebrated the enthronement of his daughter, Elizabeth II, along with Ralph Vaughan Williams' setting of Psalm 100, 'All People That On Earth Do Dwell'.

The brewer Bass produced glazed Staffordshire pottery ashtrays for the silver jubilee of King George V and Queen Mary in 1935, bearing pictures of them both. The royal coat of arms appeared as well as the coveted royal seal of approval: 'By Appointment, Bass', beneath them. 'Here's a Health unto Their Majesties' was a popular song of the period.

The jewels in the crown

Coronations in the 19th and 20th centuries were designed to embody the splendour of an Empire on which the sun never set, its rays reflected in the Star of Africa diamond embedded at the centre of the jewel-encrusted Imperial State Crown beneath a cross bearing a sapphire once worn by Edward the Confessor. The Imperial State Crown consists of over 3000 precious stones, including St Edward's Sapphire and the Black Prince's Ruby. The Star of Africa – the Cullinan diamond weighing 1.37 lb – was discovered in South Africa in 1905, the largest rough diamond in the world. It was cut into 105 gems, the largest of which, the Star of Africa, was set in the Royal Sceptre. The diamond in the Imperial State Crown, Cullinan II, was the second largest gem to be cut from the original. The Crown Jewels also included the fabulous Koh-i-Noor, the Star of India, also known as the Mountain of Light. This fabulous diamond had been presented to Queen Victoria in the 1850s after the British conquest of the Punjab during the Sikh Wars (and is today set in the Queen Consort's crown).

The 1953 coronation

For Elizabeth II's coronation troops, kings and queens and political dignitaries from all over the Empire arrived in London, including the Royal Canadian Mounted Police, 'diggers' (soldiers) from Australia, the Queen of Tonga and the Sultan of Kelantan. A week after Coronation Day the royal couple attended a Service of Thanksgiving at St Paul's Cathedral given by the people of the Commonwealth, and there were street parties all over the world. In Tasmania people met in the grounds of the Governor's House in Hobart, while at Blenheim Palace in Oxfordshire, home of the dukes of Marlborough, Winston Churchill (a descendant of the 1st Duke) attended a garden party for Commonwealth visitors.

The conquest of Mount Everest by Edmund Hillary in coronation year was seen as a sign of Britain's continued imperial vigour, and the start of a new Elizabethan age:

And if people looked for an omen, what better one could there have been than the news that greeted us all on the very morning of the Coronation, the news that a British expedition had finally conquered Everest. Once again a 'Briton' (and it was the New Zealand Premier who, significantly, called his compatriot that) had been the first to do what no other had done …

In her Coronation broadcast, Queen Elizabeth said:

Many thousands of you came to London from all parts of the Commonwealth and Empire to join in the ceremony, but I have been conscious too of the millions of others who have shared in it by means of wireless or television in their homes … I have behind me not only the splendid traditions and the annals of more than a thousand years but the living strength and majesty of the Commonwealth and Empire: of societies old and new, of lands and races different in history and origins, but all, by God's will, united in spirit and in aim.

LONDON: AN IMPERIAL CAPITAL

The world's largest Empire required a suitably grand capital. London fitted the bill admirably, from Westminster Abbey to the elegant Mall separating Buckingham Palace from Admiralty Arch and the imposing square beyond, commemorating a victory of imperial proportions at Trafalgar. Trafalgar Square was home to some of the Empire's most important high commissions, Canada House and South Africa House flanking the National Gallery. Leading off from Trafalgar Square and the gimlet eye of Nelson, high on his 185-foot column, were some of London's major thoroughfares including Pall Mall, the heart of London's clubland. On the opposite side of Trafalgar Square was the Strand, which connected Westminster to the City of London, home to the banks that had established Britain's financial hegemony throughout the world, and St Paul's Cathedral, the parish church of the British Empire. Whitehall, another broad avenue leading from Trafalgar Square, was home to Lutyens' Cenotaph, the Empire's central monument for those who had fallen in battle, as well as the Colonial Office, the War Office, 10 Downing Street and a range of military statues. It was also the location of Horse Guards Parade, where the Trooping of the Colour took place each year on the sovereign's official birthday. Whitehall connected Trafalgar Square to Parliament Square and the Palace of Westminster, a fittingly majestic Victorian home for the famous 'mother of parliaments'.

Not far from Trafalgar Square, on Victoria Embankment, stood Cleopatra's Needle, presented to Britain by Mehmet Ali, Turkish Viceroy of Egypt, in 1819. It had originally been erected in Heliopolis in 1475 and appeared on the banks of the Thames 403 years later. It was adorned with plaques describing its history and praising the British Empire. Guarded by sphinxes, its hieroglyphics chart the reigns of the Pharaohs Thutmose III, Ramses II and Cleopatra herself. Beneath the monument was buried a time capsule containing examples of Victorian objects including newspapers, coins, pins, razor blades and Bibles in different languages, an interesting reflection on Victorian values.

In May 1937 the *Illustrated London News* showed a picture entitled 'The "Heart of the Empire" Decorated for the Coronation: Piccadilly Circus as Seen from Piccadilly':

The familiar description of Piccadilly Circus as the Heart of the Empire has taken on new significance during the Coronation celebrations. Within the last few days sightseers, including overseas visitors from all over the world, have assembled there as the start-point for a tour of the decorated streets in the West End. The rather haphazard methods used at the time of the Silver Jubilee have given place to the greatest coordinated scheme ever attempted in London, and the streets have thereby retained their natural dignity. The islands in Piccadilly are decorated with blue, white, gold and red; the pavement masts with red, white, and gold; and the buildings with blue and white.

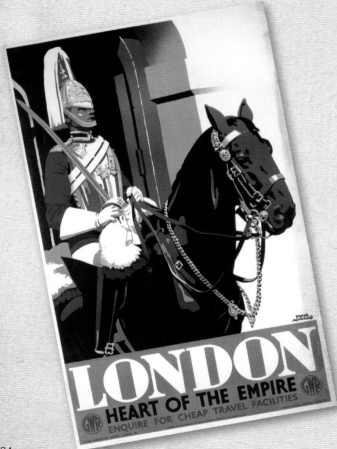

LEFT Frank Newbould's 1939 lithograph used the image of a mounted Life Guard performing ceremonial drill to advertise cheap return tickets to London aboard Great Western Railway trains.

RIGHT The *Illustrated London News* first appeared in May 1842. The first issue contained pictures of the British campaign in Afghanistan, a shipwreck in Canada and a fancy dress ball at Buckingham Palace, setting the tone for its blend of domestic, foreign and imperial news that continued until the 1970s.

THE EMPIRE, DECORATED FOR THE CORONATION

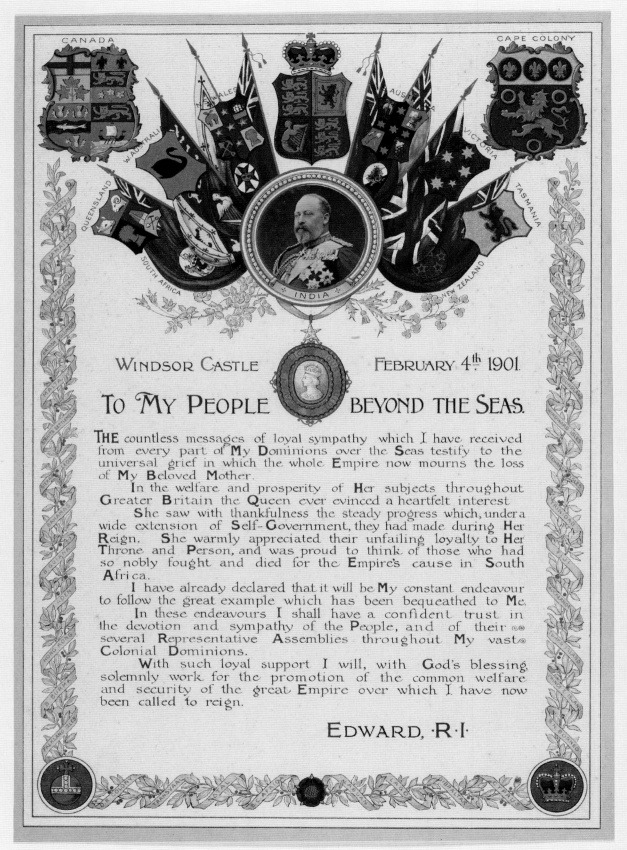

WINDSOR CASTLE   FEBRUARY 4th 1901.

TO MY PEOPLE BEYOND THE SEAS.

THE countless messages of loyal sympathy which I have received from every part of My Dominions over the Seas testify to the universal grief in which the whole Empire now mourns the loss of My Beloved Mother.

In the welfare and prosperity of Her subjects throughout Greater Britain the Queen ever evinced a heartfelt interest. She saw with thankfulness the steady progress which, under a wide extension of Self-Government, they had made during Her Reign. She warmly appreciated their unfailing loyalty to Her Throne and Person, and was proud to think of those who had so nobly fought and died for the Empire's cause in South Africa.

I have already declared that it will be My constant endeavour to follow the great example which has been bequeathed to Me.

In these endeavours I shall have a confident trust in the devotion and sympathy of the People, and of their several Representative Assemblies throughout My vast Colonial Dominions.

With such loyal support I will, with God's blessing, solemnly work for the promotion of the common welfare and security of the great Empire over which I have now been called to reign.

EDWARD · R · I ·

British Dominions beyond the Seas'. This was the iconography and symbolism that lay at the very heart of the British Empire.

Focus of fierce loyalty

The monarch was the focal point of imperial loyalty and the wellspring of all imperial proclamations, all appointments and all honours, from Knight Commander of the British Empire to the Star of India. Being part of the web of empire, in liege to the British monarch, was the major source of legitimacy and power for rulers and administrators throughout the British world. Though the British monarch had little political power, he was indispensable as a symbol of authority, the apex of a global political system, reigning supreme whilst others ruled on his behalf. Parliaments in Britain and the Dominions legislated on behalf of the King with Royal Assent; governments were formed at his invitation and dissolved only with his permission. Viceroys and governors represented the person of the King in their colonial fiefdoms and yielded to no one but him in precedence; maharajahs and mullahs paid homage to the King by paying homage to his plumed and bespurred proconsuls. Imperial administrators were appointed personally by the monarch – Sir Gawain Bell received his Commission of Appointment as Governor of Northern Nigeria signed and smudged by Queen Elizabeth II in person. Military officers held commissions granted by the monarch, received medals from him in recognition of their service, and the might of the Royal Navy assembled at Spithead off the south coast of England to be inspected by him. British citizens travelled the world requesting entry into foreign lands In the Name of His Britannic Majesty.

Loyal toasts were a feature of dinner tables throughout the country and in residences, messes and lodges overseas, as was the National Anthem, played at all manner of public events from football matches to theatre and cinema performances. The Empire's public school administrators encouraged native elites to seek honours whilst maharajahs, sheikhs and African kings competed for gun salutes and hankered after uniforms. Many indigenous rulers yearned for imperial honours and used the occasion of imperial commemorations, particularly coronations, to demonstrate their loyalty and their position within the imperial hierarchy. The Maharajah of Jaipur, for instance, travelled to London for Edward VII's coronation with 125 officers and attendants aboard a privately chartered ship. The Sultan of Perak attended the coronation of Edward VII, whilst the Sultan of Zanzibar trumped all his fellow rulers by attending the coronations of George V, George VI and Elizabeth II.

Queen Victoria and the imperialization of the monarchy

On succeeding her uncle William IV in 1837 Victoria was unknown, even by name, to most of her subjects, a retiring 18-year-old thrust to the apex of society. But by the time of her death in 1901 she had become the best-known figure in the world and its most powerful monarch, and had given her name to an age. Over the

'To My People Beyond the Seas'. A message to the Empire from the new king, Edward VII, dated 4 February 1901, two days after the funeral of his mother. Victoria died with her son, the future king, and her grandson, the German Emperor Wilhelm II, at her bedside. As she disliked black funerals, London was draped in purple and white as she was laid to rest in Windsor Great Park alongside her long-dead husband Albert.

THE SPLENDID ANACHRONISM OF ITS PAGEANTRY AT THE TIME OF GEORGE V'S SILVER JUBILEE AND GEORGE VI'S CORONATION WAS DELIBERATELY PROJECTED AS A POWERFUL AND REASSURING ANTIDOTE TO THE HIGH-TECH PARADES AND SEARCH-LIGHT RALLIES IN MUSSOLINI'S ITALY, STALIN'S RED SQUARE AND HITLER'S NUREMBERG.

– *David Cannadine*, Ornamentalism: How the British Saw Their Empire

course of her 64-year reign she became the centre of a new cult of imperial, national and monarchic devotion and rhetoric. Victoria's reign witnessed a renaissance for the British monarchy and cemented its position at the head of this distinctly imperial great chain of being. The monarchy became a truly imperial institution, most powerfully symbolized by the passage of the Royal Titles Act in 1876 which created Victoria Empress of India, thenceforward the British sovereign sitting as an Eastern potentate, successor to the Mughal emperors of old. During this period books and other publications lionizing the Royal Family became common, gentle but effective propaganda that introduced people to their rulers as private individuals and family-oriented men and women possessing the common touch, enjoying hobbies and sports and pursuing careers familiar to many of their people. This was all part of the domestication of the monarchy that began during Victoria's reign, the sovereign in all her splendour and power brought to the hearth and home of her subjects and firmly attached to the values of a burgeoning middle class.

Victoria's reign coincided with a massive expansion of British power as islands were claimed in the Pacific, Southeast Asia was gathered to the Union Jack, Russian and Turkish ambitions were checked in the Mediterranean, the final wars of conquest took British suzerainty to the entire Indian subcontinent, and Britain emerged from the Scramble for Africa with all the plums. It was not until the reigns of Victoria's successors, however, that large numbers of people overseas got to see their monarch as grand imperial tours became a recognized part of the job.

Empire tours

Empire tours were a key feature of the imperialization of the monarchy, although the sedentary Victoria never managed to visit her imperial subjects save for two trips to Ireland. In the 20th century it became an expected job for the monarch, or his close family, to tour the Empire, leading to remarkable progressions accomplished aboard battleships, trains, open-topped Land Rovers and caparisoned elephants. Official visits from senior members of the Royal Family provided a visible symbol of imperial unity and reinforced the fact that kings and princes in Britain were also kings and princes in Trinidad, Malta, Ceylon, New Zealand and a host of other colonies. King George V set the pace for others to follow, a duty energetically taken up by Queen Elizabeth upon her accession in 1953.

As Duke of Cornwall and York and later as King, George V took imperial touring to a new level as he travelled to the other side of the world on the business of empire. In 1901 he went to Australia to open the Federal Parliament of the new Commonwealth that had united the colonies of New South Wales, Queensland, South Australia, Tasmania, Victoria and Western Australia. A decade later, and

An illustration from *The Prince of Wales' Eastern Book* portraying a scene from the royal tour undertaken by the future Edward VIII in the early 1920s. Entitled 'Arrival of the Prince's White Car through the Strange Cleft', it shows Edward visiting Aden Colony in November 1921. The open-topped sedan is the same vehicle that appears in the photograph on the title page of this book.

Continued on page 92

IMPERIAL HONOURS

Honours were an important feature of the web of empire, helping to cement British authority and bind the political and administrative élites to one another and to a shared duty to the Crown. Accepting an honour put colonial administrators, army officers and rulers in a subordinate relationship to the British monarch, and welded the élites of the white Dominions, India and the colonies into a multiracial imperial ruling class. Reigning kings and queens set great store by the creation of new imperial orders and their administration; George VI was most at ease at investitures, and revived the installation ceremonials associated with the Order of the Garter and the Royal Victorian Order, while Victoria, Edward VII and George V were closely involved in designing and naming the new orders inaugurated during their reigns.

Orders of merit

These imperial orders included the Most Distinguished Order of St Michael and St George, founded in 1818 by the Prince Regent for services rendered during the Napoleonic Wars by the people of the Ionian Islands and Malta. Later in the century, with the Empire expanding rapidly, the Order was made available to those who had rendered distinguished service in the colonies and in foreign affairs. The Order of St Michael and St George, limited to 750 members, became the pre-eminent order of chivalry for those who governed and lived in the British Empire. The Order was based at the Colonial Office in Whitehall with its chapel in St Paul's Cathedral. Luminaries of the Empire could steadily progress through the ranks, from the CMG to the GCMG by way of the KCMG. Prime Ministers of Australia and Canada as well as native rulers such as James Brooke, the White Rajah of Sarawak, Queen Salote of Tonga, the Kabaka of Buganda, Sultan Idris of Perak and the Sultan of Zanzibar all held the Order's highest rank.

The Royal Victorian Order came into being in 1896 to reward personal service to the Crown. In 1917 King George V inaugurated the Most Excellent Order of the British Empire consisting of five classes (GBE, KBE, CBE, OBE, and MBE) and a separate British Empire Medal. Originally the Order's insignia depicted Britannia in the centre, but in 1937 it was altered to incorporate the crowned effigies of Queen Mary and King George V. In 1902 Edward VII instituted the Imperial Service Order, a junior branch of the Order of St Michael and St George. Notable people could expect to 'develop' their collection of honours as their careers progressed. Thus in 1925 Sir Hugh Clifford, an imperial administrator, added the GBE to the GCMG he already possessed; in 1917 the Maharajah of Mysore added a GBE to his Grand Commander of the Star of India; in 1937 the Kabaka of Buganda was given a KBE to add to the KCMG; and Queen Salote of Tonga progressed from DBE (1932) to GBE (1945), GCVO (1953) and CGMG (1965).

Honours in the Raj

In the Raj, an empire within an empire, a whole new system of honours was devised to complement the Order of St Michael and St George in the colonial empire and the Dominions. The Most Exalted Order of the Star of India was established in 1861 and embraced viceroys, Indian Civil Servants and the subcontinent's native princes, the Begum of Bhopal, for instance, posing for photographs in the same elaborate robes and decorations as the Viceroy, Lord Curzon, himself. The Most Eminent Order of the Indian Empire was founded by Victoria in 1878 after she had adopted the title Empress of India, hence the motto 'Imperatricis Auspiciis' – 'Under the Auspices of the Empress'. This was a junior order to the Star of India. The Imperial Order of the Crown of India was introduced in 1878 as an award to ladies only. The Knight Grand Commander was the grandest of all the Indian orders, awarded to the Viceroy and the Indian Princes. The Order's motto was 'Heaven's Light Our Guide', and the decoration itself was made of gold and enamel set with diamonds. The Kaiser-i-Hind award was introduced by Victoria in 1900 for those, irrespective of nationality, colour, creed or sex, who had performed useful public service in India.

Ennoblement also associated the Empire with its social and political hierarchy. Imperial locations began to appear in the titles of ennobled subjects: the Marquess of Dufferin and Ava; Field Marshal the Earl Kitchener of Khartoum and Broome; Earl Roberts of Kandahar, Pretoria and Waterford; Lord Twining of Godalming and Tanganyika; and Lord Mountbatten of Burma. Overseas meanwhile, knighthoods and royal decorations abounded. This was all part of the web of empire, and it is little wonder that Burke felt compelled to publish a *Genealogical and Heraldic Dictionary of the Peerage and Baronetage of the British Empire*.

A photomontage from the late 19th century shows a group of the principal maharajahs of the British Raj in all their finery. The first row (left to right) depicts the rulers of: Gwalior (in the white cape with the Star of India) Hyderabad (white turban and sash) and Mysore. In the second row (l to r) stand the maharajahs of Bikaner, Jodhpur and Karoli.

WE ARE UP A LITTLE EARLIER THAN USUAL THIS MORNING, IN ORDER TO GET A GLIMPSE OF BEAUTIFUL CEYLON AS SOON AS POSSIBLE … UNDER THE USUAL SALUTE FROM THE WARSHIPS AND THE FORT WE PASS INTO THE SPACIOUS HARBOUR, AND ARE MOORED AHEAD OF THE *HIGHFLYER*, THE FLAGSHIP OF ADMIRAL BOSANQUET, COMMANDER-IN-CHIEF OF THE EAST INDIES SQUADRON. AT NOON THEIR ROYAL HIGHNESSES GO ASHORE, THE DUKE IN WHITE NAVAL UNIFORM. THE ROYAL BARGE THREADS ITS WAY QUICKLY AMONG THE IRONCLADS, GAILY DRESSED AND FIRING THE CUSTOMARY SALUTE … AT THE LANDING-STAGE THE DUKE AND DUCHESS SHAKE HANDS WITH THE GOVERNOR, SIR WEST RIDGEWAY, THE ADMIRAL, AND OTHER CHIEF OFFICIALS, CIVIL, NAVAL AND MILITARY, AND ARE CONDUCTED TO A LARGE PANDAL OF THE RECEPTION-HALL TYPE, THRONGED WITH ALL THE LEADING PEOPLE OF THE PLACE. THE NATIVES ARE IN A DECIDED MAJORITY, AND THEY CONTRIBUTE BY THE VARIETY AND BRILLIANCY OF THEIR COSTUMES, MUCH MORE THAN THE EUROPEANS, TO THE PICTURESQUENESS OF THE SCENE. THE MOST INTENSELY ORIENTAL PART OF THE CROWD IS A LARGE GROUP OF BUDDHIST PRIESTS, WITH SHAVEN HEADS AND SAFFRON ROBES.

– Sir Donald Mackenzie Wallace, The Web of Empire: A Diary of the Imperial Tour of Their Royal Highnesses the Duke and Duchess of Cornwall and York in 1901

To commemorate the 1924 Empire Exhibition, Lipton's produced a brass tea caddy showing an image of the British Lion and bearing the words 'British Empire Exhibition 1924'.

now as King, he travelled to India. In the company of his Queen, Mary, George broke all precedent and took centre-stage at the iconic pageant of the Grand Durbar (see page 94). Even the idea of permanently stationing royals in the Dominions was mooted. While this was never formalized, senior royals did serve overseas. The Duke of Connaught, Victoria's favourite son, served as Governor-General of Canada from 1911 to 1916, the Earl of Athlone served as Governor-General in both Canada and South Africa, and the Duke of Gloucester, the King's younger brother, became Governor-General of Australia in 1945. Royal tours also presented opportunities for high-level state diplomacy, such as George VI's visit to Canada and America in 1939 which helped woo the American public towards Britain's side in the forthcoming conflict with Germany.

Acknowledging the Empire's great sacrifice

Two of the most memorable Empire Tours were undertaken by George V's sons, the future kings Edward VIII and his more retiring, stammering brother Prince Albert, who became George VI after Edward abdicated in 1936. These globetrotting ceremonial and diplomatic pageants were celebrated in lavish photo-books published for popular consumption. In the early 1920s, still the carefree playboy prince, Edward toured the Empire aboard the battlecruiser HMS *Renown* for a series of highly-publicized tours intended as a 'thank you' to the Empire for its stalwart support during the First World War.

During *Renown*'s four-month voyage the Prince of Wales visited Newfoundland, every province of the Dominion of Canada from Nova Scotia to British Columbia, and made a two week visit to New York and Washington DC. Pictures show the Prince dressed as an Indian Chief, inspecting war veterans, placing wreaths, addressing vast crowds, receiving gun salutes, fishing at the Virgin Falls, canoeing down the Nipigon, watching cowboys rope steers at the Saskatoon Stampede, laying the cornerstone of Parliament Buildings in Ottawa, and receiving a tickertape welcome in New York.

The Prince's second Empire Tour was dedicated to Australia, New Zealand and the colonies of the West Indies and the Pacific. His third and final tour was the longest of them all, lasting for eight months, during which time the Prince covered 41,000 miles (65,600 km) by land and sea. A full four months were spent in India and one month in Japan, Britain's Eastern ally during the 1914–18 war.

During the outward and homeward voyages, the Prince visited all the British possessions strung along the great highway between Gibraltar and the Pacific. He inaugurated the new Constitution at Malta, and saw the work accomplished by good government in such remote places as Aden and Borneo. He was guest of the King of Egypt at Cairo and of the American government in the Philippines. He traversed India from sea to sea and from Madras to the borders of Afghanistan; he travelled through the heart of Burma and into the mysterious kingdom of Nepal.

Globetrotting in grand style

Later in the 1920s it was the turn of Edward's younger brother, Prince Albert, to become a royal globetrotter. Like his brother, Albert's voyages were widely reported in newspapers, cinema newsreels and through plush commemorative books published at home and overseas. Service in the Navy had given the Prince his first experience of the vast Empire over which he would one day rule, including visits to Cuba, Bermuda, Newfoundland, Tenerife, Barbados, Martinique, Jamaica and other West Indian islands. The Duke's first tour took place in 1924 when he visited Kenya, Uganda and the Sudan in the company of his new wife, Elizabeth. Alighting from the P&O steamer *Mulbera*, they were welcomed at Mombasa by Kikuyu stilt-walkers and presented with an elephant's tusk with an Arabic address of welcome inside and a gold coin on a red ribbon.

Then came the wonderful journey to Nairobi past the 17,000-ft (5180-metre) high Mount Kenya, through game country where herds of giraffe, antelope, wildebeest and elephants could be seen from the train, with another huge mountain, Kilimanjaro, visible in the distance … At Khartoum – the streets of the new city laid out in the form of a Union Jack – there was much excitement, with illuminations and entertainments, and the desert said farewell in a blinding sandstorm, which detained them on the Suez Canal for 12 hours.

In May Albert and Elizabeth reached Canberra and the great white Parliament House, where 50,000 attended the ceremonial opening, performed by the duke with a golden key. The duke unveiled a statue of his father, George V, who, on the very same day in 1901, had opened the first Federal Parliament of Australia. Albert carried with him a present from the king in the form of two

The lyrics of 'God Save the Queen' appeared on the reverse side of Raphael Tuck & Sons commemorative bookmark, produced as a souvenir of Queen Victoria's Diamond Jubilee in 1897.

Continued on page 96

JUBILEES AND DURBARS

Victoria's status at the centre of the Empire's ceremonial life was symbolized by two great imperial extravaganzas; the jubilees of 1887 and 1897. Her Golden Jubilee centred on a thanksgiving service in Westminster Abbey attended by representatives from all over the Empire. Services were held at the same time in chapels, churches and synagogues around the world. From St George's Chapel, Windsor, the Queen pressed an electric button which telegraphed a Jubilee message around the Empire: 'From my heart I thank my beloved people. May God bless them'.

The spectacular Diamond Jubilee
The jubilee of 1897 marking the 60th anniversary of Victoria's enthronement was even more splendid. The Queen's position at the centre of the British Empire was captured in a popular poster that showed her unlovely face surrounded by scenes from Canada, South Africa, Australia and India. The Queen processed through the bunting and flag festooned streets of the imperial capital, attended by 50,000 troops drawn from her imperial domains. A Thanksgiving Service was held on the steps of St Paul's Cathedral. Edward Elgar composed an 'Imperial March', which later became 'Pomp and Circumstance, March No. 1'. From the telegraph office at Buckingham Palace on 22 June Queen Victoria sent a message to her subjects across the globe before joining the procession through the streets of London, flanked by representatives from all over the Empire. The Prime Minister of Canada was knighted; an Imperial Fête took place in Regent's Park; and an Imperial Ballet was performed at Her Majesty's Theatre. Similar events were held, and triumphal arches erected, throughout the Empire.

Paying homage to the monarch over the seas
Durbars were held to commemorate the coronation of new British monarchs and originated during Victoria's reign ('durbar' meaning a court or state reception, from Hindi *darbar*; in Persian a ruler's court, *dar* – portal, *bar* - court). These were massive and splendid affairs in which all ranks of the Indian nobility and of colonial society presented themselves, in strict order of precedence, to the King-Emperor or his viceregal representatives. The Prince of Wales had visited India in 1876, and the Proclamation Durbar marking Victoria's accession as Empress of India took place on 1 January 1877. The event was organized by the Viceroy, Lord Lytton, son of the novelist who had Gothicized Knebworth House and the perfect choreographer for this neo-traditional extravaganza. In 1903 a durbar was held to proclaim Victoria's successor Edward VII, an even more splendid affair organized by Viceroy Lord Curzon.

The 1911 Delhi Durbar
These early efforts, however, were completely overshadowed by the durbar organized for George V. For the pseudo-medieval spectacular of the 1911 Coronation Durbar a temporary city was constructed outside the old Mughal capital at Delhi, a sea of tents and caravans with a purpose-built amphitheatre, decorated with banners, coats of arms and bunting. The 1911 Durbar was attended by the new monarch, George V, himself, and he used the occasion to announce the construction of a new capital city for the British Raj, to be designed by Sir Edwin Lutyens and Sir Herbert Baker and named New Delhi. For the ceremony the King insisted on wearing the newly-made imperial crown crafted by Garrard & Company, the Crown Jewellers. The Imperial Crown of India cost £60,000 to make and was covered with emeralds, rubies, sapphires and over 6100 diamonds. It weighed about two pounds, and hurt the King's neck (and has not been used since). After the spectacular durbar ceremony, the Royal couple appeared on the balcony of the Red Fort, where they were fêted (or at least, seen) by over half a million people. These durbars became associated with the bestowal of honours, occasions on which the monarch awarded decorations and medals to deserving subjects. The 1877 Durbar was marked by the inauguration of the Empress of India Medal, and on the occasion of the 1911 Durbar 200 gold and 30,000 silver medals were distributed.

Pure theatre
Durbars were moments of high imperial theatre and symbolism, and were replicated all along the chain of imperial authority. During his tenure as Viceroy of India, for example, Lord Curzon decided to strengthen Britain's presence in the Persian Gulf in the face of growing Russian influence. To this end he toured the Gulf sheikhdoms in 1903, Edward's VII's durbar year, intent on demonstrating British power and prestige and reaffirming the alliances that secured British paramountcy. The Sultan of Oman and Muscat swore 'eternal devotion and fidelity' to the Crown, and a durbar was staged aboard HMS *Argonaut*. Photographs of the event show Curzon enthroned upon a dais beneath a canvas awning, flanked by advisers laden with medals and ceremonial swords, while the Gulf sheikhs sit barefoot on the floor before them.

All colonial territories went in for durbar-style public events to mark royal occasions and strengthen the links between indigenous rulers and élites and the great unifying sovereign in Britain. On their return journey from the Indian durbar in 1911, for example, the king and queen visited the Sudan. Here British imperial symbolism was used as a catalyst for large-scale imperial display, later reworked into the unique annual spectacle known as King's Day. Further south the 1911 Coronation was also marked in Northern Rhodesia, where the governor summoned all the Ngoni chiefs to a Coronation Day fête involving the native police band, a robed Anglican priest and a saluting flag. 'There were four huge bonfires, around which some hundreds of dusky natives capered and danced'.

For the 1937 Coronation Edward Twining organized celebrations in Uganda involving a military tattoo and a firework display, during the course of which the governor pressed a button which set off 50 rockets. A bugler sounded the retreat into the darkness and then 40 spotlights, floodlights and footlights shone out. Then schoolboys performed the 'Parade of the Toy Soldiers' wearing red tunics and white pillbox hats, and 120 warriors in leopard skins and ostrich feathers, wielding spears and shields, performed a war dance. There was then a showing of 'From Savage to Soldier', describing the process of turning natives into soldiers. 'The central event, and the sensation of the evening, was a relay of the voice of the new King-Emperor, broadcast to the gathering through concealed loudspeakers'.

Members of the royal party, including the Viceroy of India, Lord Curzon, are carried high on howdahs mounted on elephants' backs during the Imperial Durbar held at Delhi in 1903, which celebrated the coronation of King Edward VII and Queen Alexandra as Emperor and Empress of India. The durbar comprised two weeks of festivities. Edward VII did not attend but sent his brother the Duke of Connaught as his official representative.

dispatch cases exactly like those used in the House of Commons. On the return voyage *Renown* put in at Mauritius, hosting the Governor and select dignitaries beneath a sun awning on the deck, before following the coast of Africa to the Red Sea and Suez Canal, with last stops at Malta and Gibraltar. *Renown* anchored off Spithead on 27 June, ending a tour of six months' duration. The battlecruiser deposited its royal passengers and a menagerie of new pets for the princesses, including 20 parrots. As had been the case for his brother Prince Edward, large crowds and a public ceremony of welcome awaited Albert and his wife when they reached London.

As King George VI, Albert undertook a new world and Empire tour that began in America and Canada in the summer of 1939. However, the worsening situation in Europe meant that the tour had to be broken off. It resumed in 1947 when the royal family visited South Africa, the High Commission Territories of Basutoland, Bechuanaland and Swaziland and Southern Rhodesia, travelling north from the Cape on board the White Train. At Lobatse in Bechuanaland, restyled 'Royal Lobatse' for the occasion, the royal family alighted, and were met by the Governor and Chiefs Tshekedi Khama and Bathoen II, both attired in ornate uniforms modelled on those of the Life Guards. Ill health prevented George VI from further tours, though on her accession to the throne in 1953 his daughter Elizabeth took up this duty with great determination. No sooner had the coronation been completed, than the Queen and Prince Philip embarked upon a lengthy imperial tour.

Maintaining a hallowed tradition

Queen Elizabeth II has subsequently toured overseas more than any previous monarch. Though the British Empire had largely disappeared by 1977, the Queen's Silver Jubilee was a remarkably global affair, celebrated throughout the Commonwealth and the numerous remaining colonies, now officially referred to as dependent territories. This was because she had devoted herself to Commonwealth affairs. As *The Country Life Book of the Royal Silver Jubilee* put it:

> *Both the Queen and Prince Philip are Commonwealth minded. The bonds that exist between Britain and the overseas Commonwealth countries are strengthened by personal ties forged by the royal family's many visits. Previous sovereigns did not make anything like so many of these tours.*

So the imperial monarch was a central feature in the rhetoric and representation of the British Empire, the maypole around which all of the Empire's ruling princes and governors circled. On the ground, however, the monarch was represented by a host of administrators working in tandem with indigenous chiefs, princes, sultans and sheikhs, and it is to the level of direct imperial rule that we now turn our attention, in order to investigate the manner in which the British perceived their Empire and governed it.

The Queen and Prince Philip began a tour of the Empire as soon as the coronation, and a tour of the British Isles, had been completed. On a visit to Nigeria in 1955 she met emirs in the north of the country. This photograph of the event appeared in the 1957 *Commonwealth and Empire Annual.*

A World to Govern: District Commissioners, Chiefs and Whitehall

LIKE THE ROMANS, THE BRITISH RULED THEIR EMPIRE through proconsuls, provincial governors, district commissioners and clerks, backed up by scattered platoons of troops and, somewhere nearby, the reassuring presence of a sloop or cruiser.

His Excellency the Marquess of Linlithgow, in his robes of state as Viceroy of India, with Lady Linlithgow and their princely attendants. Linlithgow, who was governor-general and viceroy from 1936 to 1943, presided over a period of growing tension between the British administration and the Indian Congress Party. His unilateral commitment of India to the Second World War without consulting nationalist leaders sparked a damaging campaign of civil disobedience – the 'Quit India' movement.

The classic image of British rule in the colonies is provided by the District Commissioner, usually visualized in pith helmet and bush shorts, or perhaps a Governor, resplendent in the white dress uniform of the Colonial Administrative Service. But there was more to the civil services that ran the British Empire than baggy shorts, plumed helmets and *stengahs* on the verandah as the sun went down. Moreover, the notion that administering colonies was all about beating the natives by day and working through a bottle of spirits by night is wildly inaccurate, though the belief that the Empire was 'nasty, brutish and in shorts' has been a difficult one to counter. It is fortunate, therefore, that so many former district officers and provincial governors have set down their memoirs, leaving a precious record of day-to-day imperial administration. This is not, of course, to suggest that there were no discreditable aspects of colonial administration. For some, indeed, colonial rule, no matter how benign, could never be anything other than iniquitous and immoral. The writer George Orwell, himself an employee of the colonial state, serving in the Indian Imperial Police in Burma, was of this opinion:

> *I had already made up my mind that imperialism was an evil thing and the sooner I chucked up my job and got out of it the better. Theoretically – and secretly, of course – I was all for the Burmese and all against their oppressors, the British.*

Perks and drawbacks

Colonial administration was not easy or lavishly paid work, though the idea that administrators were handsomely paid to lord it over the natives has proved a hardy one, dating from the early days of the East India Company when 'shaking the pagoda tree' was an accepted form of self-enrichment. This episode in British colonial administration came to an end in the early 19th century when it became a contentious moral issue in Britain as well as a question of power, because *nouveau riche* nabobs could convert their ill-gotten guineas into country houses and broad-acred estates at a time when land equalled political power. By the 20th century,

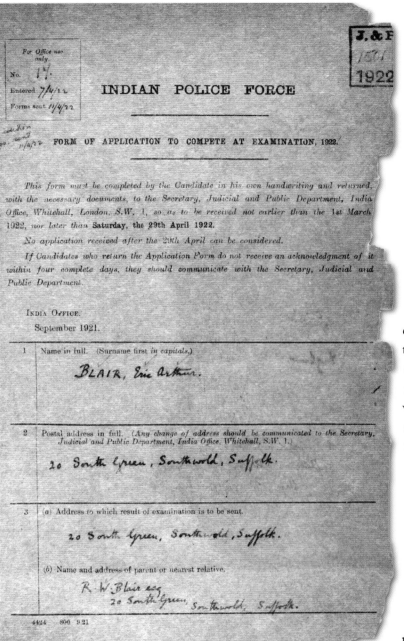

George Orwell's application form to join the Indian Imperial Police in Burma in 1922, under his real name of Eric Blair. A successful applicant, Eton-educated Orwell served in Burma from 1922 to 1927. The time he spent there inspired the novel *Burmese Days* (1934) and the essay 'Shooting an Elephant' (1936), in which he gave vent to his ambivalent feelings about imperial rule: 'With one part of my mind I thought of the British Raj as an unbreakable tyranny, as something clamped down … upon the will of prostrate peoples; with another part I thought that the greatest joy in the world would be to drive a bayonet into a Buddhist priest's guts'.

colonial civil servants were well rewarded for their work, but still led less luxurious lives than expatriate business communities and faced numerous trials – of separation and illness – that were alien to their confreres in the home civil service, banking or industry. There might be numerous perks – a verandahed house with servants and a large garden, local leave on Zanzibar reached by dhow from the Swahili coast – but there were also considerable drawbacks. Homesickness was a constant companion, as was lengthy separation from children and innumerable threats to health. The graveyards of Britain's former colonies still bear testament to the high mortality rates that cut off many of these overseas Britons in their prime. In particular, until effective anti-malarial drugs were developed, West Africa was known as the white man's grave because of the heavy toll that it took on British civil and military personnel stationed there.

Millions governed by hundreds

Colonial civil servants dispatched from Britain formed a dedicated, hard-working and highly professional cadre that successfully governed millions of people, in the process creating proto-nations and leaving behind political structures that endure to the present day. For generations the Colonial Service, the Indian Civil Service and specialist organizations such as the Sudan Political Service, provided a distinct career path for young Britons and their peers born in the Dominions. For this

SUDDENLY A PUFF OF WIND, A PUFF FAINT AND TEPID AND LADEN WITH
STRANGE ODOURS OF BLOSSOMS, OF AROMATIC WOOD, COMES OUT OF THE STILL
NIGHT – THE FIRST SIGH OF THE EAST ON MY FACE. THAT I CAN NEVER
FORGET. IT WAS IMPALPABLE AND ENSLAVING, LIKE A CHARM, LIKE A
WHISPERED PROMISE OF MYSTERIOUS DELIGHT.

– Joseph Conrad, Youth *(1902)*

select band of young men the Empire offered the most challenging and exciting
job imaginable, governing and administering diverse peoples in alliance with
indigenous political authorities such as the sultans of protected Malay states and
Northern Nigerian emirs who had accepted British residents or advisers on the
Indian pattern. These élite civil services were always small in size, though they
relied upon a host of indigenous officials. The ICS was staffed by a maximum of
1250 British officers (in the 1930s), ruling over a population of 353 million. The
1931 census, however, recorded as many as a million Indian government employees.
In the 1930s British Africa's population stood at 43 million, the
Colonial Service at 1200 officers.

This form of patron–client relationship was the cornerstone of
British colonial rule, and all round the world the British sought to
ally with native aristocracies, desirous of a form of enlightened
feudalism as the bedrock of settled administration. Arthur
Hamilton Gordon, Governor of Ceylon between 1883 and 1890,
treated high-born members of the Goyigma caste as a traditional
aristocracy and vested them with power as paramount chiefs. Much
later, this vision of traditional Ceylonese society had changed little.
Patrick Gordon Walker, Secretary of State for Commonwealth
Relations (1950–1), compared the extremely rich landowners
wielding local power and influence with Whig landlords in the
era of George III. As well as finding comfort in social structures
that they thought they recognized and could work with, the
image of the lone white man bringing peace and justice to
benighted natives preened the vanity of the British, and
confirmed their belief in their own indispensability. As
Winston Churchill wrote of the District Commissioner at
Embo in 1908:

*150 soldiers and police. Two young white officers – a civilian
and a soldier – preside from this centre of authority, far from
the telegraph, over the peace and order of an area as large as
an English county, and regulate the conduct and fortunes of
some 75,000 natives, who have never previously known or
acknowledged any law but violence and terror.*

A Yoruba wooden caricature
(*c*.1930s) of the District
Officer of Ondo Province
in Nigeria. The figure, seated
at his desk and shown in
avuncular pose, smoking a
pipe, is believed to be Mr
B.J.A. Matthews, although
the (unknown) carver has
given him pronouncedly
African features.

Continued on page 104

101

BRITISH RULE AND TRADITION

British rule projected onto Africa, Asia and Pacific islands a view of a stable, hierarchical society such as had supposedly existed in a more ordered English past when God was in his heaven, the rich man in his castle and the poor man picturesque and deferential at his gate. Colonial societies were seen as traditional and organic and governed by time-hallowed social relations of the kind that the Industrial Revolution and mass democracy had eroded in Britain, and that therefore had to be preserved overseas and protected from the ravages of modernity.

Benign feudalism

It was an image of *noblesse oblige* in an idyllic rural setting. When encountering societies overseas as yet 'untainted' by modern urban life, the British heart skipped a beat. When they identified a 'natural' aristocracy or monarchy, they thought only to ally with it, and use it as the basis of their benign rule. Where they could not find such a system, they strove to create one. Romantic escapists gushed about the nobility of Marsh Arabs or the Bedouin. They looked to utilize pre-existing kings and rulers – the Ashantehene in the Northern Territories of the Gold Coast, the sultans of Malaya and India's nizams and maharajahs. Where suitable rulers did not exist, the British created them, actually founding new monarchies through which to rule in Middle Eastern lands such as Iraq and Jordan and creating 'blanket' chiefs among African societies to which central authority was unknown. Given this patronage, it was no surprise that these rulers, bolstered and in some cases actually invented by the British, became their staunch allies. King Faisal II of Iraq was known for his British ways, his cars, aircraft, clothes, hunters, foxhounds and even his swans, while Chief Tshekedi Khama of the Bangwato in the Bechuanaland Protectorate realized that it was British rule grafted onto traditional African ruling structures that gave him his power.

The upshot of all this chief- and king-making was the creation of a global élite and an ordered system of administration and rule, subject to the overarching presence of the British monarchy. Yet this reliance on chiefs and kings ended as decolonization gathered pace, and the British turned to the educated élites and demoted their erstwhile partners. This marooned previous allies as the nationalists gained the keys to the political future.

Thus, for example, the King of Buganda, Sir Edward 'Freddie' Mutesa II, was deposed and exiled from Uganda by the British governor in 1953, a move designed to encourage the

ABOVE A drawing of a Maori chief and his wife printed in the *Pictorial Review* in 1846. At this time wars were being fought in New Zealand as settlers encroached onto Maori land.

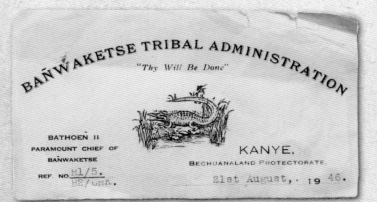

LEFT A letterhead from the desk of Chief Bathoen II, hereditary ruler of the Banwaketse tribe in the Bechuanaland Protectorate, sent in the 1940s from the tribal capital of Kanye. Note the tribal motto – 'Thy Will Be Done' – reflecting the success of the London Missionary Society in this part of Africa; and the crocodile, the tribal totem. Chief Bathoen II and his headmen worked hand-in-hand with the District Commissioner Kanye as they administered the Banwaketse Reserve. This was how colonial rule operated at grassroots level.

LONG LIVE THE KABAKA
KABAKA MUTESA II

POLICE

1100 404

Amid popular jubilation, the motorcade of the Kabaka of Buganda, Mutesa II sweeps into Kampala on the monarch's return to Uganda from exile in Britain in 1955.

growth of Ugandan national identity (as opposed to Bugandan separatism) as a prelude to eventual independence and rule by the educated élite. Freddie's 2-year exile, subsidized by the British government, was spent in a suite at the Savoy Hotel. He soon resumed some of his old Cambridge ways and became a familiar sight in Mayfair's swankiest bars and clubs. But his popularity had been boosted by his clash with the governor, and he returned to rule Buganda in 1955 and become independent Uganda's first president in 1962.

Wrong-footed by nationalists

Britain's failure to properly manage this shift from colonial states ruled by chiefs to nation-states under democratically elected leaders lies at the root of the post-independence problems of many of today's nations. Elsewhere, British-backed rulers were swept away by the rising tide of nationalism in the 1950s. In the Middle East, the rise of 'the colonels' destroyed monarchies and hence British collaborative arrangements in Egypt, Iraq and Libya.

Ruling by proxy

In Africa the practice of working through indigenous élites and their 'native administrations' came to be known as Indirect Rule, a system enshrined in the writings of Frederick (later Lord) Lugard in Nigeria. Indirect Rule, which was later extended to other parts of British Africa, was a classic case of the British elevating a necessity (ruling in alliance with chiefs because they were too few to do it alone) into a virtue (Indirect Rule was cast as a masterstroke demonstrating the natural ability of Britons to rule 'lesser' races). This approach also owed much to centuries of experience in India, where, in David Cannadine's words, the British had 'latched on to caste as the analogue of their own carefully ranked domestic status hierarchy'. This led them to embrace the 500-plus princely states, essentially feudal kingdoms, the British choosing men of property and rank to act as the leaders of society, British residents and political agents operating as discreetly as possible in the background. The princely states ranged from Lilliputian princi-palities to the vast domains of Hyderabad and Kashmir and constituted some two-fifths of Indian territory. In the Middle East meanwhile the British displayed a deepening attachment to the Arab world and its patrician values. On the Arabian peninsula and in the Persian Gulf the British made treaties with the Sultan of Muscat, with the Sheikhs of the Trucial Coast of Oman, with the ruler of Bahrain and with the sheikhs of Qatar and Kuwait. Here men with a 'a lifelong craving for barbaric splendour, for savagery and colour and the throb of drums', with a 'lasting veneration for long-established customs and ritual' and a 'deep-seated resentment of western innovation in other lands', could find their place. These were just the men wanted as colonial administrators the world over, hand-picked by the likes of Sir Ralph Furse, the Colonial Service's recruiter-in-chief, who viewed society as hierarchical and rural, a man of yesteryear's squirearchy building anew in Britain's overseas fiefdoms.

A piece of regimental silver, crafted by the London firm of Asprey's, and presented to the Joint Services Command and Staff College by His Majesty King Hussein I, ruler of the Hashemite Kingdom of Jordan, on the occasion of his visit in April 1981. King Hussein's dynasty was created by the British after the First World War. Hussein went to school at Harrow, where he was friends with his cousin, King Faisal II of Iraq, another British monarchical creation. He later attended the Royal Military Academy at Sandhurst.

Becoming a district commissioner

What inspired men to seek to make their careers overseas? For some, it was the simple desire for adventure and to get away from Britain. Bill Harrison, who became a tin prospector in the jungles of Malaya and Siam, wanted 'to escape from offices, factories, streets of houses and the general hubbub of life in England. I was looking forward to another kind of adventure – to seeing foreign places, climbing mountains, sailing up rivers and exploring.' Most young

men entered the civil services which ran the Empire without really knowing what they were doing. It was likely that a casual suggestion from a tutor, an eye-catching advertisement, or a youth spent reading the *Boy's Own Paper* first turned one's thoughts towards an imperial career. John Ainley, later a Colonial Service agricultural officer, learned of an opening in East Africa through an advertisement placed by the Crown Agents in the *Farmer and Stockbreeder*. Others cited the film *Sanders of the River* as having exerted a powerful influence when they pondered what on earth to do with their lives after university or national service. Sometimes it was a relative who offered encouragement. In the late 1920s Sjovald Cunyngham-Brown mentioned to his uncle and friends the possibility that he might win an Eastern Cadetship (for service in Ceylon, Hong Kong or Malaya) and was told:

> *Good God, if you're offered that, take it. The great island empires of the East. The Eastern archipelago, Malaya, half unexplored; a land of adventure: beautiful people, charming surroundings, tigers, elephants … All the riches of the East, loaded with romance and with things still worthwhile doing. Take it if you get the chance.*

Even most well-educated Britons, however, knew little about the Empire and its basic geography. John Baxter left a London office after a successful interview and bumped into an old school friend, who greeted him thus:

'Hullo, John, what are you doing?'

'I've just got a job in North Borneo.'

The Prince of Wales, the future King Edward VIII (far right), tiger shooting from the back of an elephant in Nepal during his second Empire Tour, 1921 (see page 93). This photograph appeared in *George V and Edward VIII, A Royal Souvenir*, by F.G.H. Salusbury, published by the *Daily Express* to mark the latter's coronation in 1936.

'Where's that?'

'I'm going off to get a map to see.'

In 1925 Edward Banks had just completed his degree at Oxford. A professor said, 'Well, they need a curator out in Rajah Brooke's museum in Sarawak. Does anybody want the job?'. Banks applied, knowing nothing about it or where Sarawak was. Nonetheless, he was interviewed by the Rajah's brother, and got the job.

Recruitment and interview

In the case of Harry Mitchell, a District Officer in Sierra Leone, the Colonial Service was a second choice after a desired opening in the Foreign Office had failed to materialize. As it turned out, it was a very good second choice, saving this particular individual from the horrors of a career selling ladies' underwear for Marks and Spencer. For some men the Colonial Service was a very deliberate career choice, and at top universities it was a leading recruiter with good connections to colleges, individual tutors and careers services. The Colonial Office application form was sent off in a speculative frame of mind, and time and time again the candidate who entered 'Cyprus or East Africa' when asked to express a preference for a posting ended up in Guiana or Malaya. Once the Colonial Office had made up its august mind, the candidate was informed of the decision ('You have been allocated Uganda') and given instructions on how to proceed.

The interview involved a visit to London and what Harold Macmillan described as 'the cool dignity of the old Colonial Office in Downing Street … The vast caverns of the Colonial Office building, where light seldom penetrated and ghostly steps echoed down the lofty corridors as in the aisles of some great cathedral.' The young hopeful would face a tweed-suited figure and perhaps a sun-tanned DC home on leave. If fortunate enough to be selected as a cadet following the interview there was a 'strip down to your underpants' medical, followed by a return home and a period of anticipation, heightened by receipt of the letter confirming appointment as a cadet District Officer at the starting salary of around £350 per annum (at 1940s prices).

ON TOUR

Touring was very important and supposed to occupy at least three months per year. Memoirs linger over the joys of the first safari, the first encounter with the 'real' Africa or India, an unforgettable experience for young men fresh from suburban Britain and the universities and public schools.

By camel, elephant and horse

District officer Michael Longford, of Westminster and Trinity College Cambridge, soon learned not to go on safari with his plasters, antiseptic cream and aspirin secured in a chocolate tin bearing the brand name 'Black Magic'. In Sind the camel was used for district tours; David Symington, an assistant collector, had seven baggage camels and one for riding. Others went by elephant. On the North-East Frontier Geoffrey Allen toured the Himalayas on foot accompanied by hundreds of porters. Cuthbert Bowder, touring in India's Great Plains, wrote:

The tents were rather like big tops … After breakfast you got on to your horse and you rode off to inspect the canals. Then you came back at about one o'clock and lunch would be ready for you. You'd probably have a pink gin or something just before, and then you'd read the papers and rest until half-past-two when you went to your office table and conducted interviews with various people, peasants and the landed gentry, until four o'clock. At four o'clock you took the gun and a couple of men and you got the odd partridge or pea-fowl or hare, just enough to keep the pot boiling … Then you came back and had a grand tea of hot buttered toast before a roaring fire. The sunsets were very beautiful but very short-lived and almost immediately after darkness clamped down. After tea, back again to the office table where I used to work until dinner.

A dozen or more local cooks, servants, guides, district messengers, tribal policemen and hired porters made up the caravan of the British official on tour. In Africa, the colonial official of the First World War era was armed and used to life in the saddle: Captain E. Salmon, patrolling in October 1914 in the Okavango Delta and the Caprivi Strip, travelled with a party of 50 NCOs and men, a Maxim gun, 19 African porters, two boats, a wagon and 20,000 rounds of .303 Lee Enfield ammunition. His inter-war successor was unarmed, usually rode in a truck and was increasingly deskbound.

The many delights of safari

Life on tour held many delights – the joy of being in the bush, the splash in the canvas washstand and the hiss of the Tilley lamp after a tiring day's march, and then turning in for the night, to the distant cry of the hyena and the quadraphonic call of the bullfrogs. And so to sleep, listening to Africa (as opposed to 'seeing Africa', a euphemism for urinating).

From the 1940s the Land Rover became a ubiquitous feature of life on tour, with 'DC Kasomba' or whatever it might be stencilled on the door. Some DCs even managed to obtain aircraft. Yet in many parts of the Empire things remained pretty basic right up until independence. Telephones were a rarity; until the end of empire, the bush telegraph was usually the fastest way to send a message, while foot safaris remained important and canoes, camels and motor launches kept their place as essential modes of transport for the colonial administrator on walkabout.

Pictured in early 1936, as tensions along the border with Abyssinia (Ethiopia) rose following the Italian invasion of that country the previous year, a Somaliland Camel Corps detachment patrols the frontier, led by a British officer.

LORD CREWE AND THE CONCUBINES

In 1909 the Colonial Secretary, bowing to public pressure concerning the morals of British officials overseas, issued the famous 'concubinage circular' or 'immoral relations memo'. The Purity Campaign argued that in the interests of racial survival and 'setting a good example' to the natives nothing less than the most conspicuous sexual restraint was necessary. A high-profile case involving a Kenyan district official, native women and letters to *The Times* further spurred the government to comment, if not particularly strenuous action. At the start of the 20th century, according to the imperial historian Ronald Hyam, 'although concubinage with local women was no longer the fashion in India and the white dominions, it was still widely practised in certain parts of the empire by members of the British colonial services, as well as by white traders, railway engineers and unmarried settlers'.

Lord Crewe's memorandum forbade the practice of keeping 'native women', the 'sleeping dictionaries' or 'talking pillows' that provided companionship, local education and sex. This was the final nail in the coffin for an older tradition of cohabitation that had developed in India early on, when East India Company men wore indigenous costume and lived with indigenous women. Yet Victorian values were bound to erode such freedom and cross-cultural intercourse. As Lord Crewe wrote:

These illicit connections have at times been a cause of trouble with native populations ... I regard such conduct as both injurious and dangerous to the public service ... It is not possible for any member of the administration to countenance such practices without lowering himself in the eyes of the natives, and diminishing his authority.

During the Victorian years this sentiment had become more generally accepted. Institutions such as the Army, though never enshrining it officially, applied similar standards, and even as late as the 1980s officers of the Brigade of Gurkhas were forbidden from marrying non-white women.

Kitted out for the colonies

Joining the ranks of those destined to govern Britain's vast imperial estate brought a great many surprises, and they could begin even at this early stage. In the 1930s men bound for Ceylon still received a document entitled 'Eastern No. 126 Notes for the Information of Candidates Appointed to Ceylon'. Among other things, this advised them to 'purchase a horse on arrival in Ceylon; bowler hats never worn – buy an Ellwood helmet with puggaree or a pigsticker helmet, evening dress, a deck chair, a rifle, a motor cycle and a camp bed'. Instructions were followed as closely as the budget allowed, as white colonial service uniform, shorts, safari suit, sola topees, cummerbunds and canvas this-and-that were purchased.

Gieves of Old Bond Street was a favourite destination for those seeking pith helmets, Palm Beach suits and duck clothes, while those up at Oxford had a tropical outfitters on their doorstep in the form of Walters of Turl Street. Many a callow recruit was sold a good deal of superfluous equipment by colonial outfitters and equipped with expensive 'must haves' that were subsequently never used.

Before progressing to his appointed colony, from the 1930s the young cadet would usually spend a year at Oxford, Cambridge or London universities taking a

'Devonshire' course (named after a sometime Secretary of State for the Colonies), which offered a basic introduction to key subjects such as law, custom, language and the history of the region for which he was destined. A constant feature of a young cadet's early career was the need for private study in order to learn local languages and pass exams in this and subjects such as 'native law and custom'. Transfer from probationary status depended upon these tests, as did future promotion.

Finding one's feet

The raw recruit fresh off the boat had to hire and manage servants and begin running his own household after years spent in institutional accommodation. He might also need credit, and here the local branch of Barclays, Dominion, Colonial and Overseas Bank was eager to help. There were relationships to be forged with new servants, as well as the awkwardness of getting used to having them and strange foods to encounter, often during socially delicate meetings and negotiations when the first 'delicacy' (eyeball/insect/intestine) was offered in honour of the District Commissioner's presence. Bachelors lived in their chummeries, where chicken curry and mulligatawny soup were served with great regularity by the communal bearer, the great fixer and general factotum who ran the lives and households of thousands of imperial Britons. Here the official could study with the *munshi* for the language exams, and plot his social life.

Numerous surprises awaited the new colonial administrator, such as tin baths and the thunderbox 'for the daily task'. One renowned official in Malaya was the proud owner of a double-barrelled thunderbox, with a photo of the Government Chief Secretary on the wall opposite, and thought it the height of good manners to join his guests when about their seated business. Colonial officials were not permitted to marry until they had spent some years in the job. Those who did marry usually brought their wives to live in the colony of their employment, where they faced the challenge of learning enough 'Kitchen Swahili' to enable them to manage the house and of breaking into a masculine world in which their husbands had already established close relations with colleagues and native servants. Some adjustments were more pressing than others; upon arriving in India to join her husband, Katherine Griffiths was horrified to find that he was being dressed and undressed by his bearer.

The administration of law and collection of tax remained mainstays of the colonial official's life. But deskbound boredom was not the lot of the generic colonial official, and there was always room for the unusual, such as being asked to pay out money for severed monkeys' heads as part of a drive to protect crops. One

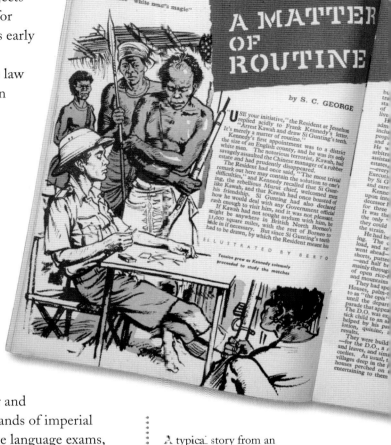

A typical story from an Empire annual, glamorizing the role of a colonial administrator in British North Borneo. In this tale, young Frank Kennedy runs a district 'the size of an English county, and he was its only white man'. Despite his youth and solitary position, Kennedy manages to outwit the 'notorious terrorist, Kawah' by using 'white man's magic', as he pursues Britain's imperial mission of bringing law and order to 'backward' lands.

A MOST IMPRESSIVE SIGHT … THE LUTYENS STATE ROOMS ARE QUITE FAIRY-LIKE LIT UP AT NIGHT. [AT DINNER] FIFTY KHITMAGARS AND CHAPRASIS IN SCARLET AND GOLD LIVERY, ONE BEHIND EACH CHAIR, WHO SALAAMED WITH BOTH HANDS AS THE GUESTS CAME IN. DINNER MORE OR LESS IN MY HONOUR TO MEET THE GOVERNORS … I WAS GIVEN AN EXACT NICHE IN ORDER OF PRECEDENCE, AND FOUND THAT I WAS RANKED AFTER THE GOVERNORS OF BOMBAY, MADRAS AND BENGAL … [THERE WAS] MUCH MORE POMP AND CIRCUMSTANCE COMPARED TO THE SIMPLE LIFE THE KING AND QUEEN LEAD BACK AT BUCK HOUSE.

– Admiral Lord Louis Mountbatten, Supreme Allied Commander Southeast Asia, writing in his diary following a state banquet at Viceroy's House, Delhi (1943)

DC in Northern Rhodesia was asked by the Governor to 'accommodate' the territory's most important nationalist leader, Kenneth Kaunda, as a government restriction order came into effect. Colonial administrators were the quintessential jacks-of-all-trades: for example, Richard Broome, appointed District Officer on Christmas Island, four days' steaming south of Singapore, was also gazetted Harbour Master, District Health Officer, Magistrate, Coroner, Chief of Police and Inspector of Machinery. The role of magistrate featured prominently in the lives of British overseas civil servants, in all sorts of settings; Guy Madoc remembered the courthouse at Kuala Selangor with its roof of jungle fibre. 'Occasionally at important moments when I was addressing the magistrate on the bench in great fluency, I would look up and staring through the roof would be the faces of three or four monkeys'. In all of his undertakings, the colonial administrator depended on the help of indigenous officials and government employees, from chiefs to native court clerks, district messengers, drivers and houseboys.

The social round

Social life was a prominent feature of the colonial administrator's world, usually because of its absence on anything like the scale that he was used to – no white people for miles around, no television, nothing. But in an age where 'entertaining yourself' was a recognized leisure pursuit, the administrator was able to cope in a way that few today could manage. Reading was a standard way of filling solitary hours in the district commissioner's bungalow, and sundowners were a universal British tradition. For some, the gramophone brought Mozart or the big band to the tropical night. The *Times Weekly Airmail Edition* and similar publications brought news from home, as did ubiquitous and out-of-date editions of *The Field*. From the 1950s the wireless and the BBC spun a new web around Britain's colonial world. In today's society, glutted with electronic devices, it is almost impossible to imagine the ineffable thrill of hearing one's first ball-by-ball Test Match cricket commentary coming over the ether, as John Ainley did in Tanganyika in 1956.

Where there was a European community there was inevitably a club, a hub of social life offering a well-stocked bar, dances and card games (the institution of the club is considered in a later chapter). Sport was officially encouraged, and

ranged from tennis to hunting. There were, of course, many private innovations; Mike Williams, a Cambridge squash Blue serving as district commissioner in the lonely Kalahari outpost of Tsabong in the 1950s, spent evenings on his verandah taking on the local bat population with his racquet.

Imperial proconsuls

Imperial proconsuls were the governors, high commissioners, consul-generals and viceroys who ruled over entire territories, subcontinents, or island groups scattered across the world's oceans. These élite imperial administrators were men of consequence and power, dispensing great authority on behalf of the sovereign. They yielded to no one in precedence, except for a visiting monarch, as they were the direct representatives of the king or queen. Civil servants and native allies on the administrative rungs below them were all linked by this royal thread: the district commissioner answered to the governor, and the governor answered to the

All the creature comforts of home: sketch of a bungalow, probably the Deputy Commissioner's house, at Jullurdur (also known as Jalandhar), Punjab, in 1888. The building has an arched verandah in the classic Indian style, with blinds to keep out the sun. In the foreground a rustic wooden seat stands among plants and shrubs.

king. As men of substance, representing the monarch, they lived accordingly. As Governor of Tanganyika Sir Edward Twining progressed around his vast country in a Rolls-Royce or a steam train bedecked with Union Flags. The pomp and ceremony attached to the office of Viceroy of India and the 12 provincial governors of the Raj was so splendid that it contrasted sharply with the relatively drab existence of the occupants of Buckingham Palace.

A power in the land

Evelyn Baring, Earl of Cromer, Consul-General of Egypt from 1883 to 1907, became known as 'the maker of modern Egypt'. Although officially Egypt was still an independent country, following the British bombardment of Alexandria in 1882 Cromer was, effectively, the ruler of this strategically located land, 'the greatest ruler that Egypt has had since the days of the Pharoahs', according to a contemporary issue of the *Spectator*. Like other leading imperialists such as Lord Curzon, Viceroy of India and later Foreign Secretary, and Sir Alfred Milner, High Commissioner to South Africa and later Colonial Secretary, Cromer regarded imperial territories as central to Britain's global standing. Having first served in Egypt in 1877, he returned as Consul-General in 1883. Baring realized that the British required greater control of the country if it was to be governed properly. He overhauled the tax and revenue system and formed new government departments, and in 1897 initiated the military campaign that recovered the Sudan, abandoned after General Gordon's death at Khartoum 12 years earlier. This led to the crushing Anglo-Egyptian victory over the Mahdi at Omdurman the following year.

The residencies of imperial proconsuls were centres of power and authority and symbols of imperial splendour, frequently hosting the itinerant movers and shakers in the imperial world as well as foreign heads of state and dignitaries. This role was reflected in their design and décor. Most splendid of them all was Viceroy's House, India, employing 6000 servants at its peak in the 1930s. Government House, Nigeria was an imposing three-storey structure on the Lagos Marina. It acted as a diplomatic and political hotel, as the Governor hosted all manner of travelling dignitaries. Elaborate dinners were a regular feature, and Government House staff had to be prepared to meet flying-boats first thing in the morning as Nigeria was on a major flight path connecting Britain with the Americas and the East, and to run around after eminent guests. A typically busy night occurred in March 1942 when the Governor, Sir Bernard Bourdillon, hosted a dinner for the Nigerian Legislative Council involving 50 guests and their wives. Simultaneously, Government House was hosting numerous birds of passage. Upstairs, King George

I GREW UP IN BRIGHT SUNSHINE, I GREW UP WITH TREMENDOUS SPACE, I GREW UP WITH ANIMALS, I GREW UP WITH EXCITEMENT, I GREW UP BELIEVING THAT WHITE PEOPLE WERE SUPERIOR.

– Charles Allen (ed.), Plain Tales from the Raj *(1985)*

CALLING CARDS AND PRECEDENCE AT DINNER

British ex-pats the world over gathered about them the accoutrements of gentility, from fox hunting and garden parties to cricket and tennis, country houses, family silver and, in some cases, scores of servants.

Keeping up standards

Dressing for dinner and such formalities raised guffaws at home, where these customs had long since died out. But by doing things 'properly', the colonials maintained, the British managed to rule a quarter of the Earth's surface with a handful of men and little use of overt force. As one observer noted:

> *There was a subconscious awareness of this that involved continual effort and expressed itself in all kinds of ways – from insisting on absolute precision in military drill to the punctilious observance of outdated etiquette, or a meticulous insistence on a knife-edge crease to khaki shorts.*

Vere Birdwood, who spent many years in India, recalled that 'all household servants wore uniforms, usually white with bands on their turbans and cummerbunds in the colours of their sahib's service'. Great emphasis was placed on protocol and hierarchy, which 'had its roots in Hindu and Moslem culture as much as British'. Precedence decided one's place at court. The Prince of Wales is reported to have said that he had never realized what royalty really was until he stayed at Government House, Bombay in 1921. Winston Churchill attended a dinner of the Colonists' Association in Nairobi in 1908. It featured 'long rows of gentlemen in evening dress', and the King's Birthday Ball given by the Governor 'revealed a company gay with uniforms, and ladies in pretty dresses, assembled upon a spot where scarcely ten years before lions hunted undisturbed'.

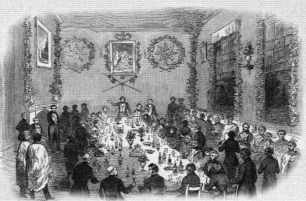

Engraving in the *Illustrated London News* of 1850 showing a banquet on the occasion of the Queen's portrait being presented to a hospital in Wellington, New Zealand. Colonial officials and Maori chiefs were in attendance.

Strict pecking order

When entertaining, the wives of British officials decided who sat where by consulting the Civil List and the Blue Book to see the order of seniority. The wives themselves automatically assumed the status of their husband's office, so the wife of the public works head of department would perennially lose out to the district commissioner's spouse. Dishes such as Brown Windsor soup and caramel custard remained firm favourites, as did ornate flower arrangements and table decorations carved from ice. The custom of ladies withdrawing after dinner was maintained, and in their absence the men set about their port and cigars and bored each other with the important matters of the day, such as rifle calibres and batting styles.

Away from official circles, colonial social life could be more informal. A prominent feature of planter life in Malaya was the Sunday curry tiffin, given in turn by managers or senior assistants in the district. The main dish usually consisted of chicken, though occasionally might involve flying foxes.

A gentleman caller

One quaint convention that clung on in India long after it had died out in Britain was that of leaving calling cards. A newly-arrived officer, civil or military, would don all his finery and call on the senior people in the district – knowing that he would not be received (even if the people were at home). He duly left his card with the servants, and if the senior officer had a daughter, a second card with the right-hand corner turned down. He would in due course be invited for dinner, an invitation that would never come unless this procedure was adhered to. Far from being a token of stuffy colonial life, this convention was a key element in British ex-pat communities' welfare service for new arrivals. Within a very few weeks the newcomer became known and in turn knew other people.

of Greece and his prime minister were dining separately and, as if this wasn't enough, lamented Bourdillon's hard-pressed ADC, 'unluckily, Sir Stafford Cripps arrived on his way to India'. Cripps, en route to offer independence to India as soon as the war ended, insisted on joining the Legislative Council dinner, and asked for a poached egg on spinach to be prepared as his vegetarian repast.

In addition to maharajahs, generals and admirals, guests at Government House, Lagos during the Second World War included King Peter of Yugoslavia and his entire Cabinet; Princess Olga of Yugoslavia; King George and Prince Peter of Greece; the prime ministers of Australia and New Zealand; Henry, Duke of Gloucester; the imperial historian Sir Reginald Coupland; General Charles de Gaulle; Lord Swinton, Resident Minister for West Africa; Lord Moyne, Secretary of State for the Colonies; Sir Kinahan Cornwallis, British Ambassador to Iraq; Captain James Roosevelt; and Lord Louis Mountbatten.

Separation and 'home'

Many Britons were born in India and the colonies, and early memories were of mosquito nets, ponies rather than prams, of 'father killing a snake in my bathroom' and of 'nanny getting smallpox'. Growing up in India and cared for by a native *ayah* (nanny), preoccupations differed from those of children back 'home' in Britain. The children of administrators usually returned to England at an early age to attend boarding school, and long separations resulted. Some, even before leaving India or the colonies, spent more time with their nanny than with their parents (a caricature of this is to be found in *The Secret Garden*'s haughty heroine Mary Lennox, unable to dress herself because her *ayah* had always done it for her). Common pets included mongooses or cubs; measles was less of a concern than cholera and rabies, and 'we were never allowed out in the sun without a topee on our heads'.

Differences in upbringing were revealed in all their complexity when, as inevitably happened, the African- or Indian-born child was sent to school in England. Settling in was difficult, as Nancy Vernede recalled: 'we had nothing in common with our new friends. They'd never heard of the brain fever bird or the sound of jackals, and they'd never ridden an elephant.' Furthermore, 'home' was usually very different in reality than in the imagination. Britain was associated with letters, parcels and shopping as Christmas brought catalogues from the Army and Navy Stores and Whiteaway's and Laidlaw's, mail order catalogues being a major institution in the British Empire. Spike Milligan envisioned England as:

> A land of milk and honey that used to send us Cadbury's military chocolates in a sealed tin once every four months. England was the land that sent us the Daily Mirror and Tiger Tim comics. England was a land where you could get chocolate and cream together for a penny, that's what my mother told me. But it never happened like that – England was a gloomy, dull, grey, land.

While British rule largely relied upon consent, acquiescence and alliance with indigenous political groups, it was based ultimately upon force, as vividly shown in

THE PITH-HELMET AND QUINTESSENTIAL KIT

The pith helmet, or sola topee, or sun helmet, or Bombay bowler, was usually made from cork or pith, typically made from sola (hence sola topee – not 'solar'), an Indian swamp growth. It was covered with cloth and lined with dark green, and often had a cloth band on the outside (a puggaree). They appeared from the 1840s, though it was in the 1870s that they became the ubiquitous tropical headgear for imperial soldiers, settlers and officials and emblematic of the British Empire.

During the Zulu War soldiers dyed their pith helmets with tea for camouflage. The Royal Marines still wear pith helmets with their Number One Dress, the Wolseley helmet (Home Service) dating from 1912.

Resplendent in the headgear named after him, Garnet Joseph Wolseley (1833–1913) was commander-in-chief of the British army from 1895 to 1900. He won a VC in the Indian Mutiny, and led the relief of Khartoum in 1884–5. This caricature of him by 'Ape' (Carlo Pellegrini) appeared in *Vanity Fair* in 1874, the year in which he led British forces attacking Kumasi, capital of the Asantahene in what became the Northern Territories of the British-ruled Gold Coast.

many parts during the days of conquest and 'pacification'. While the select band of administrators provided the 'steel frame' supporting the imperial edifice, soldiers scattered around the Empire provided the *cold* steel. The Royal Navy, meanwhile, was the lynchpin of British global power because it ensured that Britain's foes could never dominate the high seas and invade Britain or sever her vital imperial arteries. It is to a study of the armed forces of the Empire that we now turn.

CORONATION REVIEW OF THE FLEET

BY
HER MAJESTY THE QUEEN
AT SPITHEAD ON MONDAY 15TH JUNE 1953

OFFICIAL SOUVENIR PROGRAMME PRICE 2/-

Published under the Authority of the Commander-in-Chief Portsmouth

Soldiers of the Queen: Gunning for the Empire on Land, Sea and Air

PLUCKY SUBALTERNS, BRAWNY SERGEANTS AND GUN-LADEN BATTLESHIPS were British cultural icons, and the public's fascination with the nation's military forces lasted long into the 20th century. Popular culture was heavily influenced by images of martial endeavour, a phenomenon of the late 19th century that was still powerful in the 1970s, when many boys grew up on a diet of Airfix kits, Action Man figures and *Warlord* comics.

The Fleet Review was a chance for the nation to revel in its naval power, and to show it off to foreigners. Fleet Reviews dated from the 15th century, Henry V, for example, reviewing the fleet off Southampton before sailing for France and victory at Agincourt in 1415. Fleet Reviews were often held to commemorate royal coronations or jubilees, 17 taking place during Victoria's reign alone. The flagship at the 1953 Coronation Review was Britain's last battleship, HMS *Vanguard*, seen here dressed overall.

Military pageants such as Trooping the Colour, the Royal Tournament, the Spithead Naval Review and a host of air shows, military music performed in seaside bandstands and popular literature and art, all kept the warriors of the British Empire in the public eye. Kipling's yarns from the outposts of empire and *Boy's Own Paper* stories of Jack Tarr gave way after the Second World War to *Commando*-style comics glorifying war, and television comedies such as *Dad's Army* and *It Ain't Half Hot Mum* poking affectionate fun at an institution – the British Army – with which the public was very familiar. Thus the British imperial soldier remained a familiar cultural presence, as did the 'grey guardians' of the Royal Navy and the pilot aces of the Royal Air Force, epitomized by Biggles and surviving long into the age of the jet engine. This chapter explains the workings of the British military and the duties of the army, the navy and the air force in protecting the Empire, a task always pursued with the help of warriors drawn from the four corners of the world.

Noble deeds and frontier skirmishing

The British armed forces were constantly in action around the world. The Royal Navy was a reassuring presence, always vigilantly protecting the home islands and patrolling the trade routes of the world. By doing this, the navy, as the public were frequently told, upheld international law and the freedom of the seas, thereby

> IT IS UPON THE NAVY THAT, UNDER THE GOOD PROVIDENCE OF GOD, THE WEALTH, PROSPERITY AND PEACE OF THESE ISLANDS AND OF THE EMPIRE DO MAINLY DEPEND.
>
> – *British Articles of War*

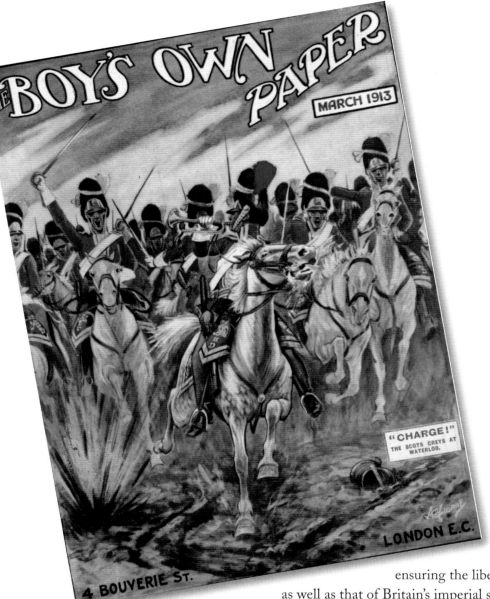

THE BOY'S OWN PAPER

MARCH 1913

"CHARGE!"
THE SCOTS GREYS AT
WATERLOO.

4 BOUVERIE ST.

LONDON E.C.

Stirring tales for British boys:
The *Boy's Own Paper*,
published from 1879 to 1967,
served up a rich diet of
conspicuous courage and stiff
upper lip to generations of
Empire builders. Here, the
cover of the March 1913
edition shows the charge of
the Scots Greys at Waterloo.

ensuring the liberty of Americans and Germans
as well as that of Britain's imperial subjects around the world. Where
appropriate, the navy imposed Britain's will through gunboat diplomacy and the
more civilized diplomacy associated with dressing ship and dispensing cocktails on
the quarterdeck whilst the Royal Marines band played *A Life on the Ocean Wave*
and other favourite tunes.

The army, meanwhile, though occasionally involved in European frays such as
the Napoleonic Wars and the Crimean War, was a specialist imperial police force,
and even 'European' conflicts were dramatically imperial in terms of battlefronts
and strategic intent. As has been seen in an earlier chapter, war on land and sea
had been one of the main engines of the expansion of the Empire. 'Small wars'
produced epic art, usually served up on exceedingly large canvases, such as Begg's
Sons of the Blood, Lady Butler's *Charge of the Light Brigade*, Robert Gibb's *The Thin
Red Line* and G.W. Joy's *General Gordon's Last Stand*. Military heroism and the
martial spirit also inspired popular poetry, which reached boiling point as the First
World War approached, and Kipling's tales 'of tough and two-fisted Tommy

Atkins and of noble young subalterns, of faithful Indian troops and gallant Afghan foes' inspired generations of Britons to respect the armed forces and their work.

Heroes and martyrs

The armed forces provided many of the imperial heroes and martyrs that built the national myth, including Clive, Gordon, Kitchener, Nelson, Wellington and Wolfe. The popular image of the armed forces contrasted the stoical behaviour of troops during the Indian Mutiny – heroic deaths at Lucknow defending the colours and the flower of British womanhood – with the supposed barbarity of subject races. It also contrasted the unpleasant nature of European, industrial warfare with 'good' colonial wars, which not only extended the borders of civilization but, in an age heavily influenced by Social Darwinism, were good for 'the breed'. Colonial wars and naval actions extended an international order based on British-imposed peace. From the late 19th century 'small wars were big box office'. Much of the interest in war, and the lust for medals that characterized the military caste, derived from the work of war correspondents reporting from the front as well as the writers of

Homage to the Fallen (1923) by Sir Frank Salisbury. The setting is the Tomb of the Unknown Warrior in Westminster Abbey. The wedding bouquet belongs to the Duchess of York (later HM the Queen Mother). This picture was exhibited at the Royal Academy in 1924 while a 10 x 8 fresco of the painting was displayed at the Wembley Empire Exhibition in the same year. The King's orderlies are Subadar Major Bir Singh MC, 2/8 Punjab Regiment; Subadar Harnath Singh MC, IOM; Risaldar Rewat Singh MC, 18th Cavalry; and Risaldar Jiwan Singh IDSM, 7th Light Infantry.

GIVE ME A LAD WITH PLUCK AND SPIRIT, AND I DON'T CARE A SNAP OF THE FINGERS WHETHER HE CAN CONSTRUE EURIPIDES OR SOLVE A PROBLEM IN HIGHER MATHEMATICS. WHAT WE WANT FOR INDIA ARE MEN WHO CAN RIDE AND SHOOT, WHO ARE READY AT ANY MOMENT TO START ON A HUNDRED MILE JOURNEY ON HORSEBACK, WHO WILL SCALE A HILL FORT WITH A HANDFUL OF MEN, OR WITH HALF A DOZEN *SOWARS* [ANGLO-INDIAN: NATIVE HORSED SOLDIERS] TACKLE A DACOIT AND HIS BAND.

– *G.A. Henty,* Through the Sikh War *(1894)*

A series of 150 cigarette cards issued in the 1920s, entitled 'Army Corps and Divisional Signs, 1914–18'. From top to bottom: 3rd Indian Corps (a symbol deriving from the crest of its commanding officer, Lt-Gen Sir Ralph Egerton); the famous Silver Fern of the New Zealand Division; and the fleur-de-lys of the 7th Indian Cavalry Brigade.

military fiction. G.W. Steevens, who died of enteric fever aged 31 while covering the Boer War as a correspondent, grew up on the *Boy's Own Paper*. As a correspondent for the *Daily Mail* he was imperialist, bellicose and a Social Darwinist, believing that war on the fringes of empire weeded out the weak and ensured the survival of the fittest. As John Mackenzie writes, war made him 'childishly happy'; it was like a 'coming of age', turning boys into men, 'the only quite complete holiday ever invented'.

Guarantor of security

The armed forces underpinned the British Empire and, indeed, the security of the world. The army and navy could project force almost anywhere in the world, and won maritime supremacy against rival Great Powers and defeated indigenous foes as the Empire expanded. Britain fought a series of world wars stretching from the 17th century to the Second World War as it sought to overhaul European rivals and, once this had been achieved, to defend its position of hegemony in diverse parts of the world. Of course, apart from world wars – against the Kaiser and Napoleon as well as Hitler – the British military's primary task was imperial policing. Its job was to defend the Empire's borders, guard its lines of communication and suppress insurrection among its people.

Meanwhile the navy kept Britain's Great Power rivals in check – glowering from its bases in Scotland and the north of England at the German High Seas Fleet across the water, bottling up the Russian fleet in the Black Sea, or hunting down French frigates in the days of sail. Aside from this, the navy's main task was to constantly patrol the sea lanes of the world protecting imperial and international trade, its many fleets and squadrons operating from strongholds such as Malta and Singapore and a host of other strategically-positioned colonies.

In addition, from the First World War onwards, the Royal Flying Corps, rechristened the Royal Air Force in April 1918, became a key imperial tool, owing its independent existence to its ability to police remote and inhospitable places such as Iraq and Somalia more cheaply than the army, and maintaining squadrons in Egypt, the Mediterranean, Iraq and Malaya as well as in Britain and the Dominions.

A Second World War poster showing a soldier of the Royal West African Frontier Force. The legend 'Our Allies the Colonies' and the listing of dozens of territories comprising the Colonial Empire emphasized the fact that, even without Great Power allies, Britain was far from alone in facing the Axis dictators.

Do you realize what you have there on your chest is an illustrated history of the British Empire?'
– Colonel Square to Corporal Jones of the Walmington-on-Sea Home Guard in Dad's Army

More cards from the 'Army Corps' series. From top to bottom: the Anzac Emblem; the 17th Indian Division, represented by the Assyrian Man-Lion of ancient Babylon; and the Lion and Sun emblem of the Persian Line of Communications.

Enhancing the British Army's reputation

The British Army's reputation was transformed over the course of the 19th century. In 1800 British soldiers – Wellington's infamous 'scum of the earth' – were renowned for their rapacity and ill-discipline. By 1900 they has become soldier-heroes by virtue of their service overseas and their association with national glory, the proud embodiment of a nation capable of striking terror into the hearts of enemies and intervening around the world. The Empire burnished the reputation of the British Army, as well as sparking Britain's fascination with 'irregular' warfare and special forces. The need to conduct 'irregular' warfare on the fringes of Empire led to the creation of units such as the Special Air Service, the Long Range Desert Group and the Chindits.

'Irregular' war became a part of the British Army's tradition and training, and it developed as a specialist counterinsurgency force because of its imperial experience, particularly in the terminal decades of empire when wars of counter-insurgency were fought in Aden, Borneo, Cyprus, Kenya, Malaya, Northern Ireland and Palestine.

During the heyday of the British Empire public interest in the army was maintained through a combination of regular overseas ventures in dramatic

The Forgotten Patrol and '5.5-inch Guns in Action' (from *The Wonder Book of the Army*): Examples of novels and short stories in children's annuals that took wars – in both these cases, North African desert battles in the Second World War – as their theme. War stories remained standard fare in juvenile literature until the 1970s.

settings fought against colourful enemies, and the largely bloodless nature of these skirmishes that made for pleasing reading when *The Times* or the *Illustrated London News* was digested at the breakfast table. Hero-myths came to surround the Empire's soldiery, from the mystic appeal of General Gordon, the martyr of Khartoum, to the common soldier brought to life by Kipling's Tommy Atkins and national adulation of VC winners. This transformation of the military's reputation was due to the fact that during the hundred-year stretch from Waterloo to the First World War the British soldier was removed from his uncomfortable closeness to the British public. In 1800 the pressgang was still a legitimate recruiting technique and the British soldier was as likely to ride the public down, as during the Peterloo massacre of 1819, as he was to save it from foreign invasion. But by 1900 he was billeted on the frontiers of a romanticized Empire, soldiering where the watching public saw no blood but read of the glory. As Thomas Hardy wrote, 'war makes rattling good history, but Peace is poor reading'. The expansion of Empire and its subsequent policing meant that the British military got rather a lot of the former, while the public at home were able to revel in their exploits because of a surfeit of the latter.

Global commitments

During the Empire's heyday the British Army remained surprisingly small, numbering around 200,000 men in times of peace. The largest army commands were India Command and Middle East Command, with headquarters in Delhi and Cairo. There were other commands, such as East Africa Command, Malaya Command and Persia and Iraq Command. Divided into about 140 battalions, the army was positioned all around the world. In the 1880s, for example, garrisons of up to 2000 men were stationed in the Bahamas, Barbados, British Guiana, British Honduras, Canada, Ceylon, Cyprus, Gibraltar, the Gold Coast, Hong Kong, Jamaica, Malta, Mauritius, St Helena, Sierra Leone, Singapore and Trinidad. Garrisons of between 2000 and 6000 men were maintained in Bermuda, Cape Town, Gibraltar and Malta, while the bulk of the British Army – over 160,000 men – was stationed in Britain, India and Ireland.

Throughout the 19th and 20th centuries this army and its indigenous allies fought innumerable 'small wars' all over the world, from New Zealand and the New Hebrides to China, Burma, Iran, Afghanistan, the Caribbean, the Americas and all over Africa. Medals were struck for all sorts of campaigns on the frontiers of empire – Ashantee, Basutoland, Burma, China, Java, Kabul, Kandahar, Nepal, Sind – and the Victoria Cross was instituted by Royal Warrant in 1856. Colonial wars might involve little more than a single column of troops teaching a recalcitrant tribe that not paying hut tax, or stealing livestock, was unacceptable, to expeditions involving tens of thousands of men and animals. Of course, although the 'glorious' side of the army's activities was always the dominant feature in its public image, policing the Empire sometimes involved what today would be considered the illegitimate use of force. British forces and their native allies used techniques such as farm burning and food denial, the Mau Mau revolt in Kenya was brutally suppressed, napalm was used in Malaya and 'imperial terror' was, according to some historians, visited upon Indians during the notorious military action in support of the civil power that led to the 1919 Amritsar massacre.

Nevertheless, these occurrences were seldom reported or made known to the public, who received a rather sanitized version of bracing campaigns on the imperial frontier and the judicious use of the gunboat as a tool of diplomacy, one that was usually effective by being seen rather than heard. The classic Victorian campaign was General Kitchener's reconquest of the Sudan (1895–8). His Anglo-Egyptian army, equipped with the latest Lee Enfield rifles and Maxim machine-guns and supported by river gunboats on the Nile, progressed south at the same time that a military railway was laid. At the iconic battle of Omdurman the

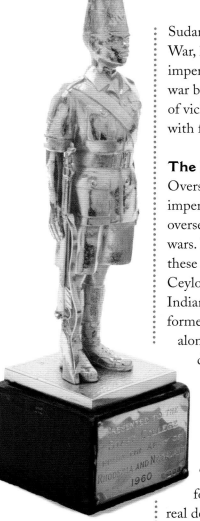

The mess was a central feature of military life in Britain and throughout the Empire. Formal dinners, at which the table would glitter with an array of mess silver, battle mementos, decanters and cut glass, were ubiquitous. This statuette of an African *askari* was presented to the British Army Staff College by the Army of Rhodesia and Nyasaland in 1960, a military formation comprising the combined forces of Northern Rhodesia, Southern Rhodesia and Nyasaland during the shortlived Central African Federation (1953–63).

Sudanese lost over 11,000 at the cost of 48 British fatalities. The Second Boer War, however, proved less of a picnic for the British. Involving nearly half a million imperial soldiers, this was the largest, costliest, most politically damaging colonial war by far. The British suffered heavy defeats and victory only came after a period of vicious counterinsurgency warfare and the international contumely associated with farm-burning and concentration camps.

The Indian Army and colonial regiments

Overseas manpower was central to the success of British arms over the centuries of imperial activity. There was extensive employment of indigenous men formed into overseas regiments, supplementing the British Army in local campaigns and world wars. Rarely did a colonial war take place in which the British Army fought without these indigenous allies, and they usually outnumbered them. Britain conquered the Ceylonese kingdom of Kandy and invaded Burma with thousands of African and Indian troops supporting the redcoats; Indians fought on the Western Front and formed the lion's share of General Slim's famous Fourteenth ('Forgotten') Army, along with entire divisions of African troops; most of the 130,000 troops who died or went into the Japanese bag on the fall of Singapore were Indian, with tens of thousands of Australians and Malayans too; and in Borneo and Malaya in the 1950s and 1960s, Australians and New Zealanders were heavily involved along with Dyak trackers and indigenous soldiers.

These locally-raised units ranged from crack infantry and cavalry to ceremonial soldiers maintained more for show than for martial purpose. The latter category mainly contained the State Forces of India, the formations that the princely states were permitted to maintain which had no real defensive purpose because British rule ensured their security from external attack. In the main, however, locally-raised units had real military purpose, and included specialized sapper and pioneer regiments, garrison artillery recruited to man the coastal defences of British islands and ports and defence forces and levies intended to repel enemy raids or supplement the manpower of an RAF station or British Army garrison. The Empire was home to dozens of these fighting units, including the West Indies Regiment, the Trans-Jordan Frontier Force, the Aden Protectorate Levies, the Somali Camel Corps, the King's African Rifles, the Ceylon Planters' Rifles Corps, the Hong Kong and Singapore Garrison Artillery, the Seychelles Defence Force, the Royal West African Frontier Force and the Tanganyika Volunteer Naval Reserve.

The armed forces of the Dominions were a mainstay of imperial defence, boasting famous fighting units such as the Transvaal Scottish, the Princess Patricia's Canadian Light Infantry and the Australian Light Horse. A contingent of 800 men and 200 horses left New South Wales in March 1885, seen off from Sydney by 200,000 people, bound for Suakin where they were to join British forces attempting to reconquer the Sudan and avenge Gordon's death. During the Boer War, and again in both world wars, Dominions' forces rallied to the colours.

Canadian troops landed in Britain before Christmas 1939, and Canada provided an entire army for the D-Day landings. Montgomery's Eighth Army included famous Australian, New Zealand and South African divisions, while at sea His Majesty's Australian and New Zealand ships were to be found all over the world, and Canada ended the war with the world's third largest navy.

Until the 1940s India was the greatest overseas seat of British military power, the 'barracks in an Oriental sea' from which imperial might was dispatched to China, the Dutch East Indies, Malaya, the Persian Gulf, the Middle East, Africa and even Europe. The British officer in India had privileges of rank and regiment, and rare opportunities for sport, hunting and action in the field. 'India was the soldier's paradise. If you were in the Army you could do anything.' It was in India that the young Winston Churchill earned his spurs during a frenetic career as a subaltern, managing to win the inter-regimental polo trophy – a holy grail for British and Indian cavalry regiments – and come under fire during campaigns on the North-West Frontier. He managed to do all of this while writing articles about his experiences for the newspapers back at home, and publishing, in double-quick time, books such as *The Malakand Field Force* chronicling his time fighting tribesmen on India's borders.

Army life in India was centred on the cantonment and the mess. We 'felt ourselves a class apart, a samurai class'. The officers mess was the centre of regimental life, a world of out-of-date newspapers and magazines, mess silver, passing the port, signing chits at the bar and high-jinks after dinner, playing hard

A supplement to *The Graphic* of 7 July 1888 shows 'Types of the Bombay Army'. The Bombay Army was one of three armies of which the Indian Army as a whole was comprised (the others being the Bengal and Madras armies). It was made up of a total of 32 regiments.

A silver Bengal Lancer, on top of a cigarette box (not shown) presented to the Staff College by officers of the Bengal Cavalry in 1896. The tip of the soldier's lance has had to be bent over because of its propensity to snag the uniforms of diners as they reach across the table for the salt or the snuff.

ALTHOUGH THE EXPERIENCES OF THE GREAT WAR HAVE STRIPPED THE TRADITIONAL GLAMOUR FROM THE SOLDIER'S TRADE, OPPORTUNITIES FOR ADVENTURE AND ROMANCE STILL EXIST IN THE FAR-OFF CORNERS OF THE EMPIRE. BRITISH OCCUPATION OF BACKWARD TERRITORIES BRINGS IN ITS TRAIN PROGRESS, LAW AND ORDER, BUT ON THE DISTANT FRONTIERS THERE ARE STILL SAVAGE KINGDOMS WHERE CHAOS REIGNS, AND THE ONLY EFFECTIVE RULE IS THAT OF THE RIFLE AND SWORD.

– Major W. Lloyd-Jones, 'Hunting Abyssinian Slave-Raiders' in The Boys' All-Round Book of Stories, Sports and Hobbies *(1934)*

and drinking hard. Sport was an army shibboleth in India, units such as the Bengal Lancers as well as British cavalry regiments placing a high premium on horsemanship and polo. For the other ranks, barracks life could be drab, parading to draw rations, parading to draw stores, parading for everything. It was a world of mosquito nets, char-wallahs with big silver urns, and staggeringly smart uniforms for in India an unlimited workforce allowed 'bulling' to reach new heights, producing the Empire's smartest soldiers. For the other ranks, not speaking to a woman for the duration of an eight or nine year tour was common, as were periodic spells of fighting 'on the grim', skirmishing with the tribes of the North-West Frontier region or campaigning into Afghanistan.

Showing the flag

Military pomp and display was an important element of soldiering overseas, where showing the flag and demonstrating military capability reminded potential foes of the power at the disposal of the government, as well as giving the men something to do. 'The New Year always began with a burst of military splendour, the King-Emperor's Parade on New Year's Day, when on every parade ground in India cavalry and infantry were to be observed marching, trotting past or even galloping past in lines of squadrons.' The comedian Spike Milligan (1918–2002) was born in Ahmadnagar, the son of a sergeant-major in the Royal Artillery. He recalled an Armistice Day Parade in Poona, where elephant gun-batteries 'paraded in phalanxes of six in a line, all polished up, all their toes whitened up, with leather harnesses and the regimental banner hung from the forehead of the middle elephant'. This was 'the Army in India seen in all its glory', a sight few watched unmoved, as Vere Birdwood described when recalling her husband's cavalry regiment passing the saluting base: 'There was a great deal of jingling harness, the cavalry regiments with pennants flying from their lances and their horses tossing their heads, all beautifully groomed. I doubt if there was a man in the regiment who was under six foot.' Display was also an important part in recruiting tours throughout the Empire: in India 'at the entrance to the village you'd probably be met by the local village band, big drum, pipes, side-drums ... Then you'd be received by your head host, generally one of the senior ex-army officers, and brought out under the great village tree, the peepul tree, under which the whole village would come and sit.' 'In Africa, when recruiting for the Royal Pioneer Corps, the Bechuana Drum and Bugle Band, wearing leopard skins, would tour the villages with military acrobats and firepower demonstration teams enticing men to enlist. At an Exhibition in Colombo in December 1942 the military provided entertainment for the public: there was a Physical Training display by a complete battalion of the Ceylon Light Infantry (over 700 men), an aerial ropeway demonstration by the Royal Navy, a demonstration of 'Artillery in Action', RAF aerobatics displays, African tribal war dances and music from massed military bands.

The vital role of the Senior Service

Maritime power was at the very heart of Britain's national self-image and the familiar 'island story' of its rise to greatness. Raleigh, Drake and Nelson were just some of the more illustrious names in Britain's seafaring pantheon, and by the 19th century the Royal Navy was universally regarded not just as the nation's 'sure shield' against any challenger, but the main guarantor of the freedom of the world

This magnificent recruitment poster was devised in Colombo during the Second World War and demonstrates an ingenious ability to harness indigenous nationalism – the appeal to mother Lanka – in order to elicit support for Britain and its world war. The Lion of Lanka appears today at the centre of the national flag of Sri Lanka.

In 1938 John Player and Sons (part of the Imperial Tobacco Company) issued the 'Military Uniforms of the British Empire Overseas' cigarette card series and a threepenny album in which to display them. The series captured the array of different imperial regiments, their uniforms and traditions. The left-hand page shows the uniforms of the 17th Dogra Regiment, the 10th Gurkha Rifles and the Indian Mounted Artillery, with the Victoria Memorial Calcutta pictured at the foot, while the right-hand page depicts the Alwar State forces and the Bahawalpur State Forces, and the Marble Cenotaph at Alwar.

This line of thinking was rammed home again and again through all sorts of events and media, from the annual Spithead Naval Review (a regular parade of Britain's naval might before the monarch in the sheltered eastern stretch of the Solent), to popular literature, parliamentary debates, the vaunted 'Singapore strategy' and history books. As one standard history of Britain, *King Edward's Realm*, put it:

> *Nothing is more interesting in the story we have to tell than the daring exploits of our seamen, by which we have risen to the command of the seas, and we are able to sing Rule Britannia with the proud happy feeling that Britannia does indeed still rule the waves and that as far as in us lies it shall never cease to do so, since it is only by thus 'ruling the waves' that we can look to the sea as a friend that unites the whole family of English-speaking peoples, and enables them to aid one another.*

The age of the dreadnought

The main burden of defending the British Isles and every imperial territory around the world belonged to the Senior Service, and it was fitting, therefore, that until the later years of the Second World War, Britain had the largest navy in the world (in order to protect commerce, trade and international freedom, as the British were

THE YEAR IS 1910 – OR 1940, BUT IT IS ALL THE SAME ... THE KING IS ON HIS THRONE AND THE POUND IS WORTH A POUND. OVER IN EUROPE THE COMIC FOREIGNERS ARE JABBERING AND GESTICULATING, BUT THE GRIM GREY BATTLESHIPS OF THE BRITISH FLEET ARE STEAMING UP THE CHANNEL AND AT THE OUTPOSTS OF EMPIRE THE MONOCLED ENGLISHMEN ARE HOLDING THE NIGGERS AT BAY ... EVERYTHING IS SAFE, SOLID AND UNQUESTIONED. EVERYTHING WILL BE THE SAME FOREVER AND EVER.

– George Orwell, 'Boys Weeklies' (1939)

The Royal Tournament was first held in 1880 in Islington, a popular pageant in which different services and units competed in various martial tasks, from gun carrying to climbing the rigging and dancing the hornpipe. The Tournament moved to Olympia in the early 1900s and then to Earl's Court after the Second World War, where it remained until the Labour government axed it in 1999, thus bringing to a close what had been the world's largest military entertainment. This poster (c.1910) shows a Royal Marine gazing out to sea, as a battleship steams by.

at pains to emphasize, rather than for any warlike purpose). It was an imperial navy like no other, maintaining fleets and squadrons all over the world along with all necessary port installations, shore bases, support units and ancillary vessels, from destroyer and submarine depot ships to boom-laying vessels and survey ships. Overseas naval bases included HMS *Tamar* in Hong Kong, HMS *Cormorant* at Gibraltar, HMS *St Angelo* in Malta, HMS *Alert* in the Persian Gulf and HMS *Terror* in Bermuda. The Royal Navy's warships, that had bested the Spaniards, Dutch and French, kept up with modern technology, wood and sail giving way to iron and steam before the arrival of the super-ship, HMS *Dreadnought*, in the early years of the 20th century, and Winston Churchill's conversion of the fleet from coal to oil (which required the construction of a pipeline connecting the 'British' oilfields of Iraq to Haifa in order to fuel the Mediterranean Fleet).

Until it was eclipsed by the aircraft carrier, the battleship remained the supreme arbiter of Great Power status, 40,000 tons-worth of armour plating and massive turrets bearing 16-inch guns that could hurl a shell the size of a car over a distance of 20 miles (32 km). At the end of the Second World War – and despite having lost 451 warships of all categories – the Royal Navy's strength stood at 15 battleships and battle-cruisers, seven fleet carriers, four light fleet carriers, 41 escort carriers, 62 cruisers, 131 submarines, 846 destroyers, frigates and sloops, 729 minesweepers, over 1000 landing craft and minor war vessels, 40 Royal Naval Air Stations supporting 69 Fleet Air Arm squadrons and 150 shore bases.

A man's life in the Royal Navy

Full information concerning any of the branches of the Royal Navy or Royal Marines can be obtained from your nearest R.N. & R.M. Recruiting Office or by writing to D.N.R. Dept. 2x2, Admiralty, London, S.W.1.

A typical advertisement for the armed forces, this one appearing in the *Boy's Own Paper* in the late 1950s. Boys' comics and magazines continued to carry adverts for careers in the armed forces into the 1970s.

Guardian of the high seas

This mass of grey steel and protruding gun barrels was grouped into fleets and squadrons dotted all over the world, protecting Britain's diverse imperial interests. Based on ports in England and Scotland, the Home Fleet and Western Approaches Command (created in February 1941 to fight the Battle of the Atlantic from headquarters in Liverpool) were responsible for the defence of Britain and the Atlantic along with the Reserve Fleet that, in 1939, numbered as many as 133 vessels. The Mediterranean Fleet was based at Alexandria following its removal from Malta during the Abyssinian crisis of 1935–6. The task of this fleet, second in strength only to the Home Fleet, was to protect the vital Suez

IMPERIAL SHIPS' NAMES

Be they river gunboats chugging up the inland waterways of China, vintage cruisers searching for German raiders in the Indian Ocean, battleships repairing at Alexandria, submarines laying mines off the coast of Malaya, corvettes riding like corks atop mountainous Atlantic swells or ancient monitors skulking in Malta's Grand Harbour – by the 20th century the ships of the Royal Navy bore names that told of the navy's global heritage and its long association with Empire. An earlier fashion for warlike sounding names – *Impregnable, Inflexible, Terrible, Thunderer, Vengeance, Warrior* – gave way to other naming traditions, though the occasional *Revenge* or *Warspite* remained into the late 1940s. Reflecting the navy's imperial heritage, there were 'Tribal' class destroyers (such as HMS *Afridi, Ashanti, Hakka*), 'Colony' class cruisers (HMS *Mauritius, Nigeria, Trinidad, Uganda*), and 'Ruler' class escort carriers (HMS *Khedive, Nabob, Rajah, Shah*). Many colonies and cities had ships named for them – HMS *Cairo, Calcutta, Cape Town, Colombo, Jamaica, Kandahar, Khartoum* – providing a touch of colour alongside the *Cornwalls, Devonshires* and *Sheffields* of the fleet. Australian ships bore the names of the Dominion's cities, such as HMAS *Adelaide, Ballarat, Bendigo, Hobart, Perth* and *Sydney*.

Canal artery of the Empire, and to at least equal the power of the strongest navy in the Mediterranean. Patrolling South American waters and the Caribbean were the vessels of the Americas and West Indies Station. The African coast from West Africa to the Cape was important for shipping bound between east and west, and facilities were developed in the region, particularly at Freetown, for convoy assembly and escort. This region was the responsibility of South Atlantic Command. The Indian Ocean was patrolled by the warships of the East Indies Station. Headquartered in Colombo and with shore bases in the Persian Gulf, the Red Sea and East Africa, its remit stretched from the Swahili coast to the Bay of Bengal and the Malacca Straits. Policing the waters of the Far East was the responsibility of the China Station, which operated from Hong Kong, Tientsin and Shanghai, while in the Pacific the Australia and New Zealand Stations comprised warships of the Royal Navy and its Dominion allies.

'The Navy's Here!'

The navy was presented to the public as the crucial foundation of British and world security, and frequent lessons in seapower and the beneficence of British maritime activity were delivered through literature and the media. *The Navy's Here!* was typical of the kind of informative propaganda that offered the British public imperial lessons in peace as in war. It illustrated the manner in which modern struggles – even the near-fatal struggle against Germany, Italy and Japan – were cast in the light of a maritime heritage that stretched across the centuries and featured intermittent struggles against deadly foes fought across the waters of the world:

> *'The Navy's Here! This was the joyful cry from hundreds of British seamen captured from sunken merchant ships when the crew of HMS* Cossack, *armed with cutlasses and rifles, sprang on board the German prison ship* Altmark *in a frozen Norwegian*

The Navy's Here! was a colourful piece of Second World War propaganda pressing home the importance of the 'grey guardians' to the survival of the British world. It linked the latest global struggle to a history of maritime warfare as Britain's enemies sought over the centuries to sever the trade and communications lifelines underpinning the Empire.

Fjord, and set the prisoners free. Since this glorious episode the Navy has been here, there, and everywhere throughout the Seven Seas which it must rule as in the days of old if Britain is to remain great, and Britons free.

The British Empire is what is known as a maritime Empire. Because Britain, the heart of the Empire, is an Island; and because more than half of what is eaten by the 45 million inhabitants who live in this Island has to be brought to us over the sea, the Navy has to protect these sea-routes from an enemy who tries to starve us by sinking our merchant ships.

That is what Germany is trying to do in the Atlantic Ocean now. But defending our foodships is only part of the Navy's mighty work. It has also to defend the transports and supply ships which carry the soldiers and their weapons across the seas and oceans from the great Dominions and Colonies to fight the enemy in Europe and Africa, and perhaps elsewhere. Remember that there are 80,000 miles of ocean trade routes between England and the different parts of the Empire. No wonder that we need a great

British naval might was a popular subject for children's literature, as exemplified by the *Wonder Book of the Navy* and the *Wonder Book of Sailors*. There was also a *Wonder Book of the Army* and a *Wonder Book of the Royal Air Force*. The *Wonder Book of the Navy* taught people all about the organization and purpose of the navy, and why Britain depended upon it. Its colour plates depicted the surrender of the German High Seas Fleet in 1918 and the graceful battleship HMS *Hood*, the 'world's largest warship'. The book informed children of the different badges of rank and different types of warship, the life and routine of a warship, airships, seaplanes and flying-boats, naval customs, navigation, mines and torpedoes and convoys.

Navy to defend us, if we in England are to be fed, and our armies are to be transported about the world … The British must rule the seas if the British Empire is to remain great and free. This is why we always have had the greatest Navy in the world.

Wings across the globe

Though the junior of the three armed services, the Royal Air Force soon gained ground because of the glamour associated with flight and flying machines, from the early days of biplane experimentation to the 'chivalry' of Battle of Britain dogfights and the post-war world of the jet engine. From the 1920s boys' annuals and comics displayed a fixation with airpower, and the fascination lasted, boys still making a sticky mess of Airfix kits and reading about missiles and jet engines in the 1980s. Books such as Ladybird's *The Airman* continued to glamourize service in the RAF and children's comics and magazines continued to carry adverts offering careers in this exciting and thoroughly modern sphere. As late as 1988, *Warlord* featured a dramatic cover picture for its 'Harrier Squadron' story.

From its foundation the RAF was associated with the British Empire, and owed its independent existence to its ability to effectively police imperial territories. At the end of the First World War, with both the army and navy vying to absorb this 'upstart' service, the RAF won the battle in Whitehall over which service could most cheaply and effectively police barren imperial frontiers such as Iraq and Somalia. Fought during Winston Churchill's tenure at the Air Ministry in the early 1920s this battle saved the RAF from being taken over by its jealous rivals.

A new generation of writers promoted the air hero in juvenile literature in the years following the First World War. Popular literature's most famous airman was Squadron Leader James 'Biggles' Bigglesworth, 'the British Empire's finest pilot adventurer'. Writers tapped into the 'technological excitement of speed, the freedom provided by the air, the chivalric image' which ensured the 'instant mythification' of the airman and the RAF, 'the cavalry of the clouds'. Meanwhile the Hendon Air Pageant, staged annually from 1920 until 1937, offered aerobatics displays and demonstrations of the potential of air power, hailing the 'triumph of technology over primitive opponents' and the social cachet of flying, symbolized by the attendance of members of the Royal Family at air shows up and down the country. These air shows were awesome spectacles, the 1937 Air Pageant, for example, featuring a parade of 260 aircraft in five columns and a simulated bombing of 'native' villages.

The Ladybird Book entitled *The Airman* illustrates the popular appeal of the Royal Air Force, even as the Empire itself was contracting rapidly. Dating from 1967, the book explained the rank system and the air force's insignia, as well as the training and manifold tasks of the modern air force.

A Ladybird 'Easy-Reading' Book

'People at Work'

THE AIRMAN

in the Royal Air Force

The Boys' and Girls' Adventure Book (1935) contained stories about deserts and lost rivers, and recounted the exploits of such characters as 'Gunboat' Smith and 'Zenobia, Queen of the East'. Its cover picture is a typical glorification of the triumph of technology epitomized by air power, at a time when the RAF was assuming a key role in policing the Empire. A biplane sweeps low over the desert, its observer peering down to ascertain whether the tribesmen encamped below are 'friendlies' or 'bandits'.

Air power in the Empire

The British government was very keen on air power as a means of enforcing colonial authority in inaccessible corners of countries such as Egypt and Iraq. Kurds, Somalis, Sudanese and Afridis were all subjected to bombing and strafing as aircraft became mainstays of colonial warfare and punitive actions. In 1919 the 'Mad Mullah', Sayyid Hasan of Somaliland, was defeated by a squadron of 12 de Havillands and 200 RAF personnel. The British base at Habbaniya on the River

Continued on page 138

MARTIAL MUSIC AND LITERATURE

Military literature was part of the staple diet of British society, from scholarly and journalistic accounts of battles and campaigns to run-of-the-mill military adventure stories. Tales of derring-do were based on familiar plot lines and many authors had little difficulty in becoming prolific; George Manville Fenn (1831–1909), for example, wrote over 120 juvenile books with titles such as *Shoulder Arms!* and *Fix Bay'nets*. G.A. Henty, author of the iconic *With Kitchener to Khartoum* and *From Cape Town to Ladysmith*, drew inspiration for his popular military stories from his experience as a war correspondent reporting on colonial campaigns, including Napier's 1867–8 expedition to Abyssinia. His books were legion, and included *With Kitchener in the Soudan*, *St George for England* – the past made a servant of the present and the glories of the British nation – and *Through Three Campaigns*, which dramatized the relief of Chitral, the Tirah campaign and the relief of Coomassie in the Ashante wars. Sir Garnet Wolseley's Ashante expedition of 1874 also inspired *By Sheer Pluck*; the first Boer War (1880–1) led to *The Young Colonists*; and Henty devoted five novels to campaigns in India, including *With Clive in India*, *Through the Sikh War* and *The Tiger of Mysore*.

All of these stories had a ramrod moral running through them, as epitomized in *On the Irrawaddy*, which justified war because of the need to liberate native peoples from appalling government. Hundreds of thousands of boys imbibed this literature and revered the work of Rider Haggard, G.A. Henty, Captain Marryat, the *Boy's Own Paper* and *Chums*. These publications, along with school history curricula, school drill, school Officer Training Corps' and the Boy Scouts, were effective recruiting sergeants for the military and the imperial idea.

Cover of sheet music for a rousing Victorian piano piece (1868) celebrating the triumphant expedition to Abyssinia of that year, in which Robert Napier routed indigenous forces and freed captured British diplomats. In the process, he earned himself the title 1st Baron Napier of Magdala.

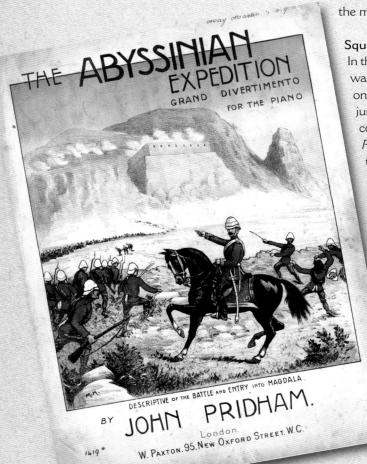

Square-jawed heroes

In the post-Second World War era comic books glorified war in a dramatic and highly visual manner. Be the action on the Rhine or in blistering African deserts, the jungles of Southeast Asia or the stormy Atlantic, comics such as *Battle Picture Library*, *Commando*, *War Picture Library*, *Warlord* and *Victor* covered every theatre of conflict and regularly featured Commonwealth formations. These comics, glorifying war and patriotism, shaped the way that generations of children remembered the war, and parted schoolboys from their pocket money well into the 1990s. They included star characters such as Union Jack Jackson ('Britain's finest fighting hero') and Squadron Leader 'Killer' Kane. The pocket-sized *Commando* ('For Action and Adventure') series, launched in 1961, included titles such as *Mustang Patrol*, *Battle Wagon* and *Glider Ace*, capitalizing on real war experiences, graphic art and the accurate portrayal of equipment and uniforms. *War Picture Library* (launched in 1958) found success with a small, pocket-sized format costing a shilling each and the subject of countless playground swaps. The writing team included a former

Commando comics first appeared in the 1960s, and, while almost all similar comics have since ceased publication, were still going strong at the start of the 21st century. Stories were overwhelmingly set in the Second World War, and portrayed the grit and heroism of Britain's armed forces, and their Commonwealth allies, in defeating the evil and cruel forces of the enemy nations. This particular issue is set in Burma in 1943.

member of the Parachute Regiment, a Fleet Air Arm pilot, a Royal Signaller and a Gurkha colonel who had served in the Far East. Titles included *Action Stations*, *Fight Back to Dunkirk*, *The Iron Fist*, *Lone Commando*, *Fire Power* and *The Red Devils*.

Songs of lament and triumph

Music was a distinctive feature of the British military all over the world, from the skirl of the pipes leading Highland soldiers into battle to promenade concerts, national ceremonial, military bands and the music halls. Victorian songs such as 'The Dusky Warrior' (set in the Zulu War), 'On Guard' and 'Burnaby the Brave', mourning the death of Colonel Fred Burnaby at Abu Klea in 1885, were commonplace. The crushing Zulu victory over the Warwickshire Regiment at Isandhlwana in 1879 led to songs mourning the 'Gallant Twenty-Fourth'; victories led to even more. Music and ceremony, for example Trooping the Colour and the Changing of the Guard, were, in the words of Robert Giddings, part of an extremely powerful 'cultural grammar' that existed 'not only in costume and ritual but in music, gesture and language'. The Royal Military School of Music was founded in 1857, allegedly because the standard of military music at the time was thought to be so abysmal.

The fictional air ace and adventurer 'Biggles' (Major James Bigglesworth) helped enthuse generations of boys for flying and service in the RAF. Biggles was born in India, the son of an Indian Civil Servant. He served in the Royal Flying Corps in the First World War, and his career extended to the Second World War and after, when he flew for Scotland Yard's Special Air Police. First appearing in *Popular Flying* magazine in 1932, Biggles appeared in over a hundred stories until his career was cut short by the death of his creator Captain W.E. Johns in 1958. Johns himself had served in a bomber squadron during the First World War.

Euphrates in Iraq was typical of the overseas facilities that supported British airpower as it policed the Empire, and demonstrated the fact that – although a country such as Iraq might be nominally 'independent', British power was still omnipresent. Established in 1936, RAF Habbaniya masqueraded as a 'training' facility known as No. 4 Service Flying Training School. It was in fact home to a large number of aircraft, including in the early 1940s 32 Hawker Audaxes, 8 Fairey Gordons, 29 Airspeed Oxfords, 9 Gloster Gladiators, a solitary Bristol Blenheim and 5 Hawker Hart trainers. This establishment was supported by over 1000 RAF personnel, a number of armoured cars and 1200 RAF levies made up of British-officered Kurds, Arabs and Assyrian Christians. Early in the Second World War aircraft from Habbaniya reconnoitred Russia as the British government explored the practicalities of attacking oil wells and refineries in the Caucasus, and in 1941 had cause to take on the Iraqi army and Luftwaffe aircraft as the country rose in rebellion against the British presence.

The uniformed forces based at the Habbaniya camp were swelled by some 9000 civilian workers. This mixed bag of races made Habbaniya one of the more extraordinary outposts of Empire. Inside its eight-mile-long iron fence were hangars, two large repair shops and corrugated iron-roofed military buildings, a tall water tower, a power station, a gymnasium, a swimming pool, social clubs and tree-lined roads with names like Piccadilly. There were also 56 tennis courts, riding stables, a polo ground-cum-racecourse, many vegetable plots, a large stock farm and a golf course, and it was sited close to Habbaniya Lake (covering an area of 100 square miles [259 sq km]) on which BOAC flying boats bound for India and the Far East landed.

Baden-Powell and the Scout movement

The Boy Scout movement and its bible, *Scouting for Boys*, taught generations of children to 'be prepared' to deal with all sorts of eventualities, including mad dogs, dead bodies, suicides and dislocated shoulders. The 1870s and 1880s had witnessed the foundation of the Salvation Army, the Church Army and the Boys' Brigade complete with uniforms, titles and military ranks, and there was a great vogue for military imagery in popular hymns such as 'Onward Christian Soldiers' and 'Fight

At Croydon Airport, Palestinian Boy Scouts pose proudly with the pilot of the Imperial Airways airliner that has brought them to England for the 3rd World Jamboree in July 1929. Held at Arrowe Park, Birkenhead, this gathering brought together 56,000 Scouts from around the globe. In his closing address, Chief Scout Robert Baden-Powell told them: 'I want you all to take back to your countries a good account of Great Britain and all the boys you have met here, and the people who have tried to be good to you. Of course, any ass can see the bad points in people or a country, but a good Scout will look out for the good points in other people.'

Tunic and cap badges of James Anderson Thomson, who served with the Gloucestershire Regiment in the First World War. The 'Glorious Glosters' had more battle honours than any other British line regiment, and were unique in wearing two cap badges (the smaller Sphinx badge is the 'back badge'). They qualified for this honour, and the 'Egypt' motif, at the Battle of Alexandria in 1801, as British and French forces clashed during the Napoleonic Wars. The 28th (North Gloucestershire) Regiment of Foot distinguished itself in this engagement.

AND TO BE STRONG AND HEALTHY, YOU MUST KEEP YOUR BLOOD HEALTHY AND CLEAN INSIDE YOU. THIS IS DONE BY BREATHING IN LOTS OF PURE, FRESH AIR, BY DEEP BREATHING, AND BY CLEARING OUT ALL DIRTY MATTER INSIDE YOUR STOMACH, WHICH IS DONE BY HAVING A 'REAR' DAILY, WITHOUT FAIL … IF THERE IS ANY DIFFICULTY ABOUT IT ONE DAY, DRINK PLENTY OF GOOD WATER, ESPECIALLY BEFORE AND JUST AFTER BREAKFAST, AND PRACTISE BODY-TWISTING EXERCISES, AND ALL SHOULD BE WELL.

– Scouting for Boys *(1908)* '*Camp Fire Yarn No. 18: Health-Giving Habits*'

the Good Fight'. Public schools had their cadet corps and even state schools adopted military-style drill as an integral part of the curriculum. Beyond the playground, the Volunteers, the Militia and the Yeomanry flourished. Into this atmosphere Sir Robert Baden-Powell launched the Boy Scout movement in 1907. This was followed a couple of years later by the formation of the Girl Guides once the determination of girls to become Scouts had been recognized.

This quintessentially imperial and martial organization appealed to deep human yearnings for regulation, adventure and a sense of purpose, and quickly spread throughout the Empire and most other countries of the world. Baden-Powell, who had schooled at Charterhouse, joined the 13th Hussars in India in 1876. He proceeded to serve as a soldier in Afghanistan, Ashante, India, Malta, Matabeleland, Natal and Zululand, and became lieutenant colonel of the 5th Dragoon Guards in India in 1897 and then colonel of irregular horse during the Boer War. In this conflict he famously masterminded the defence of the long-besieged town of Mafeking, a stand-off avidly followed by the British public. The relief of Mafeking in May 1900 led to scenes of unbridled joy in British towns and cities, and the verb 'to mafik' entered the language, meaning to caper about in the street. The depth of public jubilation was signalled by the gifts that were showered upon Baden-Powell, including a general's sword 'From the Citizens of Liverpool' crafted by Wilkinson's of Sheffield, with an ivory handle and a silver scabbard. One of Baden-Powell's other jobs during the Boer War, at the behest of Lord Roberts, was to create the South African Constabulary, whose uniform became the model for that of the Boy Scouts.

Building a young man's character

Baden-Powell enthusiastically embraced the art of scouting, and in India became an expert pig-sticker, winning the Kadir Cup in 1883 and writing the definitive *Pig-Sticking or Hog-Hunting*. From the start, the Scout Movement was imperial in spirit as well as in practice for, in John Mackenzie's words, 'Baden-Powell viewed Empire as a model for world integration and peace'. His fame aided the success of his venture, though this had much more to do with its inherent allure for young boys and girls. His ideas came from skills he had gained through waging guerrilla

In 1914 Princess Mary, daughter of King George V, served as patron of a Christmas Fund that presented British soldiers and sailors with an embossed brass box. On its hinged lid appeared Mary's profile beneath the words 'Imperium Britannicum', flanked by her initials. Below were the words 'Christmas 1914', with the bow and stern of a battleship emerging at either end. The contents included a pipe, cigarettes, tobacco and a flint lighter for smokers, and a pencil and khaki writing case and acid drops for non-smokers, both accompanied by a Christmas card from the King and Queen and a photograph of the 17-year-old princess. Non-European imperial troops fighting on the Western Front received appropriate substitutes such as spices and sugar candy.

warfare in Africa and Asia, many of them learned from native 'scouts'. Scouting embodied the skills of frontier soldiering, including orienteering and tracking. Indeed, military formations on the frontiers of India often included the words 'scouts' and 'guides' in their titles. Scouting emphasized self-reliance and a code of moral conduct, as well as loyalty to country, a sense of duty and the importance of doing 'a good turn every day'.

Orienteering, camping, conservation, comradeship, farm work, cooking skills, community service, survival skills, swimming, life-saving, first aid, signalling and team work were all important Scouting activities and qualities. The martial overtones were emphasized by uniform and rank insignia, the Cub Scouts (eight to ten years old) progressing through a badge system, and the movement organized into Districts, Groups, Troops and Units led by Patrol Leaders. In *Scouting for Boys* Baden-Powell's 'camp fire yarns' – didactic moral homilies – are replete with lessons drawn from the Empire and its native peoples. 'The history of the British Empire has been made up of adventurers and explorers, the scouts of the nation, for hundreds of years.' The scouting, woodcraft and general outdoor skills of Zulus, Swazis and other people are admired throughout the book, and the Scout's War Song was a Zulu chant, its War Dance based on a Zulu dance. 'The native boys of the Zulu and Swazi tribes in South Africa learn to be scouts before they are allowed to be considered men.'

The Empire's armed forces existed to defend Britain from invasion and to protect a global presence based upon strategic strong points and sea lines of communication. This network of ports and sea routes and, from the early 20th century, civil and military air routes, was the very essence of the British world, one defined by incessant trading activity and the movement of passenger liners and cargo ships. It is to the Empire's communications that we now turn.

Steamer to Suez: Air Routes, Sea Lanes and Ports of Call

THE BRITISH EMPIRE WAS A GLOBAL NETWORK OF PORTS AND SEA LANES, augmented in the 20th century by air routes. As the Empire grew, ever more efficient communications bound it more closely together. Pioneering postal services took mail to the four corners of the globe, while submarine telegraphy and wireless brought a breathtaking immediacy to communications.

LEFT 'An early morning call'– an extremely alluring advertising poster from the great age of liners and voyages by sea. The interwar years saw artists devise the most beautiful images for the many competing airline and shipping companies.

RIGHT An envelope illustrating two vital methods of imperial communication, the postal service and air services. The map of the globe celebrates the 'first regular air service' between Australia and South Africa, with stops in the Cocos Islands and Mauritius in the Indian Ocean. Qantas stands for 'Queensland and Northern Territories Air Service', and at the time when this letter was franked in Port Louis, capital of the British colony of Mauritius on 6 September 1952, the company was called Qantas Empire Airways. The stamps, bearing the image of an aging King George VI, show Pieter Both Mountain and sugar cane, Mauritius' chief export, being transported by cart.

These technological innovations spun an all-red web around the world, making the world a smaller place and easing the passage of information between Whitehall and its distant proconsuls and enhancing the sense of shared community stretching across the British world from Toronto to Pretoria and Sydney.

Improved communications

Communications advances enabled business centres around the world to keep in touch and an international money market to emerge, and allowed news to be syndicated internationally by agencies such as Reuters and the Press Association. Better communications also increased the central authority of London, allowing the British government to communicate with its governors overseas in a matter of minutes rather than months. Meanwhile, while submarine cables were being laid between Britain, India and Australasia, refrigerated freighters strengthened the links between British markets and the world. The first cargo of frozen Australian mutton arrived in London in 1880 and was soon followed by butter and fruit transported from the Cape and sold at Covent Garden Market. These developments were at the very core of the British Empire, what it was and how it worked. The Empire was above all else a global trading

BY AIR MAIL
PAR AVION
LINKING
AUSTRALIA
AND
SOUTH AFRICA
FIRST REGULAR AIR SERVICE
QANTAS EMPIRE AIRWAYS

The General Manager,
QANTAS EMPIRE AIRWAYS LTD.,
G. P. O. BOX 489,
SYDNEY.

THE STATELY LINERS, MARVELS OF TECHNOLOGY IN THE SECOND HALF
OF THE 19TH CENTURY, WERE A VISIBLE SYMBOL OF BRITISH
DOMINANCE. AS THEY EASED THEIR WAY THROUGH BRITISH DREDGED
CHANNELS TO BRITISH BUILT BERTHS IN BRITISH COLONIAL PORTS
THEY VISIBLY AND METAPHORICALLY PUSHED ASIDE THE HOST OF
SMALLER INDIGENOUS CRAFT IN THEIR WAY.

– Michael Pearson, The Indian Ocean *(2003)*

enterprise based upon sea connections. The centrality of the sea to Britishness and
the British Empire was well captured by Charles Hose, writing from Sarawak:

*About mid-day, set high on a cape, we notice a lighthouse, and I think of what one of
Kipling's characters, in this very part of the world, says: 'You understand, us English
are always looking up marks and lighting sea-ways all over the world, never asking
with your leave or by your leave, seeing that the sea concerns us more than anyone else'.*

The age of steam

In the 19th century the age of steam ended 2000 years of travel dictated by seasonal
winds. As steam replaced sail, Britain was at the cutting edge of the communications
revolution. It led the way in the production and employment of iron vessels such as
Isambard Kingdom Brunel's pioneering SS *Great Britain*, and the demand for the
transit of passengers, mails and refrigerated foodstuffs that came in their wake.
The first steamer to arrive in Bombay docked in 1820; in 1826 the new Governor
of Bengal, Lord William Cavendish Bentinck, arrived by steamer; and in 1829 the
Hugh Lindsay made a pioneering voyage from Suez to Bombay. Ten years later the
East India Company introduced several larger vessels, 50 per cent paid for by the
British Treasury and operated by the Bombay Marine. Steam boats were used in
the First Opium War against China (1839–42), and in 1842 the Peninsular &
Oriental Steam Navigation Company began regular services linking Suez, Aden,
Ceylon, Madras and Calcutta, and a service to Sydney soon followed.

While Brunel launched his *Great Britain* and *Great Eastern*, Samuel Cunard,
a Canadian-born Briton, won the contract in 1839 to carry British government
mails across the Atlantic, his ships soon competing with those of rival lines for the
Blue Ribband, awarded for the fastest time from New York to Britain. Cunard
formed the British and North American Royal Mail Steam Packet Company,
which later became the eponymous company. Cunard's first ships included the
Britannia (1840), the *Persia* (1858) and the *China* (1862), each one faster and
bigger than the last. Faster and bigger ships were not the only factors making the
world a smaller place. In 1869 one of the most remarkable feats of 19th-century
engineering, the cutting of the canal through the isthmus of Suez, united Europe
and Asia and redoubled British interest in the Mediterranean and the Indian

THE P&O

The British Empire was a byword for cosmopolitanism. For the imperial élite, it was but a small step from the Savoy Grill to the terrace of Shepherd's Hotel in Cairo or the Long Bar at Raffles in Singapore. Companies such as P&O, Cunard, Elder Dempster, British Overseas Airways Corporation and Imperial Airways offered romantic and luxurious travel in a British-dominated world. Though international travel took far longer than it does today, it was possible to undertake journeys to the ends of the Earth without ever departing from territory over which the Union Jack fluttered, sometimes in a tropical breeze, sometimes in a South Atlantic gale. The journey to Singapore, for example, could be made without ever leaving British-controlled airspace, stopping off at familiar imperial way-stations in the Mediterranean, the Gulf and Asia on the way.

An advertisement for Black & White Whisky, dating from the 1930s, shows a black steward serving drinks to a languid European in evening dress on the deck of an ocean liner.

district commissioners on tour. Made of teak, oak or mahogany, campaign chests included numerous drawers, a writing desk or secretaire and secret compartments.

Sjovald Cunyngham-Brown, a colonial administrator in Malaya, remembered with affection his sea trips to and from Britain, the 'hot, listless days and cool, velvety nights spent gazing out over the limitless ocean as the ship rolled gently over the Indian Ocean in starlight and phosphorescence'. He spent his days on board ship talking to friends, having a good lunch, playing deck tennis or splashing in the canvas pool erected over the forehatch. At midday there was the tote on the ship's daily run, followed by lunch and a siesta ('lie-off' in nautical terms). More sports and outdoors entertainments until the evening where everyone, whether in First or Second Class, bathed and changed for dinner, wearing dinner-jackets as far as Port Said and thereafter 'the short white jacket, worn with black trousers, known as the bum-freezer, in which one went out to dinner in the tropics'.

Travelling in style

Peninsular & Oriental liners provided a 'travelling hotel' from Tilbury or Southampton to Bombay – or, if you could afford it, you could first go by rail through France on the Blue train and catch a steamer at Marseilles, thereby missing the rough Bay of Biscay. The full paraphernalia associated with travelling in style accompanied the well-to-do on their journeys, and companies such as 'Pukka' luggage manufactured suitcases, wardrobe trunks and hat boxes. The Army and Navy Stores, meanwhile, specialized in supplying campaign chests to Britons requiring furniture as they moved from city to city or from tented camp to bungalow, essential items of kit for military officers on campaign and

P&O ships were organized along very military lines, and bugles rang at all hours. 'The bugle for dinner meant sinking one's dry martini and descending into the very handsome dining-room with its great punkahs swinging, and all my friends in their mess-kits – Gurkhas, 11th Hussars, Indian civilians going back from furlough – all of us laughing and chatting, getting to our appointed places and discussing the wines that we were to drink that evening … After dinner there was dancing, with the ship's band regaling the dancers with the tunes of Cole Porter and Ivor Novello.'

Just as the firepower of Portugal had transformed the world in the sixteenth century, now in the nineteenth the steam-power of Britain was about to sweep away patterns of travel dating back more than two thousand years. Sails would not vanish from the ocean overnight, but the thumping rhythm of steam-engines, tackling the monsoons head on, was becoming the sound of a new age.

Richard Hall, Empires of the Monsoon:
A History of the Indian Ocean and its Invaders *(1996)*

Ocean, symbolized by Disraeli's purchase of a majority shareholding in the new canal on behalf of the British government. The British Merchant Navy held a dominant position in the carrier trade of the world until the Second World War, and British naval power ensured that the world's key choke points, such as the Cape, Suez and the Malacca Straits, were controlled by British warships and bases.

Carrying the mail

By subsidizing shipping lines to carry mail, the British government gained the right to requisition ships in emergencies, particularly useful for the transit of troops during times of war. Subsidized services also increased contact between Britain and the wider world to the benefit of commerce, capital, overseas settlement and the British domestic economy. For P&O, the subsidy between 1840 and 1880 made up 29 percent of operating costs and 28.5 per cent of total receipts. This relationship between private enterprise and government resulted in the maintenance of vessels and sailors that could be turned to account in times of war, as the government harnessed the resources of the Merchant Navy, the 'nursery of seamen' upon which British maritime supremacy was founded. This still applied in the Second World War, when hundreds of merchant vessels were converted into armed merchant cruisers and emergency aircraft carriers, and passenger liners became troopships and hospital ships. As late as the 1982 Falklands conflict the British government made extensive use of 'Ships Taken Up From Trade' to supplement the task force sent to regain the islands, including the liner *Canberra* and the ill-fated container ship *Atlantic Conveyor*.

So the 19th century witnessed the birth of new shipping routes and new ports, used by scheduled steamers wearing the livery of companies such as P&O, bringing mail and passengers from Britain and other parts of the world. The Scottish millionaire Sir William Mackinnon, one of the great shipping magnates of the day, built up a dominant position in the steamship business of the Indian Ocean through his British India Steam Navigation Company, winning government mail subsidies. Mackinnon was also responsible, through his Imperial British East Africa Company, for driving Britain's coastal presence in East Africa inland towards the Rift Valley and the Great Lakes. His British India company operated branch lines and smaller local shipping routes which complemented the longer-haul services provided by P&O, its steamers plying their trade between islands, up and

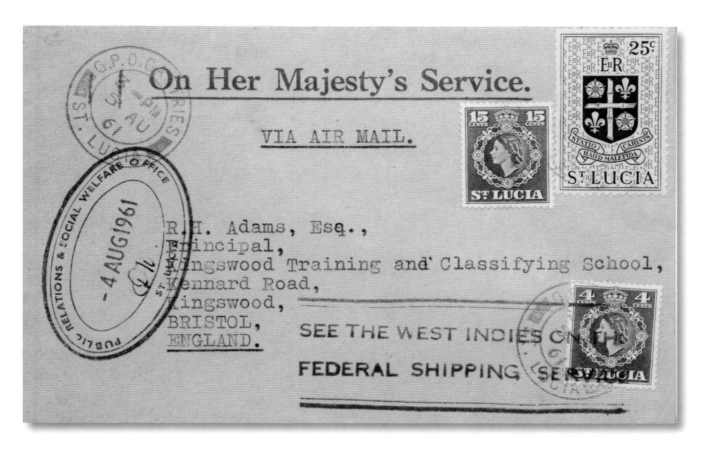

'On Her Majesty's Service' heralded official mail around the world. This letter was posted in the British colony of St Lucia on 4 August 1961, its official point of origin being the Public Relations and Social Welfare Office of the colony's government. The frank on the right says 'See the West Indies on the Federal Shipping Service'.

down rivers and along coasts. It was the main carrier on the Bombay to Basra line, and its vessels were often chartered by the Government of India for the transit of troops. By the 1860s British India steamers connected Bombay to Muscat, Bandar Abbas, Bushire, Bahrain and Basra. From here another British-owned company, the Euphrates and Tigris Steam Navigation Company, provided the onward connection to Baghdad. Eastern merchant houses such as Jardine Mathesons and Butterfield and Swires maintained their own fleets of river steamers and China coasters. These vessels worked up and down the west or east coast of Malaya carrying general cargo and passengers on the outward run from Hong Kong or Shanghai and returned with local produce such as sheet rubber, tapioca, timber and copra.

Vying for custom

Steam navigation companies and British-dominated ports and sea routes created a very British world. The Indian Ocean region, for example, was clearly an imperial arena, and it was impossible not to notice the 'Britishness' of it all. In 'British-looking' ports such as Aden, wrote E. J. Harding, Secretary to the Dominions Commission, there were 'all the necessary appliances for buying Kodak films, Whisky, Picture Postcards and other British delights. I think it really ought to be called "the Imperial Piccadilly".'

From cross-Channel packets to the monster ocean liners, foremost among which were the *Queen Mary* and the *Queen Elizabeth*, sophisticated posters lured

A postcard from the late 1930s of the P&O liner RMS *Strathallan*. Launched at Barrow-in-Furness in March 1938, she was the largest ship in the P&O fleet at the time and was built for the London to Sydney run. Her civilian career was cut short in 1940, when she was requisitioned by the War Office as a troopship. On 11 December 1942 she left the Clyde, packed with over 4000 troops, 250 nurses and the HQ staff of General Eisenhower's new North Africa Allied command. Destined for Oran as part of the Operation Torch invasion, she was torpedoed by *U-562* in the Mediterranean on 21 December. Miraculously, all but three people survived, though the *Strathallan* was consigned to an early grave. *U-562* was sunk by the Royal Navy 8 weeks later.

the traveller to the booking offices of the many competing shipping lines. The Oceanic Steamship Company, for instance, advertised its Europe to Sydney service with an image of 'an early morning call' which showed a sleek and graceful liner moored off a palm-fringed shoreline, set against a backdrop of picturesque mountains and native onlookers. Ocean liners were symbols of modernity and luxury, and a common subject for picture postcards.

In the 1960s there were still many different cargo and passenger liner companies operating in Britain and the Commonwealth. The Union-Castle Mail Steamship Company took mail, passengers and cargo between Britain and the Continent to South and East Africa; its liners, such as the *Windsor Castle*, were a familiar sight leaving Southampton's Western Docks for Cape Town until the company ceased operations in 1977. The Cunard Steamship Company, which had its headquarters in Liverpool, took passengers, mail and cargo from Liverpool, Southampton, London, Greenock and Havre to New York and Canada, and cargo to the Great Lakes and the Mediterranean. Transatlantic passenger liners included the leviathans *Lusitania* and *Mauretania*, the British White Star Line's sister ships, the *Olympic* and *Titanic*, and Cunard's *Queen Mary* and *Queen Elizabeth*. These last two vessels, built in the 1930s, were the largest of them all. They weighed over 80,000 tons each, were over 1000 ft (300 metres) in length, and could carry

P. & O. R.M.S. STRATHALLAN, 23,500 TONS.
Carrying First-class and Tourist-class Passengers India and Australia Mail Service.

CUSTOMS IN TROPIC SEAS. AT FIVE IN THE MORNING THEY PIPE TO WASH DOWN THE DECKS, AND AT ONCE THE LADIES WHO ARE SLEEPING THERE TURN OUT AND THEY AND THEIR BEDS GO BELOW. THEN ONE AFTER ANOTHER THE MEN COME UP FROM THE BATH IN THEIR PYJAMAS, AND WALK THE DECKS AN HOUR OR TWO WITH BARE LEGS AND BARE FEET. COFFEE AND FRUIT ARE SERVED. THE SHIP CAT AND HER KITTEN NOW APPEAR AND GET ABOUT THEIR TOILETS; NEXT THE BARBER COMES AND FLAYS US ON THE BREEZY DECK. BREAKFAST AT 9.30, AND THE DAY BEGINS. THE PEOPLE GROUP THEMSELVES ABOUT THE DECKS IN THEIR SNOWY WHITE LINEN, AND READ, SMOKE, SEW, PLAY CARDS, TALK, NAP AND SO ON ... IF I HAD MY WAY WE SHOULD NEVER GET IN [TO PORT] AT ALL ... THERE IS NO MAIL TO READ AND ANSWER; NO NEWSPAPERS TO EXCITE YOU; NO TELEGRAMS TO FRET YOU OR FRIGHT YOU – THE WORLD IS FAR, FAR AWAY; IT HAS CEASED TO EXIST FOR YOU – SEEMED A FADING DREAM, ALONG IN THE FIRST DAYS; HAS DISSOLVED TO UNREALITY NOW ... IF I HAD MY WAY I WOULD SAIL ON FOR EVER AND NEVER GO TO LIVE ON THE SOLID GROUND AGAIN.

– Mark Twain on a voyage between Ceylon and Mauritius, 1896

more than 2000 passengers (a figure inflated to 15,000 when they were converted for use as troopships during the Second World War).

'A swift agent of government': air power and air routes

'Fly to Africa by Imperial Airways' proclaimed a 1930s poster picturing a Short S. 23C 'Empire' Class flying boat landing smoothly off a tropical coast, a white-tipped bow wave trailing in its wake. Such adverts represented an entirely new concept of travel to Britons in the inter-war years as for the first time overseas journeys could be undertaken without boarding a ship. Thus began the golden age of the flying-boat as a series of air routes were added to the already-congested map of the Empire's lines of communication.

The military had pioneered manned flight in the 19th century, often spurred on by colonial campaigns. The Royal Engineers used observation balloons for reconnaissance during General Sir Garnet Wolseley's occupation of Bechuanaland in 1884. The American entrepreneur, Wild West showman and inventor Samuel Cody flew his 'British Army Aeroplane Number 1' at Farnborough in 1908, and in the following year the Frenchman Louis Blériot stimulated enormous interest in powered flight (not to mention a great deal of paranoia about Britain's security) when he made the first crossing of the Channel by aeroplane. The British pilots John Alcock and Arthur Whitten Brown made the first non-stop Atlantic crossing in 1919, taking off from Newfoundland and landing in Ireland, and in 1920 two more British pilots conquered the Cairo to Cape Town route. In 1926 Alan Cobham made the first non-stop flight between London and Sydney. The first man to fly from Britain to Australia, in 15 days, was the Australian Bert Hinkler in 1928. Amy Johnson became the first woman to fly solo from England to Australia when she took off from Croydon in a De Havilland Gypsy Moth on

5 May 1930, landing in Darwin 19 days later. She followed this success, which brought deserved celebrity and a CBE, with a flight from London to Japan via Moscow in a De Havilland Puss Moth the following year. In 1932 she claimed the record for a solo flight from London to Cape Town, in 1933 she crossed the Atlantic and in 1934 she flew to India. She died while flying for the RAF in the Second World War.

The S. 23C 'Empire' class was a passenger and mail flying-boat weighing 23,500 pounds and with a wingspan of 114 feet. Powered by four Bristol Pegasus engines, with a streamlined hull and high cantilever wings, Imperial Airways ordered 28 for service on Empire air mail routes. The first aircraft entered service in September 1936 and was soon ranging far and wide to Australia, Bermuda, Durban, Egypt, Malaya, New York, East Africa and South Africa. The 'Empire' class spurred significant developments that illustrated the close relationship between civil and military technological progress. Its proven lineage contributed to the Air Ministry's decision to order production examples of a successor, which developed into the famous Short Sunderland

28
HYDRAVIONS TYPE 'EMPIRE'
VITESSE : 320 KILOMETRES HEURE
IMPERIAL AIRWAYS
EUROPE   AFRIQUE   INDES
EXTREME-ORIENT   AUSTRALIE

Like shipping companies, airlines produced glamorous posters promoting their technologically advanced machines. This Imperial Airways advertisement shows a Short 'Empire' class flying-boat. Flying-boats heralded a new dawn in civil aviation, though their heyday was confined to the 1930s as world war, and then more advanced passenger airliners, overtook them.

flying-boat. The Sunderland saw service with the RAF around the world during the Second World War, playing a vital anti-submarine role in the Battle of the Atlantic.

As with sea voyages aboard British ships sailing between British ports across the world, airlines of communication were also very 'British' in character by virtue of the size of the Empire. In July 1941 the veteran American war correspondent Cecil Brown took off from the Nile. 'Before dawn, we took off and flew the entire way to Bahrain Island over the Persian Gulf at ten to eleven thousand feet altitude.' The following day the flying-boat 'paralleled the Ganges' and landed at Calcutta before striking out across the Bay of Bengal for Akyab Island and the flight down the slender finger of Southeast Asia. 'The steward woke me for tea to announce we would be in Singapore in twenty minutes. For five days of flying, from Suez to Singapore, at almost every stop we had touched on water under the protection of the British flag. It was a stunning reflection on Empire.'

Civilian air routes assumed strategic importance during times of war. The Takoradi Air Route, running from the Gold Coast to Egypt, was pioneered as a civil air route by Imperial Airways (in 1938 Imperial Airways merged with British Airways to form British Overseas Airways Corporation, BOAC). Its strategic potential was noted at the time, and when Italy went to war with Britain in 1940, making the Mediterranean supply route hazardous, it was decided to use the trans-Africa route to reinforce the Western Desert Air Force. Over 40 airfields supported this route across the belt of Africa, and it delivered over 2000 American and 4500 British aircraft to the Middle East war theatre.

The Royal Mail and postage stamps

Letters and parcels carried aboard mail packets connected the world, and from the 1840s postage stamps became the method of paying for this service. British Empire postage stamps were miniature masterpieces depicting scenes from across the globe, presided over by the image of the King or Queen. Stamps could exercise a powerful influence. Bill Bangs, who became a rubber planter, collected stamps as a boy and was always drawn to the Malayan stamps which showed a leaping tiger, telling himself 'That's the country I want to go to'. Rowland Hill was an English schoolmaster and civil servant, who in 1837 invented the adhesive postage stamp, an innovation for which he was later knighted. This was the year of Queen Victoria's coronation, and three years later the world's first adhesive postage stamp was issued, the iconic Penny Black, which bore the young monarch's profile and helped make her the most famous person on Earth.

The twopenny blue was launched in the same year, and the hobby of stamp collecting took off instantly, as people bought them as souvenirs and mementos. Other nations followed Britain's lead, and by 1866 there were over 2500 types of stamp in circulation, fuelling the new hobby as well as revolutionizing global communications. The first stamp albums for collectors to display their stamps in hit the market in 1862. From the British Empire came some of the rarest stamps

RIGHT The bearded profile of George V presides over this scene from British Guiana, which shows an 'Indian shooting fish'. Empire stamps were a delight for collectors, and remain highly desirable. Their geographic and design variety offered the collector the world in the palm of his hand, allowing him to fill in the numerous spaces allocated to the various dominions, colonies, dependencies, and overseas territories in his stamp album.

BELOW These stamps, from the reign of George VI, illustrate the kind of subjects that often formed the visual centrepiece of Empire stamps and contributed to their educational value and general fascination. Favourite themes were people, scenery and wildlife. On the left is Lake Naivasha (joint stamps were produced for the three East African territories of Kenya, Tanganyika and Uganda, reflecting Britain's hopes for regional federation), while an elephant adorns the stamp from Gambia in West Africa.

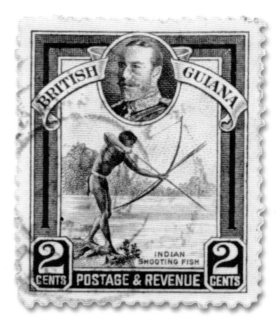

in the world, including the Blue Mauritius of 1847, the 1848 Perot stamp of Bermuda, the world's first triangular stamp issued in Cape Colony in 1853 and the 1856 British Guiana one-cent magenta.

Early postage stamps tended to feature official portraits of heads of state and politicians, though New South Wales set a trend when it launched a series of stamps bearing scenes from the colony. Later, stamps were issued to commemorate key national events, and the British Empire came to dominate this type of issue, as well as omnibus issues. This form of issue, where stamps were released simultaneously around the world, began with a series commemorating the Silver Jubilee of King George V in 1935, and has heralded royal events ever since.

Collected by commoners and kings alike

Stamp collecting developed into a hobby that was enjoyed by millions of people around the world. Moreover, it was a hobby noted for its popularity in Buckingham Palace; George V was a keen collector and amassed a particularly important collection, specializing in British and Empire stamps, that was passed on to future sovereigns.

Britain pioneered the modern postage stamp, and the country's stamps became a cipher of her imperial power. Just as in a later communications revolution

WHEN WE LOOK AT A POSTAGE STAMP WE THINK OF IT AS A TRAVELLER FROM LANDS AFAR, AND AT ONCE THERE SPRING UP IN OUR MINDS A HUNDRED ASSOCIATIONS WITH ALL THAT WE HAVE READ OR KNOW OF THE COUNTRY CONCERNED. A STAMP OF CANADA WILL BRING TO MIND BOUNDLESS PRAIRIES, GREAT LAKES, AND WIDE-FLUNG FORESTS. VISIONS OF BURNING DESERT WASTES, ACROSS WHICH WIND LONG CARAVANS OF PILGRIMS ON THEIR WAY TO THE HOLY CITIES OF ISLAM, ARE CONJURED UP BY A STAMP OF THE HEJAZ. THE TROPIC JUNGLE, THE POLAR ICE, THE HEIGHTS OF THE ANDES AND THE PLAINS OF SIBERIA ALL SPRING INTO MENTAL VIEW AT THE SIGHT OF A POSTAGE STAMP.

– Stanley Gibbons' Catalogue, 'An Introduction to Stamp Collecting'

America, by virtue of being first, was the only country not to have a 'dot.usa' suffix on its e-mail addresses, so too in this earlier era Britain was (and still remains) the only country in the world not to have the country's name on its stamps.

Edward Stanley Gibbons, purveyor of stamps and the accoutrements of stamp-collecting, conducted business from famous premises on the Strand. Gibbons had set up in business in 1856 after buying a sackful of rare triangular stamps from the Cape of Good Hope and published his first catalogue nine years later. In 1914 King George V granted his company a Royal Warrant. In 1930 Gibbons' Strand premises comprised 18 rooms staffed by 70 people. Special albums were designed for Empire stamps, such as Gibbons' 'Imperial' – 'The British Empire Album in One Volume' – which contained over 900 pages with 12,000 spaces, with 2300 illustrations. Stamp albums often contained adverts for packets of stamps for collectors. In the 'Pioneer Stamp Album' on sale in the 1940s an advert read 'Ask your Stationer for "Torch" Packets of Stamps', a range that included 'British Commemoratives', 'Old England', 'Army and Navy', 'Strategic Islands', 'the Red Sea', 'Far East' and 'Pillars of the Empire'.

Postage stamps were sold in post offices all over the world, and the envelopes and parcels to which they were attached were conveyed across continents by rail and coach after travelling overseas by steamer. The physical infrastructure of the British Empire – its grand post offices, town halls and railways – left an indelible mark on the built environment of the world, and forms the subject of the following chapter.

Despite the Great Depression, 'the number of collectors in all parts of the world has increased enormously of late' observed the 1931 Stanley Gibbons' catalogue. It offered hundreds of pages of detailed information about the Empire's stamps. Even at this period, the territories under British sway were still growing, and the catalogue noted that 'to the already extensive lists of Great Britain and the British Empire, Egypt and Hejaz have now been added on account of the British influence prevailing'.

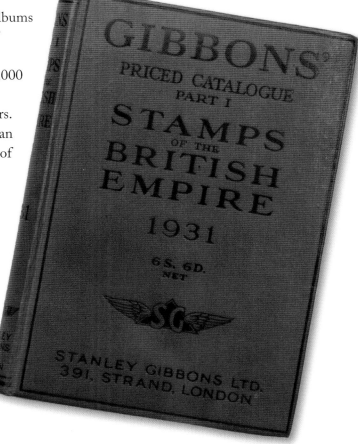

THE RHODES COLOSSUS
STRIDING FROM CAPE TOWN TO CAIRO.

Colonial Gothic and Narrow-Gauge Tracks: Architecture and Engineering

PALATIAL BUILDINGS AND FEATS OF CIVIL ENGINEERING went hand in hand with the growth of the British Empire as the built environment in distant lands was transformed. Railways, bridges, dams, verandahed houses and department stores – such as Haddon and Sly in Bulawayo and Cargill's in Colombo – were part of the fabric of the British Empire.

Wherever the British went, so they would claim, they created splendid buildings and applied the latest technology to the challenges of the natural world, damming rivers, bridging gorges, developing new ports and spanning whole continents by rail.

Construction projects such as the Victoria Falls Bridge, the Owen Falls Dam, the Lake Kariba hydro-electric scheme and the narrow-gauge railway that wound upwards to the Indian hill station of Simla, were achievements crowed over by the British, who saw them as proof of the beneficence of their rule. Grand public buildings, railways, bridges and mines were the very symbols of progress. Feats of engineering and construction, many Britons believed, were what *made* countries; through enlightened rule and the development of physical infrastructure the British actually created new nations, the ultimate justification for their rule.

Science and technology

Science and technology went hand in hand with British expansion overseas. Medicine and the study of tropical diseases, conducted at special research centres such as the London and Liverpool schools of tropical medicine, helped make it easier for people to survive overseas, and the defeat of malaria represented a major advance. Geological surveys made the British masters of what lay beneath the earth's surface as well as what lay above. New strains of crops were developed in British laboratories and botanical gardens, and pioneering geologists led the way in the search for new sources of minerals, oil and precious stones. Technological advances aided expansion, for motives had to be matched by the means. During the 19th century 'the means' developed rapidly, contributing to the speedy colonization of Africa and Asia. Technology included hardware – such as breech-loading rifles, smokeless gunpowder, Gatling guns, railways and new ports – but also 'soft', organizational technology. These included military techniques such as the use of

One of the most iconic images of Empire: in 1892, the humorous magazine *Punch* portrayed the British mining magnate and imperial entrepreneur Cecil Rhodes as a Colossus bestriding Africa. The allusion was to Rhodes' stated ambition to establish a telegraph and rail link the length of the entire continent, from the Cape to Cairo.

FROM ALEXANDRIA TO CAIRO, FROM CAIRO TO WADY HALFA, FROM HALFA TO BERBER, FROM BERBER TO KHARTOUM, FROM KHARTOUM TO FASHODA, FROM FASHODA TO GONDOKORO, OVER A DISTANCE OF NEARLY THREE THOUSAND MILES, STRETCHES AN UNINTERRUPTED SERVICE OF TRAINS AND STEAMERS.

– Winston Churchill on a visit to North Africa, 1908

The Sydney Harbour Bridge, here depicted on a jigsaw puzzle, was designed by the Australian architect Sir John Bradfield and was opened in 1932. It is 3772 ft (1150 metres) long and made of 53,000 tons of steel.

the infantry square, financial and credit innovations, currency controls, the joint stock company and marketing boards able to buy and sell the produce of an entire geographic region.

Developments in military and transport technology meant that Britons could arrive with overwhelming firepower at land-locked places such as Ava, capital of the Burmese Empire and 400 miles inland, because of shallow-draft steamers. During the first Opium War (1839–42) shallow-draft steamers towed battleships 200 miles (320 km) up river to Nanking; in Abyssinia and the Sudan the British built railway lines to aid their inexorable military progress; and from the early 20th-century fighters, light bombers and transport aircraft took munitions, warning leaflets and troops to the most inaccessible parts of the world. On the non-military side, telegraph cables and wireless revolutionized global communications. In the 1850s sending a message to India and receiving a reply took two to three months; by the 1870s, it took just five hours. At the same time, steamships and refrigeration were revolutionizing the international economy. These developments, in the words of the historian Daniel Headrick, 'turned isolated subsistence economies with limited trade contacts into parts of a single world market in basic commodities, shattering

traditional trading, technological and political relationships, and in their place laid the foundations for a new global civilization based on Western technology'.

The unstoppable march of the railways

The British Empire brought railway tracks to far-off continents and connected coastal towns to settlements deep in the interior. The extension of railway communications was presented as a triumph of achievement, opening up previously inaccessible places and permitting the movement of trade goods and troops. The King travelled aboard the White Train when touring Africa in 1947; the Canadian Pacific Railway built a nation; the Trans-Australian line began in 1912 with a 1000-mile (1600-km) stretch connecting South Australia to Western Australia; troop trains crawled across the plains of India; and Indian Civil Servants and their wives were deposited amidst the cool climes of Simla, summer capital of the Raj, by a winding narrow-gauge track driven through solid rock as it climbed the southern slopes of the Himalayas.

Railways aided imperial conquest. Lord Kitchener's ponderous but irresistible progress towards Khartoum and the Mahdi's last redoubt marched at the pace of a railway line; the kingdom of Kandy in Ceylon lost its historic impregnability once engineers had blasted a railway line into the island's central highlands; and General Sir Robert Napier's military railway in Abyssinia contributed to the downfall of

Railway workers in Salisbury, Rhodesia (modern Harare, Zimbabwe) pose in front of 'Engine No.1', which in 1909 pulled the first train from Umtali (Mutare) near the border with Mozambique to the Rhodesian capital. This stretch formed one leg of the projected 'Cape to Cairo' railway line planned by Cecil Rhodes.

Emperor Tewodoros. An army of Indian labourers built the strategic railway line that linked Mombasa and the Swahili coast to the interior of the East Africa Protectorate, the railway thereafter advertised as the 'gateway' to this wonderful new land that drew comparisons with Australia as a desirable destination for settlers. During the Second World War a military railway was constructed from Haifa to Beirut by British sappers and a host of Pioneer soldiers and specialist tunnellers drawn from Southern Africa, lest the Germans attack the Middle East from the north.

The expeditionary force sent to Abyssinia in 1867 under General Sir Robert Napier involved the conveyance of an army with all its guns and supplies 400 miles (640 km) inland from the Red Sea coast, across a desert, to the 9000 foot-high mountain fortress of Magdala. For the initial stages of the route it was decided to build a railway. To this end six tank engines, 60 trucks, 8800 twenty-four foot-long rails and 35,500 sleepers were landed from India after the Royal Engineers had surveyed the route. Construction was undertaken by the 23rd Punjab Pioneers, the 2nd Bombay Grenadiers and the Army Works Corps. In March, April and May 1867 the railway carried 14,000 troops, 10,000 'native followers', 9000 tons of Commissariat stores, 2400 tons of materials and 2000 tons of soldiers' kit.

Islands such as Ceylon and Mauritius sprouted efficient and extensive railway networks. The British government allowed Cecil Rhodes to open up Central Africa with a railway line originating in the Cape. Soon, steam engines were being used in the marshalling yards of Bulawayo's Victorian railway terminus, preparing for journeys to Victoria Falls Station or Mafeking, towing in their sooty wake elegant corridor carriages. Here first-class passengers relaxed and slept overnight in comfort, their cabins decorated with pictures showing Rhodesian scenery and cityscapes. 'RR' – 'Rhodesia Railways' – was embossed on the mirrors above the seat-cum-bunk beds and the stainless steel washstands. A porter knocked in the morning, bearing a copper pot with an elongated spout, and announced the 'morning cup'. With folded napkins bearing the company motif and waiter-served dinners in the dining car, the journey progressed. A halt for water as the track ran alongside the Wankie National Park, and an open window looking out onto a star-spangled night, brought the mournful call of a lion to the traveller's ears.

Baronial splendour in the bush

Throughout the British world gentlemen's clubs, grand hotels, railway stations, public schools, universities, provincial legislatures and Anglican cathedrals proliferated, many of them constructed in Scottish Baronial or Gothic Revival styles redolent of history, antiquity, hierarchy and tradition. The military, especially the Royal Engineers, left their mark on colonies in the form of military cantonments and family lines, and the grid system that distinguished the street layout of so many colonial towns and cities. Khartoum was laid out in the shape of a Union Jack, Bulawayo was dominated by streets wide enough for a span of oxen to turn in, Colombo and Hobart were laid out in geometrically-pleasing blocks, and onion-

THE CANADIAN PACIFIC RAILWAY

Canada was a nation quite literally created by a railway. Like Australia, Canada was an amalgamation of previously separate colonies and settlements, some of them French. Upper and Lower Canada were united in 1867, as the British habit of creating new federations developed. The construction of the Canadian Pacific Railway, extending for 2891 miles (4625 km) from Montreal to Vancouver, was a condition of British Colombia joining the federation and a move calculated to persuade the colony not to join the United States as it expanded into the prairie region. The railway, constructed between 1881 and 1885, enabled the settlers to break out of the Great Lakes and St Lawrence valley and become truly transcontinental. The Canadian government also saw the railway as a means of developing the resources of the interior and forging a sense of national identity in this vast, fledgling country. As the railway was driven inland, new towns grew up along its routes, such as Calgary and Winnipeg, and the railway company developed a unique style of architecture for its stations and its grand hotels, such as the famous Château Frontenac in Quebec.

A cigarette card of 1937 showing one of the many great engineering feats on the route of the Canadian Pacific Railway, the Lethbridge Viaduct, or 'High Level Bridge' in Alberta. It was constructed in 1907–09 as the CPR sought to improve the original track, and remains the largest railway structure in Canada.

WILLS'S CIGARETTES.

LETHBRIDGE VIADUCT.

shaped water towers and square government buildings sprouted from the camel-thorn scrub of the Kalahari as the city of Gaborone was built from scratch in the 1960s.

In many parts of the British Empire, English baronial splendour broke out from the bush, incongruous protrusions lifted from the shires and set down amidst baobab trees and elephant grass. In 1932 Sir David Duncan built a Tudor-style mansion outside Nairobi, set in 140 acres (57 hectares) of parkland. With its view of the Ngong Hills, Giraffe Manor later became a sanctuary for endangered species, such as the Rothschild giraffe, when it ceased to be a private home.

In Northern Rhodesia Sir Stewart Gore-Brown created his own feudal paradise, a sprawling country estate centred upon Shiwa House, a three-storey pink-bricked mansion that would not have looked out of place in Surrey or Hampshire. As if to signal conquest and the successful establishment of an oasis of Englishness in the heart of Africa, the house flew a Union Jack from its flagpole. Built in the early 1920s, Shiwa House concealed classic Edwardian interiors behind its stout oak door, featuring Spode china, Meissen plates, a Queen Anne desk and a canopied four-poster bed. Uniformed servants padded silently along its corridors and tended its rose gardens.

Gothic cathedrals and grand hotels

Famous architects plied their trade in Britain and across the Empire, building churches and houses, some even designing entire capital cities such as Canberra and New Delhi. Sir Herbert Baker's architectural career illustrates this progression from smaller projects to grand ones. He designed the Anglican Church in Mafeking, remodelled Groote Schuur (Cecil Rhodes' house on the slopes of Table Mountain) and designed the Prince of Wales School near Nairobi. His major projects included the 'Palladian mansion' that was Government House, Nairobi, the Anglican Cathedral in Harare and the career summits of the grand Union Buildings in Pretoria and the imposing capital city at New Delhi. Baker was the dominant force in British African architecture, and also designed Rhodes University in Grahamstown, Rhodes House in Oxford and the War Cloister at Winchester College.

New Delhi was a triumph of imperial architecture. The bust of Sir Edwin Landseer Lutyens that was erected in New Delhi in honour of the architect who laid out India's new capital was the only public monument of the Raj not to be removed by the Indian government at independence, testament to the enduring value of Lutyens' (and his co-architect Sir Herbert Baker's) design and execution. Lutyens, like Baker, had a strong British and imperial architectural pedigree. He had designed Hyderabad House in Delhi (the town residence of the Nizam of Hyderabad) as well as Campion Hall in Oxford, the British Embassy in Washington, the Cenotaph in Whitehall and the monument to the fallen of the Somme at Thiepval. Lutyens' novel take on Classical architecture embodied many elements of Indian design. The Viceregal Lodge in New Delhi, with its 340 rooms, was dominated by a drum-mounted Buddhist dome. The capital also featured the vast Parliament Buildings and Secretariat Buildings, the latter mainly designed by Baker. As well as the Mughal style incorporated into the design, the buildings' setting was reflected in the local red sandstone used in its construction.

The architecture of Anglo-India came in three basic forms, according to imperial historian John Mackenzie: palaces, public buildings and the larger railway termini, frequently 'unsuccessful attempts to synthesize the Gothic with Saracenic'. Rather more successful was the 'English Palladian style adapted to India in the latter part of the 18th century'. Meanwhile the indigenous rulers of empire built palaces and baronial halls. Lalit Malal Palace outside Mysore city was modelled on St Paul's. Maharajahs' palaces were often orientalized versions of British country houses and castles, and the Victoria Terminus at Bombay, High Court at Hyderabad and the University of Madras were reworkings of buildings in London and the Dominions.

The British also built some of the world's most famous hotels, resting places for itinerant Britons moving around the Empire once the P&O or Elder Dempster liner had deposited them and their luggage on a foreign shore. Among them was

Luggage label for the Galle Face Hotel in Colombo, Sri Lanka (Ceylon). Built in 1864, this luxurious hotel is one of the oldest in Asia and has played host to many prominent guests, including Lord Louis Mountbatten of Burma and Marshal Tito, the Yugoslav partisan leader and dictator.

the Galle Face Hotel in Colombo. Older than the Suez Canal, the Oriental Hotel in Bangkok, the Imperial in Tokyo, the Taj Mahal in Bombay, Raffles in Singapore, the Manila Hotel, the Peninsular Hotel in Hong Kong and the Victoria Falls Hotel, it was a pioneering institution, advertising itself as 'The Most Luxurious Hotel in the East'. Only a short distance from the harbour where visitors first made landfall in Colombo, its buildings were set around a palm-fringed courtyard looking directly out onto the Indian Ocean. It was the venue for regular dances and cabarets on the terrace overlooking the sea. Inside it featured early Victorian décor, lattice-work teak and cherry wood, punkahs pulled by punkah-wallahs and a nightclub known as the Silver Faun, visited by the likes of Lord Mountbatten, Prince Philip and the James Bond author Ian Fleming.

The empire in Britain

Imperial architectural influences abounded in Britain, from high-street cinemas to country houses and the interiors of London residences. Brighton Pavilion was remodelled in the 19th century in the style of a Mughal palace, with onion-shaped domes, filigrees arches and minarets, the interior decorated in exotic Chinese styles. The stately home of Sezincote near Moreton-in-Marsh in Gloucestershire, was, according to Mackenzie, built in the Oriental fashion, 'the only major essay in the Indian country house, built with a tent-room, a temple to Surya [and] Brahmin bulls'. Obelisks, pyramids and sphinxes and Egyptian mausoleums appeared on English estates and occasionally in English town squares and cemeteries from the early eighteenth century. There was an Arab Hall in Lord Leighton's house in Holland Park, one of the many Islamic interiors of Victorian England. An Indian extension was planned for Knebworth House, home of the sometime Viceroy Lord Lytton, though was never built. Other British buildings

Sectional drawing of the remodelled Royal Pavilion in Brighton, designed and executed in 1815–23 by the architect John Nash for the Prince Regent (later George IV). The exotic architecture and ornamentation of the pavilion was the apotheosis of a vogue for all things Eastern that had held the English aristocracy in thrall since the late 18th century.

told of the influence of foreign architecture and design, from the Egyptian Hall in Piccadilly to the once-common bathhouses. There were Indian-style billiard- and smoking-rooms at the Duke of Connaught's Bagshot Park and a Durbar Room at Osborne, both designed by John Lockwood Kipling and Ram Singh, the details created by his school of Indian craftsmen in Lahore. During the 20th century, cinemas often displayed touches of eastern exoticism in their architecture as well as their names, such as Alhambra, Granada, Orient and Hippodrome.

Mini-Englands overseas

Overseas, mini-Englands sprang up wherever settlers gathered. Ballarat in the Australian state of Victoria became renowned for its 'little England' character, derived from its fine buildings and wide boulevards. Fuelled by a mid-19th century gold rush, between the 1860s and 1890s the city sprouted notable shops, theatres, churches, colleges and hotels. Buildings included the Town Hall, the Post Office, the Art Gallery, the railway station and Her Majesty's Theatre. Sturt Street Gardens featured bandstands, fountains, statues, memorials, monuments and lamp-posts that would not have been out of place in a British town or city. There was even an ornamental bandstand erected in 1913 to commemorate the bandsmen of the *Titanic*, lost among the icebergs of a distant ocean the year before.

In British Colombia towns such as Vancouver and Victoria grew in size and character, and to this day retain elements of Englishness, sometimes so powerful that they appear as caricatures of a fairytale England of yesteryear. Red telephone boxes, red double-decker buses and tea at the Empress Hotel were features of life in Victoria. In Vancouver, cricket was played in Lord Stanley Park. At the University of British Columbia, the Queen Elizabeth Botanical Gardens are testament to the floral cross-pollination brought about by empire as well as the ubiquity of royal naming, as is the city's Queen Elizabeth Theatre. Canadian monarchism is further illustrated by the habit of hanging pictures of the Queen and Prince Philip in schools, common even in the 1990s when it had already died a death in Britain. Canadian Girl Guides swore allegiance to God, Queen and Country. Through North Vancouver runs the Baden-Powell Trail. Simon Fraser University in Vancouver is named after a Canadian fur-trapper and explorer who opened up vast swathes of what became British Colombia after establishing fur trading posts in the Rockies. English place names remain common: New Westminster and Surrey form part of Greater Vancouver; London Mountain was the original name of Whistler; and Kingston, St James's, King's and Queen's are all streets running off Vancouver's Lonsdale Avenue.

The foundation of Western-style cities, the development of railway networks and the bridging of gorges provided lasting legacies of Britain's imperial presence and its impact upon the world. Less tangible legacies included a range of cultural stereotypes of the non-Western world and a belief in the centrality of Britain in world affairs. These attitudes were captured and purveyed in a host of cultural media, and it is to the popular culture of the British Empire that we now turn.

DOWN THE DRIVE, UNDER THE EARLY YELLOW LEAVES OF OAKS; ONE LODGE IS TUDOR, ONE IN INDIAN STYLE. THE BRIDGE, THE WATERFALL, THE TEMPLE POOL. AND THERE THEY BURST UPON US, THE ONION DOMES, CHAJJAHS AND CHATTRIS MADE OF AMBER STONE: 'HOME OF THE OAKS', EXOTIC SEZINCOTE.

– *John Betjeman*, Summoned by Bells *(1960)*

Tasmania – A Little Piece of England

Tasmania was long regarded as one of the most 'British' of all the overseas domains. The capital city was named after Lord Hobart and English place names abound throughout the island including Launceston and Devonport, Swansea and Brighton, the River Tamar and Ben Nevis, Margate and Preston, Sheffield and Stonehenge. Bellerive, first settled in the 1820s, is a quiet village on Kangaroo Bluff, now engulfed by Hobart's sprawl across the River Derwent. In the village centre is an elegant ornamental iron lamp-post set on a stone plinth, erected as a memorial to Quartermaster Sergeant Frank Morrisby who died in the Boer War, seen off by a horse's kick. The monument bears the simple inscription 'Not for Self But Empire'. Fort Street and Gunning Street lead away from Bluff Battery, which fired its first shots in 1885, part of the defences built to protect Hobart from enemy raiders sailing up the Derwent. This English colonial village has its Britannia Place, Cambridge Road, King Street, Crown Street and Victoria Esplanade along the waterfront. Bidassoa Street was renamed Queen Street to commemorate Victoria's jubilee in 1897. Bellerive's Post Office dates from 1897, its police station and watch house from the 1840s. Bellerive's English colonial origins are also manifest in the form of the Clarence Hotel (1879), a cricket oval, a Scout Hall and streets of verandahed, English-style houses bearing names such as Bryn Mawr and Braeside.

Hobart – Home from Home

Hobart's architecture is uncompromisingly British, including the Town Hall, Colonial-Georgian town houses, the Cascade Brewery and lovely 19th-century churches. These included the English Gothic of St David's, the New Town Congregational church for the Independents of the London Missionary Society, the Wesley church for the Methodists, St Joseph's for the Catholics and St George's Battery Point with its Romanesque tower and Doric columns around the portico. The buildings of the University of Tasmania, opened in 1893, include the Gothic-style Tasmanian School of Art. Parliament House and the Customs House would not look out of place in a British town, and Anglesea Barracks was laid out during the Napoleonic Wars. Alongside Hobart's wharves ran Salamanca Place (named after a Peninsular War battle), home to chandlers, warehouses, pubs, agents' offices and a seamen's rest. Like so many English settlements, prominent buildings included the Theatre Royal, the Tasmanian Club, the Masonic Temple and a Botanical Gardens, close by the parkland of the Gothic Governor's House and the Cenotaph. A public school, Hutchins, was opened in 1846, its first headmaster selected by Dr Arnold of Rugby. Fittingly, Hutchins' Old Boys won the first two Australian VCs of the Boer War. Famous Old Boys included Pitcairn Jones, who joined the Royal Navy and rose to the rank of rear-admiral, winning the Khedive Star and Egyptian Medal and leading the naval brigade in the relief of Ladysmith during the Boer War.

Launceston – Stone from Aberdeen

Tasmania's second town, Launceston, grew in familiar grid-like fashion on the banks of the River Tamar. It was built by the British emigrants, free and convict, who poured into the island in the early years of Queen Victoria's reign. One such arrival was James Bennell, a freeman from London who arrived in this new land in 1834. He was a skilled house painter, carver and gilder. Plying his trade in Tasmania he introduced many of the features of Regency architecture then fashionable in Britain, and contributed lastingly to Tasmania's architectural heritage. Bennell built houses and shops of imitation Scotch granite, imported all the way from Aberdeen. Their Regency-style exteriors were embellished by steps and porches and sash windows, their interiors adorned with flame cedar mantelpieces with tapered pilasters and William Morris-style wallpaper. For E.F. Dease's shop on Brisbane Road Bennell built a beautiful Golden Fleece shop sign. 'Importer of British and Foreign Merchandise, Wholesale and Retail. Draper, Silk Mercer, Hosier, Haberdasher etc', it proclaimed. The roads on which these English shops and homes took root were planted with avenues of English elms and lined with cobbled gutters. In building them, the British transplanted themselves, their built environment, their mortgages and property rights, to the other side of the world.

Gum trees and gabled roofs. Only the vegetation and the intense blue of the sky belie the impression that this is an English market town: a street of restored ironstone houses in Penny Royal Village in Launceston, Tasmania.

EMPIRE OF INDIA EXHIBITION.

EARL'S COURT,

LONDON, 1895.

DIRECTOR GENERAL

IMRE KIRALFY.

OFFICIAL PROGRAMME. PRICE 2d.

Elgar and 'Chums': The Empire and Popular Culture

FROM THE PLUMMY TONES OF NOËL COWARD SINGING 'Mad Dogs and Englishmen' to adverts for Central African tobacco and the classic film *Sanders of the River*, empire was a major ingredient in British popular culture. References to empire and the strange and rather funny people who inhabited exotic locations teeming with wild beasts, primitive customs and bamboo forests were a staple ingredient of British fiction, theatre and music.

The visual arts – from colourful posters and the covers of comics to Lady Butler's stirring paintings of colonial battles – brought the frontiers of empire home to the British public. Classical and popular music – Promenade concerts, gramophone records and barrel organs – contained frequent references to empire. Flowing back in the other direction, it was contact with the non-European world that fuelled the Western taste for the Orient in décor as well as the avant garde and 'primitive' influences in 20th-century art and jazz music. Patterns, textiles, chinaware, furniture and architecture all showed lively cross-cultural exchange.

The 1890s were the high point of large-scale exhibitions in London, which became a theatrical stage for imperialism and imperial ideology. The 1895 Empire of India Exhibition's message was that British rule had created modern India. Paintings and even moving pictures were used to reinforce Victorian visions of India. As well as education, entertainment was a key theme of exhibitions, and at this one a 300-ft high Ferris wheel first appeared, offering spectacular views of London. Imre Kiralfy, a Hungarian-born British citizen, was the choreographer of this and many other exhibitions around the world, a member of the British Empire League and a Freemason.

The Empire as a cultural presence

British culture was shot through with references to empire, patriotism, the monarchy and the military. The Empire was a given in the lives of millions of people all over the world, as much a fact of international life as America is today. This was reinforced in many ways. As well as stage productions, literature and popular songs that made reference to imperial themes, BBC radio broadcasts went out to 'Listeners here, and in the Empire and the United States of America'; 'British Empire Made' was stamped on manufactured goods; and the words 'For King and Empire' appeared on the front page of the *Daily Mail*, a mass circulation newspaper that pledged to embody the imperial idea.*

Popular culture presented the British people with a distinctive view of the world and their place in it. It encompassed widely shared, discriminatory attitudes towards non-white people and greatly exaggerated the benefits brought to them by white rule. This world view was purveyed in films, newspapers, newsreels and literature that assumed the superiority of British values and institutions. Sam

* By the late 1960s it read 'For Queen and Commonwealth'.

167

Browne's famous song 'The Sun Has Got His Hat On (Hip Hip Hip Hooray)', from the 1937 musical *Me and My Girl*, illustrates the incidental and often derogatory manner in which non-Europeans were referred to:

He's been tanning niggers out in Timbuktu
Now he's coming back to do the same to you
So jump into your sunbath, hip-hip-hip-hooray
The sun has got his hat on and he's coming out today.

Schools helped embed the Empire as a fixture in the world view of the British people and their cousins in the Dominions. Al Deere, a New Zealander and Battle of Britain veteran, explains: 'In my generation, as schoolboys we always thought of [Britain] as the home country, always referred to it as the Mother Country. That was the old colonial tie … There was no question that if this country was threatened, New Zealanders wouldn't go to war for Britain.' Even people in the Empire who never visited Britain had a sense of it being 'home' or at the very least a cultural and political epicentre, and schools and bookshops in Johannesburg, Melbourne and Ontario were as choc-a-bloc with red Empire maps and literature of the derring-do, jolly old Empire variety as was the case back in Britain. This was not just a 'white' Dominions phenomenon: Connie Macdonald from Jamaica says: 'We were British! England was our mother country. We were

The Charge of the Bucks, Berks and Dorset Yeomanry, el-Mughar, Palestine, 13 November 1917 (1936) by James Prinsep Barnes Beadle RA. This painting, which hangs in the Joint Services Command and Staff College, is typical of the epic tradition in British martial painting. Beadle was born and raised in India.

THE EMPIRE CHRISTMAS PUDDING

according to the recipe supplied by the King's Chef Mr. CEDARD, with Their Majesties' Gracious Consent

1 lb Currants	Australia
1 lb Sultanas	Australia or South Africa
1 lb Stoned Raisins	Australia or South Africa
5 ozs Minced Apple	United Kingdom or Canada
1 lb Bread Crumbs	United Kingdom
1 lb Beef Suet	United Kingdom
6½ ozs Cut Candied Peel	South Africa
8 ozs Flour	United Kingdom
8 ozs Demerara Sugar	British West Indies or British Guiana
5 Eggs	United Kingdom or Irish Free State
½ oz Ground Cinnamon	India or Ceylon
¼ oz Ground Cloves	Zanzibar
¼ oz Ground Nutmegs	British West Indies
¼ teaspoon Pudding Spice	India or British West Indies
¼ gill Brandy	Australia · S. Africa Cyprus or Palestine
½ gill Rum	Jamaica or British Guiana
1 pint Beer	England · Wales · Scotland or Ireland

WRITE TO THE EMPIRE MARKETING BOARD, WESTMINSTER, FOR A FREE BOOKLET ON EMPIRE CHRISTMAS FARE GIVING THIS AND OTHER RECIPES.

Showing the provenance of every ingredient from countries of the Empire, the 'Empire Christmas Pudding' recipe was produced in the early 1930s by the Empire Marketing Board.

brought up to respect the Royal family. I used to collect pictures of Margaret and Elizabeth, you know? I adored them. It was the British influence. We didn't grow up with any Jamaican thing – we grew up as British.'

Cross-currents of influence

So cultural references to empire were part of the tapestry of life for Britons all over the world, reading news syndicated by British agencies and published in papers such as the *Bombay Times*, the *Straits Echo*, the *Sydney Morning Herald* and the *Times of Ceylon*. New media technologies made the Empire smaller by facilitating flows of information from all over the world. Such newspapers constructed cosmopolitan identities that transcended ethnicity or nation. They offered empire-wide news coverage and adverts for British goods from Huntley and Palmer biscuits to Peek Frean pies and Standard cars, whilst British papers reported on Dominions events as if they were home news as mass media brought the Empire into British homes. British presses dominated the printed word as it appeared in the colonies and Dominions, Oxford University Press opening for business in Bombay in 1912 and in Cape Town in 1915. The development of radio meant that people overseas could listen in on the news from London or to Test Match commentary from Lord's as they sat on steamy verandahs at sundown. They could also watch theatre productions transferred from the West End to the Royal Theatre Hobart, as well as American and British films from Hollywood and Pinewood.

It would be a mistake to believe that all cultural references to 'over there' were patronizing, inaccurate or disparaging. Many Britons had great respect for other cultures, sometimes to the point of romanticizing them and contrasting them with a Western way of life blighted by modernity and industrialization. Rudyard Kipling's *The Jungle Book* introduced generations of readers to the 'The Law of the Jungle', the Indian boy Mowgli and the menagerie in which he was raised, which included Baloo the Bear and Bagheera the Black Panther, Akela the Wolf and Shere Khan the Tiger. *The Jungle Book*'s popularity was taken to new heights by the Walt Disney cartoon portrayal of 1967. Written in the early 1890s, the book's success was built on a realistic portrayal of Indian village life and the struggle for survival in the jungle. Kipling was familiar with India having been born in Bombay and lived there as an adult, and gained insight into the setting chosen for the book – the banks of the Waingunga River in the Indian district of Seonee – from friends who visited and photographed the region. Other Kipling tales, such as the *Just So*

Stories, introduced thousands of people to the 'great grey-green greasy Limpopo River/All set about with fever-trees' and a host of tropical locations and native wisdom.

In the arts crude stereotyping of overseas societies was frequently rivalled by much more positive depiction of other cultures. Many intellectuals saw in the East an idealized vision of a world that had been lost in the West, and romanticized it. There were more practical reasons for valuing the non-European world; Arab horses contributed a vital strain to English bloodstock and Wilfrid Scawen Blunt (a ferocious campaigner on behalf of Irish independence) and Lady Anne Blunt (Byron's granddaughter) established an Arab stud at Crabbet Park, scouring the Middle East for new stock. In representing the non-European world to the British public it wasn't just Europeans who defined the image that was portrayed. As John Mackenzie writes, the vogue for chinoiserie saw the 'construction of an imaginary Orient to satisfy a Western vision of human elegance and refinement within a natural and architectural world of extreme delicacy … as much a product of Chinese craftsmen as of the West'.

The soundtrack of Empire

Music halls, sheet music played around the family piano, symphonic works, popular songs, brass bands playing at civic events and on the ornate bandstands that littered Britain's parks and coastal promenades – imperial themes suffused British musical life. The Last Night of the Proms became an annual festival of popular musical fervour from the inception of the Promenade Concerts by Robert Newman at the Queen's Hall, Langham Place, in 1895 (where the Proms remained until forced to move to the Royal Albert Hall by German bombing in 1941). Sir Henry Wood conducted from the very first Prom, and remained the musician most associated with the concerts. Nautical tunes in the Last Night of the Proms included 'Farewell Ye Spanish Ladies', 'See the Conquering Hero', 'Jack's the Lad' and 'The Saucy Arethusa'. The Proms always featured the music of Elgar, other regulars including Sir William Walton's 'Crown Imperial' and 'Orb and Sceptre', Hubert Parry's 'Jerusalem' – which associated Christ himself with English pastoral romanticism – Parry's 'I Was Glad', written as the processional anthem for the coronation of Edward VII and repeated at every Coronation since, and Wood's 'Fantasia on British Sea Songs'. This piece included the orchestration of 'Rule Britannia', the colourful, frenetic finale of the Last Night of the Proms ever since.

Sir William Gilbert and Sir Arthur Sullivan produced 14 operettas between 1871 and 1896, musical entertainments that attained great popularity even outside the theatre, their songs played by bands and barrel organists alike. The Savoy Operas, as they were known, featured exotic peoples and locations and nautical and military themes as they lampooned British society and a familiar Western view of the world. *The Mikado* (1885) was set in Japan at a time when it was emerging from obscurity and beginning to fascinate Western observers, fuelling the fashion for Japanese ornaments and furniture. *HMS Pinafore* was a satire on the Royal Navy which opened in London in May 1878 and ran for 700 performances.

An 1888 poster for Gilbert and Sullivan's comic light opera *HMS Pinafore*. The opera lampooned the First Lord of the Admiralty at the time, William Henry Smith, who had legal, but no naval, experience:
'When I was a lad I served a term/ As office boy to an attorney's firm/ I cleaned the windows and I swept the floor/ And I polished up the handle of the big front door/ I polished up that handle so carefully/ That now I am the Ruler of the Queen's Navy!'

The Yeomen of the Guard (1888) poked fun at 19th-century militarism through the self-importance of the Dragoon Guards. The character of 'the very model of a modern major-general' created in *The Pirates of Penzance* (1879) was an easily recognized Victorian character, the bluff, whiskered, port-reddened senior soldier leading British campaigns on the fringes of empire.

Classical musicians also took aspects of imperialism and Europe's contact with the East as inspiration. Exotic echoes are woven into William Walton's ethereal composition *Façade: An Entertainment*. This peculiar and fascinating work was a series of studies in word-rhymes and onomatopoeia written by Edith Sitwell and set to music by Walton in 1921. Amazons, bison, elephants, rhinoceros, Hottentots, Coramandel winds, a tall black Aga and Robinson Crusoe drift in and out of the composition.

... Floating on they see
New-arisen Madam Venus for whose sake from far
Came the fat and zebra'd emperor of Zanzibar
Where like gold bouquets lay far Asia, Africa, Cathay
All laid before that shady lady by the fibroid Shah.

Popular music also abounded in references to Empire. Among the many exotic imperial locations name-checked by songwriters, the Indian city of Bombay was especially favoured, as for example in the rousing wartime number 'Bless 'em All', which was written by Fred Godfrey while serving in the Royal Naval Air Service in 1917, but made famous by George Formby during the Second World War:

They say there's a troopship just leaving Bombay
Bound for old Blighty's shores,
Heavily laden with time-expired men
Bound for the land they adore.

The city also gets a mention in Ralph Butler and Peter Hart's evergreen children's song 'Nellie the Elephant' (1956):

To Bombay
A travelling circus came
They brought an intelligent elephant
And Nellie was her name.
One dark night
She slipped her iron chain
And off she ran to Hindustan
And was never seen again.

Chorus:
Nellie the Elephant packed her trunk
And said goodbye to the circus
Off she went with a trumpety-trump
Trump, trump, trump.
Nellie the Elephant packed her trunk
And trundled back to the jungle
Off she went with a trumpety-trump
Trump, trump, trump.

The head of the herd was calling far far away
They met one night in the silver light
On the road to Mandalay.

RED, WHITE, AND BLUE,
WHAT DOES IT MEAN
TO YOU?
SURELY YOU'RE PROUD,
SHOUT IT OUT LOUD,
BRITONS AWAKE!
THE EMPIRE TOO, WE
CAN DEPEND ON YOU
FREEDOM REMAINS,
THESE ARE THE CHAINS,
NOTHING CAN BREAK.

– Parker and Charles,
'There'll Always Be An
England' (1940)

173

HAVE YOU HAD ANY WORD
OF THAT BLOKE IN THE 'THIRD',
WAS IT SOUTHERBY, SEDGEWICK, OR SIM?

THEY HAD HIM THROWN OUT OF THE CLUB IN BOMBAY
FOR, APART FROM HIS MESS BILLS EXCEEDING HIS PAY,
HE TOOK TO PIG-STICKING IN QUITE THE WRONG WAY.
I WONDER WHAT HAPPENED TO HIM!

– Noël Coward, 'I Wonder What Happened to Him' (1945)

The inimitable Noël Coward

Noël Coward was an international celebrity, and his global travels and the circles in which he moved meant that he was well placed to record the life of Britain's ruling élite and the exotic settings in which they lived and worked as planters, administrators and soldiers. Coward, the son of a naval officer, worked for British intelligence during the war as well as entertaining troops all over the world and making patriotic films such as *In Which We Serve*, based on the war service of his friend Lord Louis Mountbatten. Coward visited many parts of the Empire including Canada, the Caribbean, Kenya, Rhodesia, Burma, Ceylon, Malaya, Australia and Fiji and spent his final years, like Ian Fleming, living in the British West Indies.

With biting wit Coward's songs satirized British society, its class distinctions and idiosyncrasies. He was acutely aware of the global work of the British armed forces, thanks to his lengthy association with the Royal Navy. Some of Coward's imperial experiences were reflected in his writings, including the story 'Mr and Mrs Edgehill', inspired by a visit to the British administrator of Canton Island in the Pacific. In 'Mad Dogs and Englishmen', Winston Churchill's favourite Coward song, the odd habits of the English are compared to those of people in diverse parts of the globe. Marking itself out as different appealed to a nation that revels in its quirkiness and loves to consider itself apart from the rest of the world. Coward captured that spirit:

> *In a jungle town*
> *Where the sun beats down*
> *To the rage of man and beast,*
> *The English garb*
> *Of the English sahib*
> *Merely gets a bit more creased.*
> *In Bangkok*
> *At twelve o'clock*
> *They foam at the mouth and run,*
> *But mad dogs and Englishmen*
> *Go out in the midday sun*

Edward Elgar: hymning England and the Empire

Edward Elgar is popularly associated with British patriotism at the highest point of imperial swagger, his music providing a backdrop to the golden afternoon of Edwardian empire before the First World War changed the world forever and jolted the British from their proud stride. Elgar's music, tinged with nostalgia and a sense of 'Englishness', sprang from his love of his boyhood Worcestershire, became associated with British imperial pride and the royal family, and included compositions for Queen Victoria, a symphony dedicated to the memory of King Edward VII and music for the 1924 Wembley Empire Exhibition.

Imperial March and *The Banner of St George* were composed for Queen Victoria's Golden Jubilee in 1897. Imperial March, written in a bell-tent in front of his Malvern home, catapulted Elgar to fame beyond his native West Midlands. It was performed by massed bands at the Crystal Palace on 25 April 1897; at a Royal Garden Party on 28 June; on the anniversary of the Queen's coronation by command of the Queen herself; at a State Jubilee Concert on 15 July; and by the Royal Artillery Band at the Royal Albert Hall on 24 October. Elgar spent Diamond Jubilee Day itself, 22 June, at home in Malvern. He wrote in his diary that 'after dinner, Edward and Alice to common to see bonfires', the fires lit across England on prominent hills such as the Worcester Beacon to mark the occasion.

Sea Pictures captured the nation's romance with the seven seas, first performed in 1899 by the contralto Clara Butt with Elgar himself conducting. Later that year the performance was repeated at St James's Hall, London, and days later Butt gave a command performance of *Sea Pictures* for Queen Victoria at Balmoral. Elgar was asked to compose a madrigal to mark the Queen's birthday, summoned to Windsor to meet the Queen in person.

The *Enigma Variations*, first performed in 1899, proved to be the triumph Elgar had been seeking all his life and established him as the 'coming man' of English symphonic music. Comprising portraits of his friends, one of the Variations, 'Nimrod', became a favourite at the Proms, as did *Pomp and Circumstance March No. 1*, which received a tumultuous ovation when premiered at the Queen's Hall. 'I've got a tune that will knock 'em − knock 'em flat' Elgar wrote, and to King Edward VII remarked 'I've been carrying that around in my pocket for twenty years'. This work gained enduring fame when the words of A. C. Benson's 'Land of Hope and Glory' were added to it. This created Elgar's *Coronation Ode* and what became Britain's unofficial National Anthem. According to Ian Lace 'it was the King who first suggested that the air from this Pomp and Circumstance March should be sung. It was first incorporated into the *Coronation Ode* as the Final Movements but then became a work on its own'. 'Land of Hope and Glory' swept the country in 1902.

After this, Elgar planned a symphony about the life of the Victorian soldier-hero General Sir Charles Gordon, though later insisted that the 1st Symphony (1908) was not the promised 'Gordon Symphony'. Nevertheless, the spirit of Gordon touched the creation of *Gerontius* and was part of the inspiration for both

A coloured lithograph of Edward Elgar, published in 1912. Elgar became the quintessential composer of Empire: when Britain handed Hong Kong back to China after expiry of the 99-year lease in 1997, the beautifully elegiac Variation No. 9 ('Nimrod') of the *Enigma Variations* played the Royal Yacht *Britannia* out of the harbour.

GREAT RACE, WHOSE EMPIRE OF SPLENDOUR
HAS DAZZLED A WONDERING WORLD!
MAY THE FLAG THAT FLOATS O'ER THY WIDE DOMAINS
BE LONG TO ALL WINDS UNFURLED!
THREE CROSSES IN CONCORD BLENDED
THE BANNER OF BRITAIN'S MIGHT!
BUT THE CENTRAL GEM OF THE ENSIGN FAIR
IS THE CROSS OF THE DAUNTLESS KNIGHT!

- *'The Banner of St George', words Shapcott Wensley,*
music Edward Elgar

his symphonies. As Elgar's musical career flourished, along with his acquaintance with the King, so too did his standing. He was made 'Master of the King's Musick', was knighted in 1904 and in 1911 was awarded the Order of Merit, instituted by King Edward in 1902 and awarded by the monarch personally (there can only be 24 OM's living at any one time).

Public recognition pleased Elgar's wife, on whose behalf he strove for social recognition and honours befitting her background. Alice Elgar was born in India, the daughter of a distinguished soldier who had served on the North-West Frontier under Napier and taken part in the post-Mutiny reprisals. He became a major-general and a Knight Commander of the Bath while Alice was still a young girl. Alice's family and its distinguished service in India influenced Elgar and increased his awareness and pride in the Empire. Indian artefacts featured in the Elgars' home as in so many others of the time. In the words of Jan Morris, the composer:

> *… reached middle age in the heyday of the New Imperialism, in that provincial society which was perhaps most susceptible to its dazzle, and for a time he succumbed to the glory of it all. In Elgar's Worcestershire of the nineties, the innocent manifestations of imperial pride must have been inescapable, drumming and swelling all around him … He plunged into the popular emotions of the day with a sensual romanticism … He was forty years old in the year of the Diamond Jubilee, and he saw himself then as a musical laureate, summoned by destiny to hymn Britannia's greatness.*

Elgar's naval, royal and imperial connections continued throughout the rest of his life. In 1905 he had the opportunity to view the powerful Mediterranean Fleet at close quarters when Lady Beresford, wife of the admiral commanding, invited him to join a party aboard HMS *Surprise* for a cruise round the Inland Sea. In 1912 he wrote the music for a masque called *The Crown of India*, staged at the London Coliseum to mark the Royal visit to India for the Delhi Durbar. In 1917 Elgar was approached by Lord Charles Beresford to set to music some verses by Rudyard Kipling entitled *Fringes of the Fleet*. Elgar conducted this new piece at the Coliseum from June 1917 until Kipling, still devastated by the loss of his only son John at the Battle of Loos two years before, stopped performances. At the British Empire Exhibition at Wembley in 1924 Elgar conducted the massed choirs at the opening ceremony, though by now considered 'Land of Hope and Glory' anathema. For the Exhibition he wrote *Pageant of Empire*, a setting for the songs of Alfred Noyes which included 'Shakespeare's Kingdom', 'The Blue Mountains', 'The Heart of Canada', 'Sailing Westward', 'Merchant-Adventurers' and 'The Immortal Legions'.

The wonder of the wireless

In the 1920s new wireless technology and the creation of the household radio combined with the foundation of the British Broadcasting Corporation to forge the 'empire of the air'. As with global postal and telegraphic communications the British were at the forefront of this latest innovation. According to John Mackenzie, Lord Reith, the founding Director-General of the BBC, fervently believed that the 'British Empire was the most successful example of internationalism and peaceful coexistence in modern times'. It was no surprise, therefore, that he sought to use the Corporation for imperial ends as well as forging a close association with royal ceremonial including coronations, weddings and state funerals. The BBC broadcast the King's opening speech at the Wembley Empire Exhibition in 1924, and the world first heard the monarch's Christmas Message in 1932.

The BBC began its dedicated Empire Service (the precursor of today's BBC World Service) in 1932, broadcast on short wave from Daventry in the Midlands. Broadcasting in over 40 languages, the BBC became the world's major news source, and was used as a propaganda instrument during the days of ideological competition with Nazi Germany. The BBC established a reputation for giving the unadorned facts, a core element of its success ever since. Reith himself first broadcast on the Empire Service on 3 January 1938, offering a greeting to people in Arabic countries and expressing his wish for closer ties between them and Great Britain. Radio stations soon followed throughout the Empire. Ceylon was one of the first colonies to introduce radio broadcasting a few years after its inauguration in Europe. The Governor, Sir William Henry Manning, made the first broadcast in South Asia on 27 June 1924. The Central Telegraphic Office in Colombo soon began broadcasting musical records, and English music broadcast on Radio Ceylon became a popular favourite for planters and servicemen alike. During the Second World War annual Festivals of Empire were broadcast from the Royal Albert Hall, together with Sinhalese folk songs, Tamil music and news for 'Ceylon Lads Overseas'.

The Empire on the silver screen

Empire provided a regular source of material for filmmakers, often as the backdrop to tales of romance or action. Action and adventure in the untamed wilds of the non-European world were the staple ingredients of such films, which included the popular *Tarzan* series based on the novels of the American author Edgar Rice Burroughs (the first, *Tarzan of the Apes*, published in 1912). This famous story, which inspired dozens of films and cartoons, featured the ape-raised Lord Greystoke, an English child marooned on the coast of West Africa by mutineers. *Sanders of the River*, directed by Zoltán Korda, was a classic colonial movie filmed on location in West Africa in 1935. Based on a novel by Edgar Wallace, it is the story of a British district officer keeping the peace in a remote part of Africa. The Resident Commissioner, Sanders, had established peace in the River District and built an alliance with Chief Bosambo (played by the black American actor Paul Robeson). In this story of Britain's civilizing mission in Africa, Bosambo freed a

slave convoy belonging to the 'primitive' King Mofolaba. He then took a beautiful slave girl, Lilongo, to be his wife. With Sanders away visiting the capital on the coast, however, things went awry. Mofolaba killed the deputy commissioner and recaptures Lilongo. Bosambo, in pursuit, was staked out and left to die alongside his wife. Returning to his district in the nick of time, Sanders saved the day. The film encapsulated several key elements of Britain's imperial self-image – peace secured without bloodshed; moral fibre and pluck winning the day; and enlightened British rule and loyal native allies trouncing evil foes.

Trader Horn (1931) was another well-known film set in Africa, based on a true missionary story from East Africa and Madagascar that began life as a popular book. It was the first non-documentary film shot on location in Africa. In 1939 Zoltán Korda produced *The Four Feathers* – an imperial epic in glorious Technicolor – set in the late 1890s against the backdrop of the British conquest of the Sudan. In the same year a famous story of British exploration and adventure was transferred to the screen with the release of *Stanley and Livingstone*. *Rhodes of Africa* appeared in 1936, *King Solomon's Mines*, based on H. Rider Haggard's stirring novel, in 1937. *The Four Just Men* (1939) was based on an Edgar Wallace novel about a plan to seize the Suez Canal. The American comedy *Road to Zanzibar* (1941) starred Bing Crosby, Bob Hope and Dorothy Lamour. Other African films included *Storm Over Africa* (1953), *West of Zanzibar* (1954), *Storm Over the Nile* (1955), *Zulu* (1963), *Call Me Bwana* (1963), *The Naked Prey* (1966) and *Khartoum* (1966). Even as the Empire shrank in the 1960s African themes remained attractive to filmmakers, productions including *Guns of Batasi* (1964), which chronicled the struggle of a British Army unit caught in the crossfire between African factions in the run up to independence, and the dreary *Death Drums Along the River* (1963).

Tales from the Raj and beyond

The Raj provided fertile ground for filmmakers, their output ranging from the stoutly patriotic to the hilariously irreverent. 1935 saw the release of *Clive of India* and in 1938 *Storm Over Bengal* appeared. In *Gunga Din* (1939) Cary Grant and Douglas Fairbanks Junior played lusty British Army sergeants on the North-West Frontier of India. This became a national favourite, as did *The Lives of a Bengal Lancer* (supposedly Adolf Hitler's favourite film; Hitler was fascinated by how a small British garrison could control a country of so many millions). In 1942 a film version of Kipling's *The Jungle Book* was made, and in 1951 *Kim* hit the silver screen. *Khyber Patrol*, *King of the Khyber Rifles* (both 1954) and *North-West Frontier* (1959) featured the well-known imperial theme of frontier soldiering and the intrigue of the 'Great Game'.

India provided the subject matter for a notable departure from the worthy, hagiographical approaches common in British cinema: *Carry on Up the Khyber*. Probably the best film to emerge from the 'Carry On' stable and brimming with bawdy slapstick humour, sexual innuendo and the Great British *double entendre*, it was an affectionate send-up of the British Empire. The film tells of the struggles

Colonial settings, big game, white hunters and tropical heat and lust have long fascinated movie makers: A French poster advertises the 1953 film *Mogambo*, which was set in Kenya.

Continued on page 182

RIPPING YARNS

Imperial literature is most famously associated with the great adventure novels written by the likes of John Buchan, G.A. Henty, H. Rider Haggard and Rudyard Kipling, buttressed by a massive output of imitators, children's annuals and comics. These stories featured strong white heroes acting on a white-dominated stage. There were generals fighting Sikh wars, boys exposing dastardly native plots and strong colonial types like Richard Hannay coming to the aid of the old world from the new in Buchan's classic *The Thirty-Nine Steps*. Very often these stories were based on true accounts of experiences on the imperial frontier, or were inspired by stories heard as children. During his childhood in an Oxfordshire village Rider Haggard heard tales of lost civilizations, secret runes, curses and the supernatural. What particularly stuck in his mind, writes Peter Haining, was a local curate who 'wore a thick gold ring engraved with sun symbols'. He recalled that a Reverend Graham 'told me that an old friend of his who had business in Peru had opened some burial place and in it found a chamber wherein, round a stone table, sat a dead and mummified man at the head of about a dozen other persons ranged round the table ... the man at the head of the table wore this ring upon his hand'. This scene was used in *King Solomon's Mines*, his most famous novel, which was written as the result of a bet that he couldn't write something better than *Treasure Island* (Robert Louis Stevenson's famous 1883 novel of pirates and the sea).

Worlds of adventure and intrigue

Herbert Strang novels included *Fighting With French*, *Winning His Name*, *Barclay of the Guides*, *Swift and Sure*, *Tom Willoughby's Scouts* and *In Clive's Command*. This type of literature was simply ubiquitous. As late as the 1970s and 1980s companies such as the Children's Press were still churning out books such as J.M. Downie's *The Yellow Raider*, in which Ken Webster inherits his uncle's pearling fleet in Australia and is then pitted against the 'sinister' Ah Kwee, leader of a

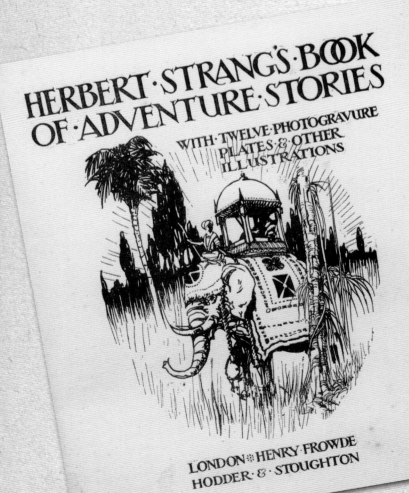

HERBERT·STRANG'S·BOOK OF·ADVENTURE·STORIES

WITH·TWELVE·PHOTOGRAVURE PLATES·&·OTHER ILLUSTRATIONS

LONDON ⁕ HENRY·FROWDE HODDER·&·STOUGHTON

A typical title page from a Herbert Strang annual (this one appeared in 1919). Strang annuals simply dripped with gripping tales of derring-do from the frontiers of Empire.

band of thugs and pirates. 'This is an exciting tale, guaranteed to delight all boys; pearl-fishers, pirates and yelling savages'. Girls were also targeted, for example in Mollie Chappell's *Rhodesian Adventure*, a story of an English family embarking 'on the great adventure of beginning a new life in a new country – Rhodesia'. The family travels by liner to the 'romantic, historical city' of Cape Town, then overland through South Africa to Rhodesia and their new home at Jacaranda House. Here the girls have adventures involving poisonous snakes, a flight to Johannesburg and a visit to Cecil Rhodes' grave in the Matopo Hills. Even novels that weren't directly about the Empire frequently made reference to commonly recognized imperial themes, including J.M. Barrie's *Peter Pan*, Arthur Ransome's *Swallows and Amazons* and Frances Burnett Hodgson's *The Secret Garden*.

Like *The Yellow Raiders*, *Rhodesian Adventure* was another story glamourizing distant parts of the world that just happened to be under the Union Flag, providing an exotic backdrop against which Europeans could enjoy thrilling adventures. Such books were still being published in the 1960s and 1970s.

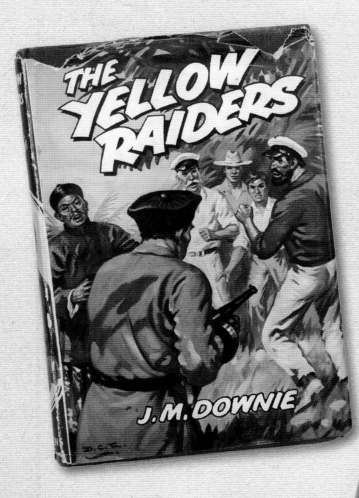

'Sinister' natives, in this case Chinese pirates, threatening Europeans, an extremely common visual image in imperial popular literature that shaped the perceptions of countless numbers of people.

of a British Governor on the North-West Frontier (Sir Sydney Ruff-Diamond, played by Sid James), where the kilted soldiers of the 3rd Foot and Mouth Regiment – the 'Devils in Skirts' – attempt to defend the Khyber Pass against the wily Khasi of Kalibar and his Burpa tribesmen. It was advertised as 'a tale of passion, greed and missing underpants set in the raging days of the Raj'.

Further east, the Boxer Rebellion and the subsequent siege of the European legations in Shanghai was the subject of *55 Days in Peking* (1963), starring Charlton Heston and Ava Gardner, and Bing Crosby and Bob Hope starred in *Road To Singapore* (1940). Other feature films covering imperial subjects included *Susannah of the Mounties* (1939), *Scott of the Antarctic* (1948), *Soldiers Three* (1951) and *Lawrence of Arabia* (1962). Cinemas occasionally showed educational and propaganda films, such as *Song of Ceylon*, *Gold Coast Cocoa*, *Cargo from Jamaica*, *Air Post*, *African Skyways* (made by Imperial Airways) and *Men of Africa* made for the Colonial Office in the 1930s. The Second World War led to a rash of films with imperial settings, including *Objective Burma*, *Desert Victory*, *The Rats of Tobruk*, *Three Came Home*, *The Purple Plain*, *Too Late the Hero*, *The Sea Wolves* and *The Bridge Over the River Kwai* which, in 1958, required the largest film set ever built. Filmed in Ceylon, the bridge alone required the cutting down of 1500 trees, dragged to the site by 48 elephants.

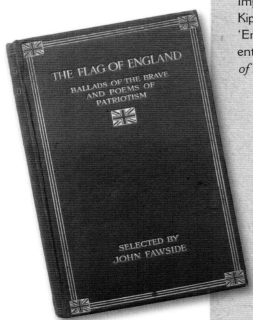

IMPERIAL POETRY

Imperial poetry ranged from the observant, even critical, verse of Rudyard Kipling, to the tendentiously patriotic and triumphant. William Watson's poem 'England and Her Colonies' was printed in an Edward Arnold volume entitled *The Tree of Empire: A Book of Readings in Prose and Verse Illustrative of the History and Development of the British Empire*:

She stands, a thousand-wintered tree,
By countless morns impearled;
Her broad roots coil beneath the sea,
Her branches sweep the world.

The rivalry and nationalism that characterized the years leading up to the First World War brought imperial versification to boiling point. Volumes included W.H. Fitchett's *Fights for the Flag* (1910) and John Fawside's *The Flag of England: Ballads of the Brave and Poems of Patriotism* (1914). Fitchett had already written books called *Deeds that Won the Empire* and *How England Saved Europe*. His volume of poetry began with Kipling's question: 'What is the flag of England? Winds of the world declare!'.

Imperial capers on the small screen

Imperial themes were also the subject of television dramas and comedies. *It Ain't Half Hot Mum* (1974–81) was set in British India and starred Windsor Davis as the fire-breathing Battery Sergeant Major reluctantly attached to the Royal Artillery Concert Party. At the more serious end of the scale, the popular 1970s drama *Tenko* told the harrowing story of women prisoners of war captured by the Japanese and interned in Singapore. The 1950s BBC TV series the *Army Game*, starring Bernard Bresslaw, Alfie Bass and Charles Hawtrey followed the exploits of a hapless bunch of National Servicemen. In the spin-off film *I Only Arsked!* (1958), they are deployed to the fringes of Britain's shrinking Empire:

> *The potential discovery of a vast oil field under an Arab nation threatens to ignite civil war. The King requests a brigade of crack British Guards. Instead, with typical army efficiency, what he received is seven men from the No. 3 Surplus Ordnance Depot, Nether Hopping! Now Bootsy, Popeye, the Professor, Cupcake, Springer, 'Potty' Chambers and The Major find themselves acting as the 'thin red line' against two thousand hostile desert tribesmen!*

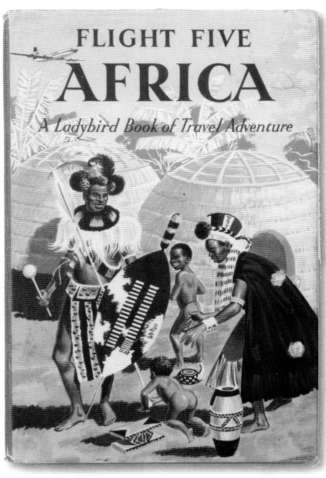

From the 1960s the British Empire became fair game for those seeking to send it up. A particularly memorable example is Terry Jones and Michael Palin's *Ripping Yarns*. The inspiration for this hilarious 1970s series was a book given by Palin to his *Monty Python* colleague Terry Jones which bore the title *Ripping Tales*, suggesting 'a comedy script which encapsulated the spirit of boy's adventure stories and tales of "stiff upper lip" from the 1930s'. The anthology featured 'unlikely or flawed heroes ... full of the propagandist pluck common in Edwardian juvenile literature'. Episodes included *Tomkinson's Schooldays*, 'a pastiche of the public school rites of passage fiction as epitomized by *Tom Brown's Schooldays* (Tom's sufferings at Rugby School at the hands of the bully Harry Flashman); *Across the Andes by Frog* (exploration) and *Roger of the Raj*, which sent up the social and sexual mores of the port-guzzling rulers of British India.

Upright heroes and shifty natives

Comics and magazines presented a visually striking view of the world in which the white man was always the active lead character – as explorer, administrator, soldier, hunter, missionary or trader – whilst native peoples formed a passive backdrop along with lush vegetation and wild animals. If Africans or Indians in these stories

The fascination with far-off lands, and dissemination of entrenched images of the world, remained strong even after empire had begun to fade. Ladybird's *Flight Five: Africa* was a 1960s educational book in which a BOAC Comet flies over the Sahara to Khartoum, where Sudanese soldiers trained by the British, and Gordon's legend, are discussed. The plane then visits East Africa, where facts are revealed about the source of the Nile and the colony's reliance on cotton and coffee exports. The Comet proceeds to the Victoria Falls and the Lake Kariba Dam in Rhodesia before reaching South Africa, flying over the Union Buildings in Pretoria, a Zulu kraal, Table Mountain and diamond mines.

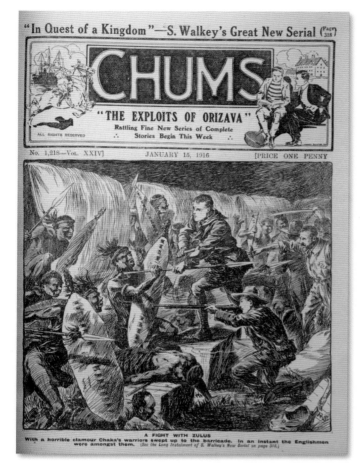

"In Quest of a Kingdom"—S. Walkey's Great New Serial (Page 318)

CHUMS

"THE EXPLOITS OF ORIZAVA"

Rattling Fine New Series of Complete
.'. Stories Begin This Week .'.

ALL RIGHTS RESERVED

No. 1,218—Vol. XXIV]   JANUARY 15, 1916   [PRICE ONE PENNY

A FIGHT WITH ZULUS
With a horrible clamour Chaka's warriors swept up to the barricade. In an instant the Englishmen were amongst them. (See the Long Instalment of S. Walkey's New Serial on page 318.)

An issue of *Chums* from January 1916: 'A fight with the Zulus: With a horrible clamour Chaka's warriors swept up to the barricade. In an instant the Englishmen were amongst them'. Note how the Englishmen look like the improbably mature schoolboys common in juvenile school literature.

were active rather than passive, it was either through their 'loyalty' or through their wickedness, and this helped ripping yarns along. A shifty native – the sinister Chinaman, the African witchdoctor, or the Mohamadan slave trader – gave the white hero something to kick against. Comics were full of 'public school stories of boys routing the natives or restoring to the throne a rightful Indian claimant who had been a schoolmate back in England'. As Orwell put it, in this literature 'foreigners are comics who are put there for us to laugh at [and they] can be classified in much the same way as insects'.

Hergé's creation Tintin, popular among British readers, ventured into imperial territory in the 1930s in a cartoon strip that embodied many of these commonly-encountered literary themes. In *Tintin in the Congo* the eponymous hero and his dog Snowy board an ocean liner as they leave Europe for a mission in Africa, kitted out with all the familiar accoutrements of travel in the tropics including mosquito net, rifle, pith helmet and khaki shorts. While wandering abroad in the Dark Continent Tintin shoots big game, collects ivory and encounters witchdoctors, sacred fetishes, unscrupulous white colonists and well-meaning missionaries. Africans are presented as feckless and backward, with only monosyllabic mastery of European language. The story ends with the natives, in their grass hut village, venerating images of Tintin and Snowy.

Between 1880 and 1918 an incredible 149 boys' papers were launched. Titles included *The Union Jack* (1894–1933), *Pluck* (1894–1924) and *Marvel* (1893–1922). In his 1939 survey of boys' weeklies, George Orwell examined a host of titles common on the shelves of Britain's newsagents, including *Gem*, *Magnet*, *Modern Boy*, *Triumph*, *Champion*, *Wizard*, *Rover*, *Skipper*, *Hotspur* and *Adventure*.

'To the boys of the Empire …'

One of the most successful of the boys comics was *Chums*, published weekly by Cassell from 1892 to 1932, then annually until 1941 when wartime paper shortages caused its demise. The 'youngsters' Bible … it was romance in black and white, stirring vague longings, spurring warm desires'. It was 'sold here and to Chums in distant colonies', and its stories were very imperial, very military and very sporty. *Chums* serialized Edgar Wallace's *Bosambo of the River*, the naval serial *The Iron Pirate* and *The Mysterious Fu Manchu* 'charting the struggle between Commissioner Nayland Smith and "the yellow peril incarnate in one man"'. From 1930 onwards *Chums* bore the logo 'To the boys of the Empire upon whom the sun never sets'. An 1898 *Chums* series featured heroes from the public schools, and 1900 brought a photographic series on military and naval life in the Empire entitled *Under the Queen's Flag*.

A regular serial writer for *Chums* was Captain Frank Shaw, one of the more influential boys' paper writers, who could churn out stories to order. For example, on the day of the American explorer Robert Peary's 'discovery of the North Pole was announced to the world, 6 September 1909, Cassell's telegraphed to ask if he could produce a 70,000 word juvenile book on polar exploration, embodying the Peary story, within a month. Shaw wrote it in a week and it was on sale by 1 November'. Captain Shaw was also responsible during the First World War for serials such as 'With Jellicoe in the North Sea'. The July 1916 issue of *Chums* in which this story appeared was absolutely typical of this genre of literature. Its stories included 'The Head-Hunters of Borneo', 'The Pirates: A Story of Adventure in the China Seas', 'Eldorado: How The Seekers of Gold Have Pioneered for Civilization', 'The Raiding of the *Sickle*: How a Young Apprentice Proved His Pluck', and a public school mystery story. Informative articles included 'How Ships Speak to Each Other', and advertisements appeared for Pears Soap and for the sports shop Gamages, the 'complete cricket outfitters'.

V-bombers, Dinky toys and pocket Brownies

This type of content lasted down to the final days of empire and beyond. In 1958 each issue of the *Boy's Own Paper* carried recruitment adverts for the Army, the Air Force and the Navy, all three services gaining new appeal in a post-war decade fascinated with technology. The Air Force advertised its new 'V-Force', elegant long-range bombers designed to carry Britain's nuclear threat to the heart of the Soviet Union and epitomized by the delta-winged Avro Vulcan. The Senior Service, meanwhile, emphasized the opportunities for young men in 'Britain's New Navy'. There were also adverts for radio operators aboard ocean liners, and a regular first-page slot for the Cadet Course at the Merchant Navy School of Navigation at the University of Southampton. As late as 1958 *BOP* was serializing 'Biggles' stories. Adverts tempted boys with model kits of aircraft such as the BOAC 'Britannia', white, black and piebald mice delivered by rail, Dinky toys, chemistry sets, Webley air pistols, bicycles from Raleigh and BSA, tents and sleeping bags, crystal sets, Kodak Brownie cameras and Cadbury's chocolate. Dunlop tyres also advertised in *BOP*, emphasizing its part in Britain's expansion overseas. Articles included news of 'Boys' Ambassadors' to the newly-independent

Look and Learn carried a surprising number of imperial strands into the 1970s, when the Empire had all but disappeared and imperial attitudes and ideologies were widely frowned upon.

Commonwealth country of Ghana, Shell's search for oil in Nigeria, a regular 'Round the Stamp World' column, 'English Searchlights on Niagara', the Empire and Commonwealth Games and 'How Rubber First Came'.

As late as the 1970s the boys' magazine *Look and Learn* was serving up a heavy diet of imperial and military items. In spring 1973 the magazine's colour covers featured imperial themes – 'Break-out on Norfolk Island', 'On the Road to Mandalay' and 'A Doctor on the Run' (about the East Africa campaign in the First World War). These 1973 issues carried tales of imperial derring-do in this markedly post-imperial decade, including 'A Skirmish in the Foothills' (Afghanistan), 'The Making of Midshipman Mann', 'The Day that the Zulus Stormed Rorke's Drift' and 'The Rum Barrel Bargain' (Niger Delta). There were also articles on the Crusades, the Great Age of Discovery, Baden-Powell, the discovery of a route to the Pacific coast of Canada, the battle for Mandalay and stamps from the Cocos-Keeling Islands.

Annuals by 'Herbert Strang'

The quintessential format for imperial adventure stories was the children's annual. Of this genre the most iconic were those by 'Herbert Strang', the pseudonym of two employees of Oxford University Press, George Herbert Ely (1866–1958) and Charles James L'Estrange (1867–1947). Herbert Strang annuals were dominated by imperial yarns, often written by former soldiers or sailors who had been involved in the actions that they dramatized for boy's consumption. Herbert Strang stories included 'Contraband: An Adventure with Opium Smugglers', 'Sunshine, Logs and Lumberjacks', 'Sledging Adventures in the Antarctic' and 'Jungle Adventures'. 'The People of the Caves: The Story of a Weird Underground War' was written by Captain E. J. Wolseley and described a minor colonial campaign against a 'tribe of pagan savages known as the Marghi who before 1907 had caused continual trouble to the authorities of Northern Nigeria by raids on the main trade route between Kuka on Lake Chad to Yola on the River Benue'. Two British subalterns commanding 'plucky Yoruba soldiers' were sent by the Resident of Bornu to deal with them. 'Our Ranch' was set in the Rocky Mountains, 'Marooned on a Sandbank' in New Guinea.

Other stories featured tigers on the banks of the Ganges, Maoris in New Zealand, war in the Solomons, a perilous crossing of the Limpopo, daring naval missions, 'Ning-Wo the Wonderful' set in Malaya, 'On the Hill Crest Patrol' set in Natal, a non-combatant's work on the North West Frontier, a fishing trip on the Molopo and a journey down the Zambezi.

'The Empire Too, What Does it Mean To You?': A Reminiscence

Richard Aston, an American citizen who was born and grew up in Wales, writes eloquently of his memories and impressions of Empire in the 1930s and 1940s, recollections that would be recognized and understood by millions of people of his generation and the one that followed:

As well as catering for the imaginations of boys, this popular comic-cum-magazine format targeted adults. *The Wide World: The True Adventure Magazine for Men* was published between 1898 and 1965. From its front cover, usually dominated by a scene of adventure or war in distant lands, it looked much like a boy's magazine. Its adverts, however, revealed its intended audience: Senior Service and Craven 'A' cigarettes, briar pipes, Canadian Club, Dubonnet, Gordon's Gin, Guinness, muscle-building equipment, hair colour, psychology courses, artificial limbs, trusses, remedies for weak bladders, wristwatches, electric shavers, houses, premium bonds and cars such as the Austin A55. The stories, however, were much the same and all, allegedly, based on verified truth.

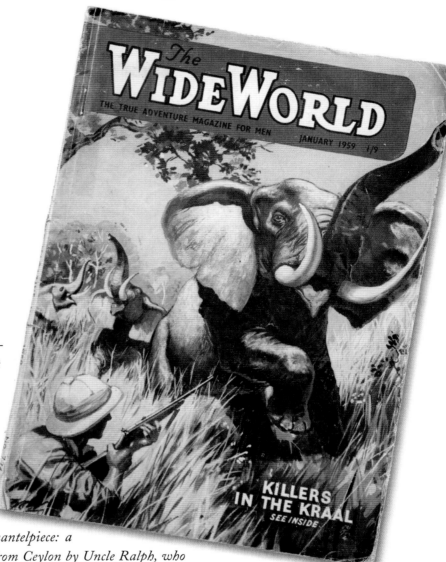

The first thing it meant to me was bare-breasted Masai girls, dancing in a row. That is one of my earliest memories; sitting in my father's lap as he turned the pages of a National Geographic *magazine, and talked of Africa, India and the rest of the pink countries.*

Like any other British home of the time, there were mementos of the Empire scattered throughout the house. On the mantelpiece: a parade of wooden elephants brought back from Ceylon by Uncle Ralph, who worked on the P&O ships; a boomerang from Uncle Bart in Australia; a Buddha from Hong Kong, a present from Uncle Frank, also in the merchant navy. Elsewhere in the house there was a carved Japanese sideboard, a stuffed tortoise with an ashtray in its back, a picture made of butterfly wings from Malaya, a brass tray from India, a knobkerrie (from Uncle William who was in the South African police), figurines, gaudy sea shells, and all the flotsam of empire brought back by aunts and uncles. And, of course, there were lots of photographs: Aunt Edith, a nurse in Calcutta, in her starched white uniform; Bart in his turned-up Aussie hat; Uncle Bill, in the uniform of a ship's engineer; men in pith helmets and Bombay bloomers [shorts]; women in cool dresses and wide sun hats on the decks of ships, lounging under palm trees, or even riding in a howdah – the kind of collection you will still find, stuffed in some old shoe box, buried in the back of a closet, in many a British home.

I distinctly remember May 24th, 1939. I was almost six. In Miss Cook's class, at Christ Church School, Weston-Super-Mare, it was Empire Day, and so there had to be a "pageant" in the schoolyard. A little girl, sitting on a chair, wrapped in a bed-sheet, holding a

EXHIBITIONS AND EMPIRE DAY

Empire Day, 24 May, became an annual event in most schools and was publicized in the *Radio Times*. The Royal Colonial Institute – renamed the Royal Empire Society in 1928 – held annual Empire Essay competitions. The public regularly encountered the Empire at the exhibitions that were a feature in British cities before the Second World War. In 1937 Trafalgar Square was home to an Empire show staged to coincide with the Coronation and the Dominions' Prime Ministers Conference. Empire exhibitions were all about showing off the Empire and why it benefited people of all classes. The famous Crystal Palace in London housed an Indian court and the 1862 London Exhibition displayed Indian crafts. London hosted a Colonial and Indian Exhibition in 1886, and as national and international exhibitions developed into a regular feature of city life they came to embrace elements of the fun fair, the educational and the voyeuristic, as people were able to gawp at 'real, live Africans' in mocked-up Zulu kraals, or admire the Native American braves and squaws brought all the way from America by the ever-popular Buffalo Bill Show.

The Greater Britain Exhibition of 1899 included motion pictures sponsored by the government of Queensland, a mining section for which Cecil Rhodes provided advice, and 200 Zulu warriors.

The most famous empire exhibition was that held at Wembley in 1924. The idea was to present the entire British Empire in miniature on a single site. Wembley Stadium was its specially-built centrepiece, approached along Empire Way (later changed to Wembley Way) which was lined with the pavilions of various colonies and dependencies. The year before the Exhibition opened it hosted its first big football match, the famous 'White Horse' FA Cup Final. The Exhibition was inaugurated by King George V on 23 April 1924, St George's Day. In the two years of its existence, the Exhibition attracted over 27 million visitors. One of them was the future Poet Laureate John Betjeman, then 18 years old. He preferred the Imperial pavilions of India, Sierra Leone and Fiji 'with their sun-tanned sentinels of Empire outside' to the Palaces of Industry and Engineering 'which were too much like my father's factory'. As he wondered, when revisiting Wembley while filming the documentary *Metro-Land* in 1972:

Oh bygone Wembley, where's the pleasure now?
The temples stare, the Empire passes by …

broomstick, and wearing a paper crown, was Britannia. Then came a procession of kids, some in strange attire, to lay tribute at Britannia's feet while reciting their lines: "I am India, I bring you tea," [a packet of Lipton's from the local Home and Colonial Stores]; "I too am India, I bring you jute," declaimed Mickey Heath, the greengrocer's son, as he dropped one of his dad's potato sacks; "I am Canada, I bring you furs from my vast forests," said one girl, as she draped her mother's tatty fox collar over Britannia's shoulder; Kenya brought coffee [a bottle of Camp liquid instant with a picture of a Bengal Lancer on the label]; I was Nigeria bearing chocolate [a bar of Cadbury's from Marks and Spencer's, where my mum worked]. And so it went on, until everyone had presented Britannia with some kind of

offering. Then we sang "God Save the King," and all went home to our tea.
Three months after this skit, September 2nd, 1939, to be exact, I was lying in a field with some friends, eating blackberries from a nearby bush, looking up at the sky, when one of the boys said, "My Daddy says, tomorrow we are going to have a war with Germany."

A year later, during school recess, while all the kids were playing in the yard, we all became aware of a distant droning. As it got louder, we looked up into the sky and counted ninety-two German bombers, flying high, glistening in the noonday sun. They were on their way to the Bristol Aircraft factory, twenty miles away. There, along with four hundred other workers, my Uncle John was killed. Within a few months Ralph was in flight school in Canada, Desmond was flying a bomber, Frank, also in the RAF, was in Iraq, Pat was in Burma, Richard in the Indian Army, and Aunty Joan was a WAAF. Not much later, Bart was torpedoed in the Timor Sea, managed to get ashore, and had walked two hundred miles through the desert to Darwin, and our house was bombed.

As I grew, so did my awareness of the Empire, driven by current events, school and reading. In school, it was pretty much a matter of "1066 and all that," with not much of the "all that." Of Clive, The Mutiny, Nelson, Wolfe, Gordon and Scott, I remember a little, but I don't recall the American colonies even being mentioned. I did win a prize in Sunday school for drawing a map of the Holy Land.

My concept of the Empire came more from reading than anything else: The Boy's Own Paper, *wherein public school boys were constantly being invited to spend "the hols" with some uncle, or princely school chum in India, Malaya, Borneo or Africa where they would be caught up in some great adventure involving man eating tigers, rampaging elephants or dastardly dacoits. Then came Henty, Ballantyne and, above all, Kim. So, Empire was equated with adventure.*

What of the real world at the end of the war? Ralph had been shot down over Germany, imprisoned, escaped, and made his way back to England. But his health was broken. At home there was little prospect of a job, so he emigrated to South Africa. Joan had been injured when the cable of a barrage balloon snapped. She didn't fancy working as a waitress, so had left for Rhodesia. Vincent married an Austrian girl and moved to Canada. Pat, suffering with severe malaria, thought the climate in South Africa would be beneficial. Mary and Eddy went to work among the Eskimos in Yellow Knife, Canada. Heather married a G.I. and went to Virginia. Bart came home from Australia, but, after a few months, said he couldn't stand the bloody weather, or the bloody people, sailed back to Australia, and was never heard from again. Food rationing became more severe than it was during the war. Interminable arguments between Tories and Socialists seemed to go nowhere. Even the weather was the worst in living memory. Almost everyone wanted to be anywhere but here. The Empire became a place to escape to.

Safari so good!

It's really grand,
This Guinness canned —
On English shore,
Or foreign strand.
Lighter to take,
It cannot break.
And what a treat
Your thirst to slake!

CANNED GUINNESS
good to drink and so sustaining

NO EMPTIES TO RETURN—VERY HANDY TO STORE

Elephant Guns and Leather on Willow: Sports and Safaris

WHILE THE PIG-STICKING SO BELOVED OF ROBERT BADEN-POWELL was a rather specialist pursuit, the British Empire took rugby, football and cricket to the masses. During the 19th century, sport in British society went from the rough to the respectable. Overcrowded, illegal gatherings for cock-fighting, ratting and gambling, usually fuelled by drink, were transformed by the Victorians and replaced by orderly leisure-time pursuits that were then transplanted around the world.

An advertisement from *Wide World* magazine which demonstrates the common currency of the word 'safari' and the image of the white man in the tropics, adventuring while also clearly occupying a superior position to the 'natives'. From 1962 onwards, thirsty safari-goers didn't even have to import Guinness to Africa, after the company established a subsidiary in Lagos, Nigeria, brewing 'Foreign Extra Stout'.

Wherever they settled, the British constructed stadiums, racetracks, cricket ovals and racquets courts. They and their indigenous allies played polo in the shadow of the Himalayas, on elephant or horse, hunted jackal with hounds on the slopes of Table Mountain, and whiled away lazy afternoons at billiards in the clubs of the Raj. The first recorded use of the sports blazer, that essential item of British kit, was by cricketers in Mexico in 1838. In Palestine, Peshawar and Lahore the British rode to hounds, dressed in hunting-pinks, just as they did back in the shires.

Aside from hunting, it was team games that the British pioneered, and their penchant for codification and order meant that they wrote rules and founded governing bodies for almost every sport they encountered. Football was taken to Brazil in the 1870s by British sailors, and thence spread throughout South America, football associations being formed in countries such as Argentina, Chile, Paraguay and Uruguay. The names of clubs, such as Corinthians in Brazil, Everton in Chile and Liverpool in Argentina, reflect the British roots of the game. Meanwhile the British formalized the rules of croquet in the 1860s and established the All-England Croquet Club, and then took the game to Australia, New Zealand and South Africa, the only countries outside Britain where the game is widely played. Reflecting the importance attached to sport and leisure time in the Raj, India was responsible for popularizing numerous modern sports including badminton. Originating in England and named after the country estate of the Duke of Beaufort, badminton migrated to India where the rules were first drawn up in 1877.

Cricket and the rules of the game

Cricket was first played in the American colonies in 1709, the year in which the first inter-county match was recorded in England. The first touring Australian side to visit England had comprised Australian Aborigines. Cricket soon became an

Johann Joseph Zoffany's 1790 painting *Colonel Mordaunt watching a cock fight at Lucknow, India,* shows East India Company officers enjoying their somewhat dissolute leisure pursuits. The occasion was a challenge match between the colonel and Asaf al-Daula, Nawab of Oudh, in 1786. In an open-sided tent, officers and administrators sit and stand under a canopy. In the foreground two cocks with metal spurs fight, anxiously watched by attendants. Various members of the surrounding Indian crowd hold their fighting cocks, waiting for their turn. This painting once belonged to Warren Hastings (1732–1818), the first governor-general of India.

Empire-wide sport. In 1853 settlers in Australia created the world's biggest cricket ground in Melbourne. An English touring team first visited Australia a decade later, the first Test Match took place in Melbourne in 1877 and Australia first defeated England in a Test Match on an English ground at the Oval in 1882. Joking that English cricket was thenceforth dead, the Australians said that they would take the ashes back home. When, in the following year, England defeated Australia on their own soil, the victors were presented with an urn of ashes to be taken home, and the tradition stuck. Other nations featured too, and in 1911 the Maharajah of Patiala captained an Indian side touring England. Cricket was not this prince's only passion, however, and he fathered eighty-eight children and died playing polo.

Character-building sport

Cricket, character and job prospects went hand in hand in the British Empire. Sir Ralph Furse, the main recruiter for the Colonial Service for over a quarter of a century, would ask would-be district commissioners during formal interviews if they played cricket. Peter Lucy's uncle had been a ship's doctor before becoming a Medical Officer in Malaya. 'The ship called in at Singapore and they played cricket against the Singapore Cricket Club. My uncle made a hundred and the Governor said, "You're the sort of man we want in the Malayan Service".' It wasn't just the colonial services that took sport seriously. The business houses of empire were the same, including large British rubber companies in the East like Dunlop's and Guthrie's. Both companies took on players of international standard to grace their respective rugby teams. John Theophilus's interview for Dunlop's consisted of one or two questions 'as to where I'd been born and what my parents were and so on' and then the interviewing director said, "What's that tie you've got on?" I said, "It's the Harlequin Rugby Club, sir". And he said, "You'll get some rugger out there" – and that was my interview.'

After inventing, adapting and regulating all sorts of different sports, the British then took them to the four corners of the globe and planted passionate sporting communities in the dominions and elsewhere, reflected today in events such as the Rugby World Cup and the location of cricketing test nations in regions formerly dominated by British rule. As Richard Tames writes, 'more than any other country, Britain contributed to making sport a codified, competitive and international phenomenon. In doing so it also significantly defined itself as a nation. Gymnastics was for Germans. Training was for Americans. The British *played*.'

Snooker and the application of technology to sport

A classic sport of the British Empire, popular in clubs and messes around the world, was snooker and associated games such as billiards and pyramids. It was from India that these games found their way into the sporting life of the metropolis, starting with the great and the good and by the end of the 19th century working their way down to the common man in the public house. An adaptation of billiards, snooker was invented at the Ootacamund (Ooty) Club in the Nilgiri Hills in southern India in 1875. Its inventors were Army officers,

Pig-sticking was a favourite pastime of British officers in India. This lithographic plate, entitled 'The Charge', was one of a series produced for the book *Hog Hunting in Lower Bengal* by Percy Carpenter (1861).

THE CONTRIBUTION OF THE BRITISH EMPIRE
TO WORLD SPORT WAS STAGGERING.
BRITONS INVENTED TENNIS, RUGBY, SQUASH, TABLE-
TENNIS, BADMINTON, NETBALL, WATER-POLO AND
COMPETITIVE DIVING; REFORMED, REGULARIZED AND
UPDATED HORSE-RACING, ARCHERY, BOXING, BOWLS,
FOOTBALL, ATHLETICS, ANGLING AND WEIGHTLIFTING;
AND IMPORTED CROQUET, POLO, SNOOKER,
GYMNASTICS, CYCLING, ROLLER-SKATING, LACROSSE
AND CANOEING.

– *Richard Tames,* **The Victorian and Edwardian Sportsman**
(2008)

prominent among them Colonel Sir Neville Bowes Chamberlain. A decade later, Chamberlain met John Roberts in Bangalore. Roberts was a billiards wizard, and he brought the new game back to England and popularized and commercialized it. Captain Rawdon Crawley's 1856 classic, *Billiards: Its Theory and Practice*, began by musing that although Cleopatra in Egypt and the Chinese claimed to have invented the game, 'its introduction into British India and the Australian Islands is certainly due to British enterprise'.

New technologies played a significant part in forging a global sporting community. New materials such as rubber and gutta-percha (tough plastic made from Malayan latex) transformed the design of sports equipment such as racquets, golf balls and tennis balls. Ivory entered mass circulation in the form of snooker balls, and snooker was further refined by the replacement of cotton or horsehair cushions by rubber ones. Rubber and the pneumatic tyre led to a craze for cycling in the 1890s, and in the twentieth century bicycles became a status symbol for Africans who could afford the price, as Raleigh and BSA (which officially stood for Birmingham Small Arms, but was colloquially rendered as 'Bloody Sore Arse') machines were exported around the world. The world's first hard tennis court, made of asphalt, was laid at St Kilda in Melbourne in 1878. The spread of the mail order catalogue and department stores around the world kitted out budding sportsmen and women. As new materials and new commercial connections interlinked the sporting world, other developments and technologies aided its spread. The opening of the Suez Canal and the growth of steamship routes made possible the globalization of sporting competition, which culminated in the first Olympic Games in 1896, revived by the French aristocrat Baron Pierre de Coubertin, who was inspired by the sporting ethos of the British public school and the worldwide spread of British games.

Schools, garrisons and imperial sport

The Victorian public school became a temple to athleticism, manliness and the team spirit, and this translated itself to the Empire and its fringes as upright, noble and muscular young boys became, in theory at least, upright, noble and muscular young district commissioners and army officers. The first purpose-built gymnasium was constructed in 1851 at the East India Company College, Addiscombe, near Croydon and team games became a school cult and a central theme in children's literature from the late nineteenth century until the 1960s. Henry Newbolt's famous poem 'Vitai Lampada' captured the spirit, telling of a schoolboy cricketer who grows up to fight for the Empire in Africa. So did Rudyard Kipling's novel *Stalky and Co*, in which a gang of public schoolboys rehearse for the greater 'game' on the battlefields of empire through team sports and high jinx (the novel, a major

inspiration for the boys comics of the day, was
dedicated to a classic imperial school, the United
Services College at Westward Ho!, Devon).

Sports spread with imperial garrisons and settler
communities and became closely associated with the
'civilizing mission' that Britons zealously undertook
overseas. As well as sports clubs and racecourses, the
public schools established by the British overseas
promulgated the modern cult of sport; Mayo College
in India, catering for the pampered offspring of the
subcontinent's princes, had five games masters on the
books, and sports days, sports prizes, rolls of honour
and trophies were as integral a feature of school life as
they were back in England.

A plethora of sporting activities

All Britons overseas, whether private soldiers
sweating out their time in India or planters' daughters
on the tea estates of Ceylon, were encouraged to play
sport and play it regularly. The Army decreed that
every overseas barracks should have a cricket pitch;
officers were expected to play polo or some other
team sport; and district commissioners were strongly
encouraged to play a set of tennis at the club
whenever they could, or go hunting for the pot if

'A boundary hit': A classic
image from a *Boys' Own
Annual* of the 1920s. This
type of image – showing a
schoolboy batsman in action
or a rugger player going over
for a try – was ubiquitous in
juvenile literature, part of the
hallowed ideal of the 'making'
of upright and talented men
through the lessons of team
work and fair play.

away from what passed as civilization. In Southeast Asia football and cricket were
played from March through August and then it was rugby and hockey. Sporting
tournaments were legion, such as the HMS *Malaya* cup for rugby competed for
by the different Malay states, and the Layton Cup in Ceylon, a boxing tournament
involving any imperial units stationed on the island. This emphasis on sport had
more behind it than a desire for healthy, manly bodies; it was also an attempt to
stop men going out of their minds with sexual frustration and to provide an
alternative to pastimes such as gambling. Anything, in short, to prevent young
sahibs going deolali (Deolali, a town 100 miles [160 km] northeast of Bombay,
was a major army base. 'Going deolali' – Anglicized to 'doolally' – referred to the
madness of troops waiting to return to England after a tour of duty in India).

Many clubs in the Empire had golf courses attached, and sports clubs
developed rituals, traditions and forms of dress. Army life for many officers
overseas featured riding in the morning, as well as hunting and shooting and
team sports. Cavalry regiments partook of almost any kind of horse-based sport
conceivable, from flat racing to steeple-chasing and polo. In India, polo was taken
very seriously indeed, as evidenced by the importance attached by Winston
Churchill's regiment to winning the inter-regimental polo trophy. Aside from

Indian Army officers and maharajahs mingle in a photo-call for the Hyderabad Contingent Polo Team in 1883. Polo originated in Persia, but was codified and popularized by the British in India. The first club was founded in Assam in 1834.

actual fighting, of which there was not always much to be had, polo was the most important thing of all. The game had been introduced into Britain in 1869 by cavalrymen from India, and was then taken around the world, forging some of the more surprising links, such as that between the British and Argentine equestrian communities, a link strengthened by the habit of sending the sons of well-to-do Argentine families to British public schools. As in the case of the ritualized hunt – a Mughal tradition – the British were adopting and then adapting indigenous recreations and making them their own.

Tonic for the troops

The military increasingly saw sport as an important supplement to formal arms drill, leading to improved fitness levels and offering an alternative to idleness, boredom and alcohol. It was also recognized that sports such as boxing, fencing, polo and shooting enhanced unit cohesion. The revelations of the Boer War – when seven out of nine potential army recruits were judged unfit for service – led to a renewed emphasis on sports and 'national efficiency'. It was widely believed that if the British breed was to survive and if the blot of urban poverty was to be removed from the national escutcheon, then sport and healthy living had to become a national preoccupation. As well as British garrisons dotted around the world, the civil services that administered the Empire became increasingly keen to have sporty types unearthed by their recruitment procedures. Brains, naturally, remained important, but not *all*-important, in the search for young men for the Indian Civil Service and the Colonial Administrative Service. The Sudan, indeed, became known as 'the land of blacks ruled by Blues' because of the prevalence in the ranks of the Sudan Political Service of varsity men who had rowed or played cricket or rugby for their university. Chris Farmer, who became a District Officer in Nigeria, saw himself 'as a typical product of the much-maligned public school system … I was head of my house, I was deputy head of the school, captain of rugger and company sergeant-major in the Officer Training Corps, exercising responsibility and learning to use the authority which went with the responsibility, so that when eventually I found myself out in the bush in Nigeria on my own I wasn't worried about it in the slightest way'.

This adoration of the intelligent outdoor type was taken to extremes by Cecil Rhodes whose will created the Rhodes Scholarships that thrive to this day. His aim was to offer the finest men from the Dominions, as well as America and Germany, a period of informal Anglicization at one of Britain's great universities in order to provide global links between men destined for great things in their respective countries. Brains alone were not enough, however, and referees were asked (and still are) to comment on a candidate's sporting abilities as well as their intellectual and social ones.

Shikars and *safaris*

Aristocrats brought hunting packs from England to their estates in the White Highlands, recreating a rural sporting scene that had grown to define the English well-to-do. For a select band of Britons the Empire was an extension of the grouse moors of Scotland, the game drives of the great estates, and the hunt meets of the English shires. For these men, bagging a brace of tigers before tiffin or taking pot shots at rhinoceros from the front of a moving locomotive – as Winston Churchill did on his visit to East Africa in 1908 – were some of the more bracing attractions of the Empire. Britons simply couldn't get enough hunting, and fortunately, so it seemed, the supply of targets was endless. As Churchill himself put it, barely able to believe the abundance of animals as he passed through Kenya and Uganda by rail, 'the plains are crowded with wild animals. From the window the whole zoological garden can be seen disporting itself.'

This imperial sporting scene was presided over by the sporting activities and patronage of royalty. Through the media and Royal souvenir volumes kings and princes were associated with sports such as cricket, football, racing and shooting. Race meetings were followed passionately by Britons and their subjects across the colonial world and the British established racecourses almost as soon as they stepped off the boat in some new part of the world, as quickly as they established churches, public schools, clubs and Masonic lodges. Throughout the Empire the

THE GREAT AFRICAN SAFARIS LASTED FOR ONE CENTURY. FROM 1836 UNTIL 1939 UNIQUE
CONDITIONS AND ECCENTRIC INDIVIDUALS CREATED A STYLE OF ADVENTURE THAT CAN NEVER
EXIST AGAIN. ABUNDANT BIG GAME, UNGOVERNED LANDSCAPES, SUITABLE WEAPONS, THE
LIFELONG HABIT OF HUNTING, A ZEST FOR DISCOVERY AND AN APPRECIATION OF BOTH HARDSHIP
AND LUXURY, ALL CAME TOGETHER THEN IN THE VAST BUSH OF SOUTH-EASTERN AFRICA

– Bartle Bull, Safari: A Chronicle of Adventure *(1988)*

British shot anything that moved, rolling back the game frontier in Southern Africa for hundreds of miles in the process, and endangering numerous species. In this matter, the past truly was a foreign country, and for Britons the world over, it was hunting country. Young midshipmen on their first overseas posting, perhaps on a river gunboat somewhere up the Yangtze, would let rip at snipe; tigers were prized in India where princes invited well-connected Britons for *shikar* ('hunt' in Urdu); while in Africa, hippos were punted to the shore by African porters after being 'bagged' by a hunter's gun as *safari* ('long journey' in Swahili) became a recognized feature of the white man's relationship with Africa. It spawned 'big game hunters' and famous devotees such as Ernest Hemingway and Teddy Roosevelt. And so the skins, hides, antlers and jawbones of beasts great and small came to adorn homes, clubs and messes from Aldershot and Addiscombe to Crater Town and Mandalay.

The imaginations of children and adults alike were captivated by the prospect of hunting adventures in the great expanses of the Empire, from lofty proconsuls such as Lord Curzon, shooting tigers with maharajahs, to the work-a-day settler or junior district officer hunting for the pot. One of the most common images purveyed in popular literature was of the white man

Former US President Theodore Roosevelt (left) sitting with Mr and Mrs Hobley, fellow members of his hunting party to Africa, on the cow-catcher of a locomotive at Kikuyu Station, on 4 August 1909. Landing in Mombasa in April with his son Kermit and a group of friends, Roosevelt led a safari involving 250 porters and guides across British East Africa, into the Belgian Congo and back to the Nile, ending in Khartoum. The expedition bagged 1100 specimens, including 500 big-game animals. He published his experiences the following year in the book *African Game Trails*.

in the bush with rifle at the ready, a man-eating tiger, rogue elephant or pot-bound kudu within sight.

The English love of hunting in the Empire clearly derived from their love of hunting at home, and the cross-fertilization was striking, partridges, peacocks and pheasants arriving from Asia as foxhounds left their crates at ports in Africa and the Middle East. Books about hunting and life on the frontiers were commonplace, including works such as R.M. Ballantyne's *The Gorilla Hunters: A Tale of the Wilds of Africa*. *The Wonder Book of the Wild: The Romance of Exploration and Big Game Stalking* was packed with photos of elephants, crocodiles, giraffes, flamingos, polar bears and moose.

Long before the coming of the Raj, the Indian nobility had engaged in *shikar* – the highly-skilled pursuit of tigers – and many wealthy princes maintained full-time *shikaris* (professional hunters). They constructed lodges, and when the British came, first as East India Company traders, later as Residents and District Collectors, tiger-hunting became a way of extending hospitality.

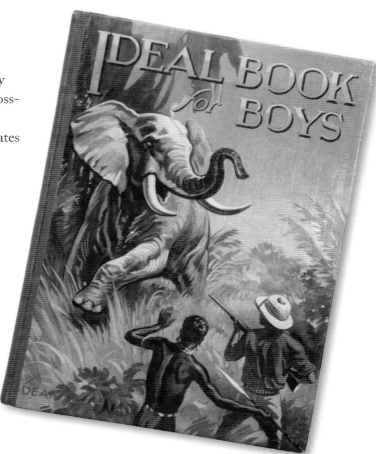

Quatermain, the quintessential hero

One of fiction's great heroes, read avidly until well after the Second World War, was Sir Henry Rider Haggard's Allan Quatermain. Haggard's mother had been born in Bombay, and told stories of India that enthralled the young man as he grew up in Norfolk, learning to ride and shoot at an early age. Given this squirearchical background, it was no surprise that Quatermain was a renowned hunter and adventurer (the model for the *Raiders of the Lost Ark* and a character in the *League of Extraordinary Gentlemen*). The character was based on a farmer in Garsington near Oxford, whom Haggard had known when a boy. 'A fine, handsome man of about fifty, with grey hair and aristocratic features, that came to him probably enough with his Norman blood.' His name was Quatermain. In *King Solomon's Mines* (1885), Sir Henry Curtis introduces Quatermain as 'one of the oldest hunters and the very best shots in Africa, who has killed more elephants and lions than any other man alive … He had short grizzled hair, which stood about an inch above his head like the bristles of a brush, large brown eyes, and a withered face, tanned absolutely the colour of mahogany from exposure to the weather.'

While sports brought Britons together across the world, important bonds were forged and maintained by institutions such as the public school, the gentleman's club and the Masonic lodge, pillars of imperial society that are considered in the following chapter.

The thrill of safari: another classic image – the white youth, facing up to the challenges of a dangerous and exciting colonial world, his technology (the rifle) trumping the spear of 'lesser' cultures. The *Ideal Book for Boys* included 'The Jungle Vet', a story of forests, tigers, pygmies and Chinese bandits set in Malaya, a tale set amidst Canadian forests, and 'The Tower of the Dead', set among the mountain peaks of North Persia where an employee of Anglo-Iranian Oil is captured by 'wandering Kurds'. There was also 'The Kunkuru Killer', a story of elephants set around Lake Victoria.

The Playing Fields of Aligarh and Eton: Schools, Lodges and the Imperial Élite

FROM PUBLIC SCHOOLS TO LONDON CLUBS AND MASONIC LODGES, Britain's imperial élite belonged to powerful institutions from childhood, and the British formed satellites of these institutions wherever they went in the world. Public schools at home and abroad trained the imperial ruling classes while clubs and lodges merged with the honours system and tokens of rank to create the Empire's ruling castes, from box-wallahs and army officers to colonial administrators, native princes and Dominions' politicians.

'Across dashed Wellgate's full-back, and dived for his knees'. A plate from *Herbert Strang's Annual*, c.1923. This illustration accompanied the story 'Nothing on Earth: A Public School Story'.

The Victorians, according to historian P.J. Rich, created a reality 'in which to an extent we still live, one of remarkable ritualism which the English public schools played a major part in producing. The story is of glittering decorations and convincingly choreographed ceremonies, but more importantly concerns the political confidence that such phantasmagoria produced.'

The social and political hierarchy and symbolic authority were part of the fabric of British and therefore imperial life, from coats of arms and crests on buildings to dress uniforms, decorations and the strict order of precedence reflected in the seating plan at dinner. Though subsequently seen as props to cultural hegemony, at the time they reflected the manner in which Britain conceived the ordering of society and arranged its business, be it military, clerical, juridical or political. Authority, it is said, needs a face, and in the British Empire that face frequently appeared squashed between a piece of ceremonial headgear and a chest laden with medal ribbons and honorific insignia.

Turning out a basically sound chap

Manning the imperial civil and military services was the job of the public schools and ancient universities, and the British transplanted these élite institutions, along with their clubs and Masonic lodges, wherever they set foot overseas. Public schools were thoroughly imperialized during the course of the 19th century, as headmasters took it upon themselves to turn out the kind of man that could knock a cricket ball for six, confidently talk to members of the opposite sex and govern New South Wales.

THERE'S A BREATHLESS HUSH IN THE CLOSE TO-NIGHT –
TEN TO MAKE AND THE MATCH TO WIN –
A BUMPING PITCH AND A BLINDING LIGHT,
AN HOUR TO PLAY AND THE LAST MAN IN.
AND IT'S NOT FOR THE SAKE OF A RIBBONED COAT,
OR THE SELFISH HOPE OF A SEASON'S FAME,
BUT HIS CAPTAIN'S HAND ON HIS SHOULDER SMOTE
'PLAY UP! PLAY UP! AND PLAY THE GAME!'

THE SAND OF THE DESERT IS SODDEN RED, –
RED WITH THE WRECK OF A SQUARE THAT BROKE; –
THE GATLING'S JAMMED AND THE COLONEL DEAD,
AND THE REGIMENT BLIND WITH DUST AND SMOKE.
THE RIVER OF DEATH HAS BRIMMED HIS BANKS,
AND ENGLAND'S FAR, AND HONOUR A NAME,
BUT THE VOICE OF A SCHOOLBOY RALLIES THE RANKS,
'PLAY UP! PLAY UP! AND PLAY THE GAME!'

– from Sir Henry Newbolt, 'Vitaï Lampada' (1897)

The public schools were instrumental in fostering this love of ritual and taking it forward into adult life, where lodges, clubs, royal patronage, honours and prizes – and the extension of such institutions overseas – were features of British life. These schools moulded 'the imperial élite, products of those curious institutions, the English public schools ... whose friendships, slangs and values often lasted a man through life. These were the nurseries of Empire.' Nearly all the young men joining the civil and military services – as well as those who went into business – shared the common background of the English public schools. According to Robert Huessler, 'the importance of the English Public Schools to the major civil and military services and even to business would be difficult to exaggerate. Their grip on the national imagination is not equalled by that of comparable institutions in any other country among the Western democracies.'

Loyalty, élitism and Christian duty

Wherever the flag went so too did ex-public schoolboys and public schools themselves. As they were transplanted to Central Africa and the Pacific they borrowed from the alma maters of their founders, from heraldry to the classic quadrangle arrangement of the school buildings. The Empire's public schools were modelled on their English counterparts in every way – quads, dorms, masters, crests, songs, special slang and the centrality of sports and games. St Michael's University School in Victoria, British Columbia, included the stars from Dulwich's coat of arms in its own coat of arms, founded as it was by an Old Dulwichian.

First prime minister of independent India, leader of the Congress Party and Old Harrovian: Jawaharlal Nehru (or 'Joe Nehru' as he was known while in England) in his Harrow School uniform in 1904, aged 15. Nehru went on to study natural sciences at Trinity College, Cambridge before studying for the bar at the Inner Temple.

ETON AND EMPIRE

Melville Macnaghten, son of a chairman of the East India Company, was at Eton between 1868 and 1873, and later rose to be head of Scotland Yard. His *Sketchy Memories of Eton* serves to illustrate the multiple imperial links provided by the public schools. One of the masters during his time there was Johnson Cory, who wrote the Eton Boating Song in 1863 with Old Boys' serving the Empire in mind – 'young men quartered in Indian hill-forts' and the like. Among hundreds of others, Cory influenced boys such as Curzon and Rosebery (respectively, a future Viceroy of India and Foreign Secretary, and a future Prime Minister at a time of dramatic imperial expansion). Macnaghten's classmates included a future headmaster of Metropolitan Calcutta, a Secretary of State for India, a man who died in Aden of wounds inflicted by a lioness in Somaliland, one who 'died unmarried at Umballa from an accident at polo', and one who discovered the prehistoric flint mines in Somaliland and the Egyptian emerald mines. There was a legal member of Council in India, an explorer who died in Uganda, an aide-de-camp to the Governor-General of Canada, the Viceroy of India, the Lord Lieutenant of Ireland, a director of education in Ceylon, a tutor to the offspring of the Maharajah of Baroda and Field Marshal Lord Roberts of Kandahar. Beyond this impressive list, Rich writes, 'there were legions of Etonian tea-planters and winners of medals in now forgotten campaigns'.

King's Parramatta in Australia sported the same crest as King's Canterbury. St Thomas' College in Ceylon was conceived on the principles of an English public school. Founded by the first Bishop of Colombo in 1851, in the early 20th century it moved to a new site at Mount Lavinia south of Colombo. The school was centred on a classical-style quad dominated by the Chapel of the Transfiguration on one side and the Library on the other, the quad completed by handsome buildings housing classrooms, dormitories and the College Hall. Big Club Grounds for school sports lay between the quadrangle and the white-crested waves of the Indian Ocean. The school consciously fostered a sense of loyalty, élitism and Christian duty. Just as in the public schools of Britain, life here in the middle of the Indian Ocean featured boarders and day boys, housemasters, games, cadet corps, school mottos, songs and the inculcation of a sense of imperial loyalty.

Some British schools, such as Haileybury, were founded specifically for imperial reasons or had Empire-related scholarships, such as the Knightley Scholarship at Tonbridge for the sons of Indian Civil Service officers, and the Lugard Scholarship at Rossall. Imperial schools included Mayo College, Ajmer; Victoria College, Alexandria; Harrison College, Barbados; Peterhouse, Southern Rhodesia; Timaru School, New Zealand; Prince of Wales School, Vancouver; Upper Canada College; Muhammadan Anglo-Oriental College, Aligarh; Gordon College, Khartoum; Geelong Church of England Grammar School, Australia (where Prince Charles spent an exchange year away from his school, Gordonstoun); Queen's College, Hong Kong; King Edward VII School, South

AS HE LOOKS TO THE FUTURE OF HIS PUPILS, [THE ENGLISH HEADMASTER] WILL NOT FORGET THAT THEY ARE DESTINED TO BE THE CITIZENS OF THE GREATEST EMPIRE UNDER HEAVEN; HE WILL TEACH THEM PATRIOTISM … HE WILL INSPIRE THEM WITH FAITH IN THE DIVINELY ORDAINED MISSION OF THEIR COUNTRY AND THEIR RACE.
– *Headmaster of Harrow, early 20th century*

Indian alma mater: La Martiniere College was the first school in the world to be awarded Battle Honours for the part its staff and pupils played in the defence of the Residency at Lucknow during the 1857 Mutiny.

Africa; and King's College, Budo, Uganda. King's College was built on the Coronation Hill of the Baganda kings, and coronation services were held in the school chapel. The Kabaka (the King of Buganda) and Sir Hesketh Bell, Governor of Uganda, attended the first speech day in 1908, and Winston Churchill visited in the same year:

> The schoolboys sang English songs and hymns in very good tune and rhythm. It was astonishing to look at the map of the British Empire hanging on the wall and to realize that all this was taking place near the north-western corner of the Victoria Nyanza.

School houses at Budo included Australia House, England House and South Africa House. Edward Mutesa became Kabaka while still at Budo, and his coronation was solemnized in the school chapel. Later in life he became a member of the Cambridge University Officers' Corp and of the Grenadier Guards, illustrating the manner in which native élites became a part of imperial élites.

Public schools cleverly enlisted religion in the service of the school spirit along with lofty ideas of patriotism, manliness, duty and loyalty. As dim light filtered into the school chapel through the stained glass, illuminating boys in various states of inattention as the Headmaster read the lesson or a mumbled hymn commenced, it was as much secular values and ideas as religious ones that were being conveyed. As Rich puts it, 'architecturally the chapel edifices emphasized school rather than Christian symbolism', not least through the veneration of old boys lost in world wars and distant imperial campaigns, as much a matter of tribal pride as were the successes of the 1st XV or the fencing team. This is not, of course, to say that public schools produced nothing other than lathe-turned empire loyalists; Richard Symonds first learned to view imperialism as ridiculous whilst at Rugby, especially when 'defeat at football meant "no jam" because the team had let down the Empire'. Nevertheless, there's little doubt that the overwhelming impact of public schools was to produce boys who looked with favour upon the British Empire, and evinced an uncomplicated patriotism. As Molesworth senior, 'the goriller of 3B', proclaims when told that 'Britain is the most heavily mechanized country in the world. It hav more traktors per acre than america or rusia': 'Cheers cheer cheers hurrah for st george and boo to everybody else ...' All of the boys at St Custard's, and most other public schools, would have heartily agreed.

The advantage of the old school tie

Recruits from public schools dominated the Empire's administrative services, as well as its military, religious and legal branches (as they did at home). In 1900 the *Lahore Civil and Military Gazette* carried an article entitled 'Which Public School Sends Out the Most Men to India'. The survey found that Clifton, Winchester, Charterhouse, Marlborough, Cheltenham, St Paul's, Rugby and Eton did. Like the imperial honours system, attendance at public school or one of the ancient British universities fashioned bonds that transcended racial barriers, and the 'old school tie' could be as useful a tool to an African or Asian as it was to a Briton. The way in which class, more than race, divided British society is illustrated by the two principal characters in Paul Scott's 'Raj Quartet' (1965–75); Ronald Merrick, the lower middle-class police superintendant and ex-grammar-school boy, is acutely aware of not having been to a public school. By contrast, Harry Kumar, though an Indian, enjoys advantages closed to Merrick from the fact that his family sent him to an English public school ('Chillingborough', possibly modelled on Marlborough).

Public schools and the networks they forged were also a way of taking 'home' overseas. Young men out in the colonies for the first time lived in chummeries, a tropical continuation of the boarding house. Every colony boasted its school dinners, university moots and Boat Race events. Such events were as important to the British sense of self amidst alien surroundings as was dressing formally for dinner in the midst of the African jungle hundreds of miles away from the nearest white man. Schools and rituals were an important part of governing and idealizing the Empire, its values and connections. The *Boys' Own Paper* produced posters showing dozens of different public school shields, distributed with the comic for boys to collect.

THE LAWRENCE MEMORIAL ROYAL MILITARY SCHOOL, NILGIRI HILLS

John Banks attended Haddon Hill, a boarding school at Nuwara Eliya in Ceylon's central highlands. After finishing primary school he was sent to the Lawrence Memorial Royal Military School (LMRMS) at Lovedale, near Ootacamund in South India, a school endowed by Sir Henry Lawrence of Indian Mutiny fame for the poorer Anglo-Indian or English people employed on the railways or in the army. It became home to numerous boys from Ceylon during the Second World War because they were unable to proceed, as was normal practice, to schools in Australia or Britain.

The journey to the Nilgiri Hills entailed a fascinating three-day journey by boat and train.

We would leave Colombo in the evening and arrive by morning at Talamanaar in north-west Ceylon. Here we would embark on a ferry for the fifty miles or so crossing of the Palk Strait to Southern India. Having made the crossing, we entrained again, after passing through the quarantine department at Mandapam Camp. Despite the heat and the steady stream of soot and grime which poured through the carriage window, the day journey through the seemingly endless plain of Southern India was fascinating for me with glimpses, however fleeting, of strange birds, desert plains and dusty villages. In the evening of the second day we reached Trinchinopoli, where we had dinner in the station restaurant. Some time next morning we would change trains at Metapolium for the long slow climb up into the Nilgiri Hills.

It was by all accounts a very martial school, as befitted its foundation. Boys spent a great deal of time parading in khaki uniform with boots, stockings and First World War puttees. They marched to church on Sundays wearing uniforms similar to the Royal Marines but with peaked caps, and on special occasions the boys carried dummy .303 rifles with First World War bayonets attached with a lump of cast iron. The school marched to church twice on Sundays behind a full-blown boys' band which played the military marching tunes of the day. Success in the annual rifle shooting competition entitled Banks to wear the coveted crossed rifles on his uniform. As in many English public schools, corporal punishment and rough justice beneath the purview of the staff was common. A juvenile form of duelling existed, known as 'Com' (short for 'combat'). 'In due course, in a secluded part of the school grounds, and surrounded by a yelling blood-thirsty throng of boys, the two would fight each other with bare fists until one of the combatants, or more often, the senior boys present, called a halt.'

The public school curriculum

Imperial history and attitudes were an integral feature of British education. Imperialism wasn't just the preserve of the public schools; in 1917 E.J. Golledge, Headmaster of St John's Boys' School, Ealing, wrote an article entitled 'How I Run My "Empire Room"', describing a classroom dedicated to imperial artefacts, maps, models of mountain ranges, sporting trophies and general imperial information. The school curriculum was an important conduit of imperial information and opinions, particularly in the fields of English literature, geography and history. H.M. Buller, an assistant master at Clifton College in the 1920s, wrote a textbook entitled *Macaulay's Essay on Warren Hastings*. Despite its historical subject matter, it appeared in a Longmans English Literature series, and children were expected to write essays on the book. Longman's 'Class Book of English Literature' series included *Robinson Crusoe, Captain Cook's Voyages, English Seamen in the Sixteenth Century, Coral Island, Where Three Empires Meet, Settlers in Canada, Life of Nelson*, and *Tales of King Arthur and the Round Table*.

As well as Empire Day pageants and the study of history, schoolchildren encountered the Empire through the study of geography, featuring the world's political boundaries, its rivers, mountains and deserts and the production and exchange of trade goods. With its emphasis on maps and distant mountain ranges, and the origins of products consumed in British factories and British dining rooms, geography gave children a working knowledge of a distinctly British world. Geography, according to John Mackenzie, had 'notable immediacy because of exploration and the consequent discussion of natural resources, character of indigenous peoples, and capacity of technology to exploit global riches'. As well as encouraging children to pore over maps, it familiarized them with products such as Australian wool and Gold Coast cocoa, shipped by the Merchant Navy to British ports, while British coal and manufactured goods travelled in the opposite direction.

Geography also introduced children to different peoples and their habits and customs. In E.C.T. Horniblow's *Wonderful Travels in Wonderful Lands*, part of a 1950s human geography series, lessons were delivered through the adventures of Tom Franklin and his Uncle Mac as they toured the world by aeroplane. 'Tom did

Young ambassadors of the mother country: public-school boys going on the Schools Empire Tour, 1933, are seen off at Euston by Dr Montague Rendall, headmaster of Winchester College from 1911 to 1924 and one of the founding governors of the BBC.

This illustration ('Jack Looks after the Sheep') appeared in Chapter One: 'Wool: On the Sheep Farms of Australia' in the 1930s school geography book *Our Neighbours: Their Work for Us*. The chapter ended with the information: 'Britain buys most of Australia's wool and the factories of Yorkshire weave it to make the clothes we wear'.

want to get older quickly. If only he could go to baking-hot Africa and icy-cold Greenland, or to the wonderful lands of India and China.' Uncle Mac tells him: 'I am going to take you to South Africa, to see how the black people there live. We call them *Kaffirs*.' In typical fashion, Africa is presented in terms of elephants and mud huts with natives wearing 'little more than a small piece of cloth hanging round their waists'. Tom and Uncle Mac then visit the home of the pygmies. Here they were less impressed.

'I'm glad I'm not a Pigmy,' said Tom suddenly.

'So am I,' replied Uncle Mac. 'They are not very nice people. Often they quarrel and fight with each other, and are very cruel. They have no God, and certainly do not have very lovable ways to each other. They are more like animals than men.'

As well as geography and literature, history was the other main vehicle by which schoolchildren learned about the British Empire. From the 1890s education codes and teacher manuals began to stress 'the importance of the Empire and its associated adventure tradition in conveying concepts of national identity and pride in schoolchildren', writes John Mackenzie. This was the age of Whig history, in which Britain's past was presented as one long march to triumph. School history emphasized two broad themes: the island story of Britain's internal history and the expansion of England into Ireland, Scotland and Wales; and Britain's imperial history, which stressed the acquisition and exploration of Empire, its extent and the positive benefits that it brought.

An uncomplicated world-view

Literally hundreds of histories along these lines were used widely in schools and homes. It was an age in which arguments over historical interpretation were almost unknown, and one, therefore, in which having a widely-accepted national history was possible. A typical example is a 1912 work by T.F. Tout, Professor of Medieval and Modern History in the University of Manchester, entitled *An Advanced History of Great Britain from the Earliest Times to the Death of Edward VII* in the Longman Historical Series for Schools, 'with 29 Genealogical Tables and 63 Maps and Plans'. The 'Maps and Plans' began with Roman Britain and moved through the voyages and states of the Norsemen, the Battle of Hastings, the crusade of Richard I, English dominions in France in the 13th century, the Battle of Agincourt, voyages and settlements of the 16th century, the English colonies in North America under Charles II, the Battles of Blenheim, Trafalgar and Waterloo, British expansion in Egypt and the Sudan, India and South Africa at the end of the 19th century, and a survey of the British Empire in the early 20th century.

According to this standard school history, the reign of Elizabeth I stimulated English maritime enterprise, the growth of plantations in New England and the foundation of the East India Company. British power expanded through the Dutch wars, the Protestant conquest of Ireland, the War of the Spanish Succession, colonial and commercial development, the Seven Years' War, European traders in Mughal India, the Battle of Plassey and the conquest of Canada. There were, of course, setbacks along the way in this narrative of Britannia's tryst with destiny. These included the dramatic counterpoints of the South Sea Bubble, the Black Hole of Calcutta, the American War of Independence and the death of General Gordon at Khartoum. But such reverses could do little to halt the onward march of progress.

THIS BOOK IS NOT INTENDED FOR YOUNG STUDENTS ALONE. IT WOULD BE WELL IF A NARRATIVE OF THE RISE OF OUR EMPIRE WERE NEEDED ONLY BY THEM. NO CIVILIZED COUNTRY TREATS ITS NATIONAL HISTORY WITH SUCH SCANT REGARD AS ENGLISHMEN. IT SURPRISES FOREIGNERS TO SEE HOW PHLEGMATICALLY WE IGNORE THE STORY OF THE GROWTH OF OUR GREAT DOMINION, AN UNCONCERN WHICH REACTS INEVITABLY UPON OUR SCHOOLS OF ALL TYPES AND GRADES. IF GERMANY, FOR INSTANCE, HAD SUCH A HISTORY AS OURS IT WOULD BE THE CENTRAL SUBJECT ROUND WHICH ALL HER NATIONAL EDUCATION WOULD REVOLVE.

– *William Woodward*, **A Short History of the Expansion of the British Empire, 1500–1923** *(school textbook)*

*Coelum Non Mutat
Genus* ('the clime does
not change the breed').

*– Motto on Freemasons' Hall,
Georgetown, British Guiana*

The global web of freemasonry

Other British institutions were propagated around the world and played a part in the networking and politicking of a global élite. Membership of a good club or lodge meant admission to the elite of any colony. These institutions were important meeting grounds for the business, military, administrative, indigenous and expatriate élites of the Empire, and fuelled British fascination with ritual as well as fulfilling practical functions such as the extension of hospitality and the provision of recreation and a communications network.

Lodges sprouted wherever the British settled, forming a vast chain around the globe. There was University Lodge, Toronto, Lagos Lodge, South Australia Lodge of Friendship, Caledonian Lodge, Uganda and Prince of Wales Lodge, Penang. Imperial lodges were also a feature of freemasonry at home. In 1897, the year of Victoria's golden jubilee, Empire Lodge included among its active members the Earl of Lathorn, Lord Saltoun, the Duke of Abercorn, the Raja of Kapurthala and the Prime Ministers of Natal, New South Wales, Victoria, Tasmania and New Zealand. In that year the Lodge initiated the Raja of Khetri and the son of the Raja of Shahpura. A few years later Viscount Hayashi, Japanese ambassador to the Court of St James, went through the chair as Master of Empire Lodge.

Lodges often reused the arms of public schools, and over 170 lodges existed for old boys of public schools. The ancient universities had their lodges too; at Oxford, Apollo University Lodge initiated men at 18 (the age of a freshman) rather than 21. It was here that Cecil Rhodes was initiated into the Brotherhood while studying at Oriel. Some colleges, such as Magdalen and Christ Church, had their own London lodges, patronized by men who had pursued professional careers in the capital. Masonry featured in popular literature about the Empire, notably the work of Rudyard Kipling, for example in the stories 'The Man Who Would Be King', 'Mother Lodge', 'Rough Ashlar', 'The Palace' and 'Banquet Night'. In his most famous novel, *Kim*, Colonel Creighton is both a freemason and a spy.

Imperial clubs: a strict hierarchy

Masonry reinforced exclusivity and buttressed the ritualism at the heart of imperial rule, most visibly extended in the honours system. The same was true of gentleman's clubs, stretching from Pall Mall to the Gezira Club in Cairo, the Muthaiga Club in Nairobi, the Salisbury Club in Rhodesia and the Sind Club. 'Ritualism and its totems, taboos and ceremonialism', according to Rich, were all 'part of the tricks of governing. Because the schools influenced the development of institutions such as gentleman's clubs, these too became rehearsal halls for the elaborate etiquette that enabled the British to keep an empire with precious little military force (in fact the military attended public schools and joined clubs with as much regularity as did the ICS).'

The British Empire was famous for its clubs, and to this day travellers are occasionally surprised when they happen upon a club still run as if the imperial masters had never departed, long bars and leather armchairs, slow moving punkahs

The "Club House", Ootacamund. 1852.

a splendid building; beautifully furnished; accommodation for about 30 members; with Library; Billiard rooms, &c. (cost a lac of rupees.) — £10,000.

stirring the heavy afternoon air, and uniformed servants carrying drinks on silver trays. The club was probably the most important social institution of the Empire. As George Orwell put it in *Burmese Days*, 'in any town in India the European Club is the spiritual citadel, the real seat of British power, the Nirvana for which native officials and millionaires pine in vain'. Even for the pukka Briton, a member of the Indian Civil Service or a swish cavalry regiment, say, clubdom at home and overseas represented a carefully graded ladder, progress along which depended upon the prestige of your employer, your seniority and the size of your purse. For one new Indian civil servant joining the club 'meant the local Gymkhana Club, as against the Sind Club which was for higher-ups'. The club exerted its power even on the journey out; entering a new imperial world as he sailed for a posting in India the new recruit would notice the white trousers and black jackets of the Punjab Club and the black coats and white trousers of the Calcutta Club.

View of the Ootacamund Club (1852) in Tamil Nadu, southern India. Its exclusive location in the hills, where only higher-ranking colonial officers decamped in the summer, earned it the nickname 'Snooty Ooty'.

SOFAS, MAGAZINE TABLES, PICTURES OF MONARCHS, VICEROYS, CLUB PRESIDENTS,
LISTS OF MASTERS OF THE OOTACAMUND HUNT ... SPORTING PRINTS, OLD
PHOTOGRAPHS OF OOTY AS IT WAS, SLIGHTLY MANGY HEADS OF HUNTED JACKALS,
PALE WATERCOLOURS, A NOTICE-BOARD FULL OF PINNED NOTES, CANE CHAIRS,
POLISHED PARQUET FLOORS, *THE TIMES*, *THE FIELD*, THE *ARMY LIST*, THE *INDIA
OFFICE LIST* ... PERVASIVE SMELLS OF CIGARS, VEGETABLES AND FURNITURE POLISH,
THESE WERE THE SIGNS AND SENSATIONS OF THE CLUB ...

– Jan Morris and Simon Winchester, **Stones of Empire** *(2005)*

Upon arriving in the colonies newcomers soon turned their attention to joining the right clubs. Penang could boast the senior club in Southeast Asia, the Penang Club, founded in 1858, an all-male preserve with a women's annexe known as the 'hen roost'. This was the *tuan besars'* (big masters') club. Members included a number of leading Asians, Muslim Indian and Chinese business tycoons and notables such as the Sultan of Kedah. For juniors there was the Penang Cricket Club. As a junior in Singapore you could join the Tanglin Club and the Singapore Swimming Club but you couldn't join the Singapore Club. In Kuala Lumpur there was the Golf Club for the seniors and the more egalitarian Selangor Club, universally known as the Spotted Dog. The Dog was the scene of such high spots in KL's social calendar as the St George's Night Ball, and was visited by the Prince of Wales in 1922. In the 1920s the Dog's 2000 members were mainly planters and people living outside Selangor State. 'We would no more have dreamt of putting our names up for the Lake Club than flying.'

The British overseas preferred to work through the day leaving an hour or so before the short tropical twilight for games and exercise. A standard routine for a British planter in Malaya might involve a visit to the club at six, driven by his *syce*, in order to have a drink with friends. He would be home by 7.30, where he would change into *sarong* and *baju* (Malayan shirt with open neck and long sleeves), swallow a couple of whisky *pahits* and then have dinner and go to bed.

The club had definite practical uses for Britons overseas – it wasn't all about necking gimlets (gin and lime) and *chotapegs* (two fingers of whisky, three fingers being a *burrapeg*). First of all, it was vital to be able to unwind away from the people among whom one worked and over whom one ruled. Letting your hair down in private enabled administrators and officers to maintain appearances in public, the secret of that precious buttress of imperial rule, prestige. Clubs also allowed people to meet and mix, to socialize in public rather than drink or brood in private, and got them to play sport. In Simla there was a racecourse and a golf course, and at the Gezira Sporting Club on the banks of the Nile hollyhocks grew alongside Tudor and Cotswold architecture and a verandah overlooking the cricket pitch.

Lodges and clubs, in the words of Rich, were 'educational institutions in their own right. Besides their informal role as a place where information was exchanged, they provided useful libraries and even map rooms that were valuable to imperial opinion makers.' The memberships of clubs and lodges grew throughout the late 19th and first half of the 20th centuries. London clubs included the Oriental, the East India, the Calcutta, the Madras and the Bombay. There was the Political Dinner Club for the Indian Political Service, and the Corona Club for members of the Colonial Administrative Service home on leave. Contrived club customs and elaborate rules, membership waiting lists and traditions, all forged collective identity and were very familiar to the largely ex-public school membership. Clubs provided an extremely useful home from home for itinerant men, and a forwarding address for mail. Clubs maintained reciprocal relationships with partner institutions overseas, offering an automatic hotel and social network for members when business took them abroad. Acting both as clubs and centres of academic endeavour were organizations such as the African Association (which became the Royal Geographical Society), the Royal Asiatic Society and the Round Table, all catalysts of British imperial growth.

The 'Happy Valley set'

Kenya's famous Muthaiga Country Club opened on New Year's Eve 1913, though within a year its membership had dwindled as men volunteered for war. The club began as a home from home for settlers making their way to Nairobi for Race Week. Nairobi's only other club was dominated by government officials, who formed a class apart and one with which the settlers were constantly at loggerheads over land policy or native policy. The idea of founding a new club, on the other side of town, was therefore mooted. Thereafter the Muthaiga Club became part of the lore of white Kenya, the unofficial headquarters of the colony's hedonistic, drink- and drug-fuelled settlers. The truth, naturally, was somewhat less brazen, and the club continued to serve the needs of the European community when visiting Nairobi. In her autobiography, *West with the Night* (1942), the Kenyan aviatrix Beryl Markham wrote of the Muthaiga Club:

> *Its broad lounge, its bar, its dining-room – none so elaborately furnished as to make a rough-handed hunter pause at its door, nor yet so dowdy as to make a diamond pendant swing ill at ease – were rooms in which the people who made the Africa I knew danced and talked and laughed, hour after hour.*

Markham, renowned for her wildness, fitted the stereotype of the Happy Valley set. Involved in a threatened law suit following her affair, whilst married, with Prince Henry, King George V's son, she was romantically involved with Denis Finch Hatton after his affair with Karen Blixen had ended.

While schools were teaching youngsters about Britain's 'glorious' imperial history, and élite institutions were churning out young men to run the Empire, probably its most familiar manifestation in the minds of many people was its role as a provider of trade goods and foodstuffs. Imperial produce was marketed as just that, as adverts inculcated 'empire mindedness' by stressing the connection between imperial goods and home consumption. This is the subject of the next chapter.

EMPIRE TOBACCO
FROM
NORTHERN RHODESIA & NYASALAND

Issued by the Empire Marketing Board.

Printed for H.M. Stationery Office by Waterlow & Sons Ltd. London, Dunstable & Watford.

The Imperial Treasure Trove: Produce and Marketing

SILKS, TOBACCO, TEA, COTTON, SANDALWOOD, OPIUM AND FURS were as central to the growth of the British Empire as strategic ambitions and the activities of missionaries and frontier pioneers. Since the 15th century the search for trade and profit had been a driving force of overseas exploration, shared by queens and commoners alike.

LEFT This eyecatching poster, showing the clear influence of modernist art, was produced by the Empire Marketing Board in 1931 to promote tobacco grown in Northern Rhodesia and Nyasaland (the modern states of Zambia and Malawi). Not everyone was as keen on southern African tobacco as the EMB: in a Commons debate in 1928, Labour member Manny Shinwell waspishly asked Colonial Secretary Leo Amery: 'Does the fact that the Rt. Hon. Gentleman is a non-smoker induce him to recommend this tobacco, which cannot be smoked?'

RIGHT Advertisers were quick to associate products with popular symbols of Empire. In the 1880s, for example, the yarn manufacturer J&P Coats capitalized on the stir generated by the recent arrival by sea in London of Cleopatra's Needle (see page 84) by commissioning this neat visual pun, showing the needle being towed on a rope made of their cotton thread.

Bristolian fishermen exploited the rich fishing grounds off North America before it was officially 'discovered' by Henry Cabot; London merchants mortgaged themselves to the hilt gambling on a successful trading voyage to India or far Cathay; Cook's voyages alerted businessmen to the abundance of whales (and therefore whale-oil) in Antarctic waters; and big game hunters struck out across Africa in search of ivory, skins and feathers for the clothing and leisure industries of England.

A veritable cornucopia

The British Empire was a cornucopia of valuable minerals, exotic luxuries, clothing fabrics and household staples. The colonies produced the sugar, tea, butter and lamb that filled British larders, the cotton and wool that clothed the masses and the whalebones and ostrich feathers that adorned and supported the dresses of well-to-do ladies. The explosion of consumer goods that resulted from British industrialization and contact with the wider world changed the way that Britons dressed themselves, fed themselves and decorated their homes, and had a vitalizing impact upon the worlds of fashion and interior design, in forms such as chinoiserie and willow-pattern tableware for the lower orders. The Empire sponsored such a revolution in global trade and finance that it cost less to import wheat from Canada by sea than to transport it by rail from Liverpool to London.

British towns and cities stood as testament to the trading wealth drawn from empire and the creation of a globalized market. Hardwood from the Nigerian Iroko tree was used to make lamp-posts and park furniture in the 1950s. The City of London's famous

I VENTURE TO ALLUDE TO THE IMPRESSION WHICH SEEMED GENERALLY TO PREVAIL AMONG THEIR BRETHREN ACROSS THE SEAS, THAT THE OLD COUNTRY MUST WAKE UP IF SHE INTENDS TO MAINTAIN HER OLD POSITION OF PRE-EMINENCE IN HER COLONIAL TRADE AGAINST FOREIGN COMPETITORS.

– George V, in a speech (Wake Up, England!) delivered at the Guildhall, London on 5 December 1901

banks and fine Palladian houses in Bristol and Liverpool were built on the revenues of empire. Country houses were erected on nabobs' fortune, and in the crowded, vibrant, docks of London and Glasgow ships from all over the world were set about by lighters, cranes, railway engines and horse-drawn wagons as the bountiful produce of a global empire was distributed to factories across the country.

Free trade and taxation

As produce from the four corners poured into Britain, much of it to be re-exported to continental Europe, British manufactures flowed in the other direction. Thus Argentinean and Australian beef, New Zealand lamb and wool, Canadian wheat and timber, West African palm oil, Indian jute and Malayan rubber and tin fed British people and provided the raw materials from which they manufactured goods. The cars they built – running on Malayan rubber tyres – and the clothes the Lancastrians wove from Bengali cotton, were shipped out from the workshop of the world. Where the British didn't own a product within their ever-expanding imperial estate, they tried to grow it, from hardy wheat varieties to tea and the opium beloved by addicts in Canton and London alike. Where they could trade in kind rather than in cash they did so, even if this meant, as in one of the more perverse applications of the doctrine of free trade, going to war. The First Opium War broke out in 1839, when the Emperor of China banned the import of opium transported from Bengal in lieu of bullion and exchanged for Chinese tea and silks. The British declared war, outraged by this brake upon the unfettered laws of supply and demand. The need to 'impose' free trade was also a stimulus for British military action and eventual rule in other parts of the world, notably West Africa. Thus profit and consumerism masqueraded as morality and principle, the British effortlessly eliding the pursuit of Mammon and the work of the Lord.

Free trade versus protectionism was a central topic of British domestic politics for much of the 19th and 20th centuries. Ministers resigned and political parties were defeated on this issue, and Churchill left the Tories for the Liberals because of it. In 1932, as a response to the Great Depression, imperial preferences (i.e. protection) finally came into being at the Ottawa Conference, the culmination of a battle of protectionists versus free traders championed, in particular, by Joseph Chamberlain. In the late 19th century, he had decided that imperial protection was vital if Britain were to remain in the global economic race with emerging powers

such as America, Germany and Japan. Cecil Rhodes had tried to rouse the public to understand that the Empire was 'a bread and butter question', not one of abstract irrelevance to the common voting man. Chamberlain went further, resigning from the Cabinet in order to go to the country and campaign for the termination of Britain's fixation with free trade that had lasted since the repeal of the Corn Laws.

Produce traded and plundered from Europe's ever-expanding frontiers was not just good news for consumers gaining a taste for sugar and tea; it was big business for government. Tax was the name of the game, and the excise levied on imported goods paid for the wars that British governments and monarchs engaged in with such constancy from the 17th century. Tax, of course, meant resolute and well-organized efforts to evade payment, and thus the golden age of smuggling developed. At one stage, 80 percent of tea drunk in Britain was imported illegally. More than this, the growth of empire and lucrative overseas trade encouraged piracy, and the operations of 'privateers' that governments, desirous of their military services during times of war, shadily sanctioned.

The imperial market place

The school geography book *Our Neighbours and their Work for Us* illustrated Britain's dependence upon imperial sources of food. It showed cocoa being shipped from the Gold Coast, stockmen (jackaroos) tending sheep in Australia, oranges

TEA CARDS

'Flags of the World' was a tea card series issued by Brooke Bond in 1967. Collectors could purchase albums in which to display their cards, providing extra information about the history of the flags and the countries from which they came.

Though the card market was dominated by cigarettes and tobacco, other products issued cards as well. In 1939 the *Wizard* and the *Rover* comics issued 26 cards showing scenes on the theme of 'Battle for the Flag'. From about the same time tea companies started issuing cards in boxes and packets of loose tea. The main issuers were PG Tips and Brooke Bond (issuing its last cards in 1999), and cards were produced not just for the British market but also for Canada, East Africa and Rhodesia and South Africa. Series included the Canadian 'Songbirds of North America' (1959) and 'Explorers of the Ocean' (1971) and the East Africa/Rhodesian 'African Wild Life', 'Tropical Birds' and 'African Birds', all launched in the first half of the 1960s.

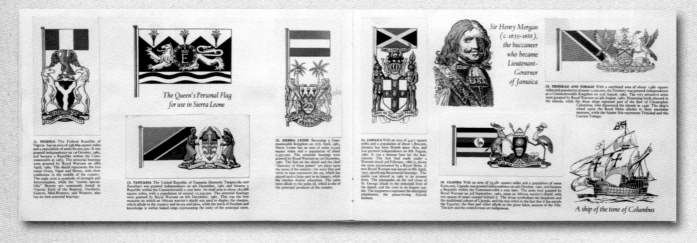

being picked by natives in South Africa and peasant women harvesting cotton in Egypt. Each chapter dealt with a different product – wool, cocoa, leather, wheat, rubber, fruit, mutton and beef, sugar, timber, tobacco, rice, eggs, silk, cotton and tea. The British Empire was seen for the tropical treasure trove that it was; Indian tanneries, Canadian prairies, Malayan forests, Jamaican cane fields, Cape fruit farms, Chinese silkworms, Burmese paddyfields, and Ceylonese tea plantations all contributing their wares to the British home.

As well as being educated about the nature of the imperial trading economy, schoolchildren and the general public were made aware of the importance of the sea lanes to national and imperial survival, in an age where a maritime awareness was second nature to Britons. Connecting the imperial market place, steaming busily hither and thither, sailed the many thousand vessels of the Merchant Navy. From the days of clippers such as the *Cutty Sark* to the massive bulk tankers of the mid-20th century, the Red Ensign dominated the shipping lanes of the world.

In the post-Second World War period imperial produce remained just as important to Britain's economy, and to its health and well-being. There was a drive to increase the production of groundnuts and other fat-yielding products as a major deficiency in the British diet, still afflicted by rationing and shortages, was addressed. Malayan rubber and tin became key dollar earning products as the government set

OH, WHERE ARE YOU GOING TO, ALL YOU BIG STEAMERS
WITH ENGLAND'S OWN COAL, UP AND DOWN THE SALT SEAS?
WE ARE GOING TO FETCH YOU YOUR BREAD AND YOUR BUTTER
YOUR BEEF, PORK, AND MUTTON, EGGS, APPLES AND CHEESE.

WHERE WILL YOU FETCH IT FROM, ALL YOU BIG STEAMERS?
AND WHERE SHALL I WRITE TO YOU WHEN YOU ARE AWAY?
WE FETCH IT FROM MELBOURNE, QUEBEC, AND VANCOUVER,
ADDRESS US AT HOBART, HONG KONG AND BOMBAY.

– *'Big Steamers', song for children by Edward Elgar (1918)*

From *Our Neighbours and their Work For Us*, this picture shows cocoa being loaded on board a freighter in West Africa. The chapter describing the production of cocoa told children of its African origin, the growth cycle of the elongated pods of the cocoa tree, and the extraction of the paste from which was made the chocolate bars that emerged from the British factories of manufacturers such as Fry's and Cadbury's.

about increasing foreign exchange earnings in an attempt to kick-start economic recovery. Empire and Commonwealth produce remained a significant feature of the British supermarket and industry for many years thereafter, from the familiar legend 'Made in Hong Kong' stamped on the base of toys and manifold plastic goods in the 1970s, to Anchor butter, Cape apples and Fyffes bananas.

A tipple and a toke

The British Empire was closely associated with drink and drugs, including opium, marijuana and good honest beer. The brewer Bass always associated its product with the Empire and the monarchy. A 1911 advert boldly proclaimed Bass 'The Drink of Empire'. 'Well Known in 1778', it claimed, above a picture of a British redcoat, 'World-Famed in 1911', above a picture of his khaki-clad latter day incarnation. India Pale Ale, according to Martyn Connell, 'was born from the desire of officers commanding the East Indiamen sailing ships to make fortunes supplying home comforts to nostalgic expatriate Britons in 18th-century India working for the East India Company'. Beer was the regular drink on these voyages because water turned brackish. Nearby the East India Company's docks at Blackwall on the Thames was Bow, and it was from here, at Hodgson's Brewery, that captains of East Indiamen bought their beer. IPA was so suitable for their purposes because:

CIGARETTE CARDS

Tobacco had first come from the colony of Virginia, though by the 20th century the Empire had developed new plantations in places such as Nyasaland and the Rhodesias. Cigarette cards were an everyday item in the lives of millions of Britons until the 1970s. They encouraged brand loyalty and provided children with a ready source of collectable, informative and swappable currency. Most brands offered albums for series of cards to be displayed in. Frequently, cigarette card series were based on imperial or military themes, such as Player's 1938 series 'Military Uniforms of the British Empire' (see page 128). In the early 1920s Player's published a giant series (150 cards) picturing the symbols of British and imperial divisions, corps and overseas commands that had served in the First World War, and in the following decade Wills issued 50 cards in the 'Life in the Royal Navy' series.

In 1914 W.D. & H.O. Wills issued a series of 12 cigarette cards showing recruiting posters for the war that had just broken out. In 1916 John Player & Sons issued a series of 25 cards depicting scenes of polar exploration. There were many patriotic First World War cigarette card series, including Wills's Specialities' (Capstan, Vice Regal, Ribbon Cut and Pennant brands) 'Britain's Defenders', showing 50 photographs of major imperial political and military leaders.

To commemorate the 1911 Coronation Godfrey Phillips Limited issued a 36-card 'Coronation of Their Majesties' series, which included the Imperial Crown of India. In 1934 J. Wix & Sons Kensitas brand – 'the *mild* cigarette – just what the doctor ordered' – issued a set of 48 'Flags of the British Empire', each card made of silk,. Three years later Kensitas issued 'Builders of Empire', a series of 50 cards including pictures and biographies of the Duke of Wellington, Florence Nightingale, Clive, Wolfe, Kipling and Kitchener.

Wills's Specialities issued the 'Arms of the British Empire' series, and its Capstan Navy Cut brand issued the 'British Empire' series which featured scenes from around the Empire. The information accompanying each image had a lesson to convey; a picture of a 'Mohamedan Mosque and Chinese Temple, Singapore' showed that 'throughout the British Empire the right to worship as they please is granted to members of every religion and every sect'. A picture of 'A Bengal Village' illustrated a 'peaceful pastoral scene [that] is typical of thousands of a precisely similar character in the Bengal Presidency. The wants of a Bengali peasant are easily satisfied, and providing he has a few oxen and a fair crop he is content'. Many other series included pictures from around the Empire. Pennant's 'Riders of the World' series, for example, included a Boer farmer on horseback; Havelock cigarettes' 'Royal Mail' series included 'An Outstation Post Office, Cape Colony'.

Clockwise from left: 'Mohameden Mosque and Chinese Temple, Singapore'; 'An Outstation Post Office, Cape Colony'; and 'A Bengal Village'.

… the slow, regular temperature changes and the rocking the beer received in its oak casks as the East Indiamen ploughed the waves had a magical maturing effect. By the time the beer arrived in Bombay, Madras or Calcutta, having gone via Madeira, Rio de Janeiro, St Helena, Cape Town and the stormy Mozambique Channel, it was as ripe as a brew six times its age that had slumbered unmoving in an English cellar.

By the early 19th century Hodgson's beer was 'in almost universal use' in India. It wasn't long before other companies, including big brewers such as Burton upon Trent's Allsopp's and Bass, muscled in on this lucrative market. By 1823, Bass had 43 percent of the yearly beer trade to India, amounting to some 12,000 barrels.

Early British experiments with hashish took place in India. The first systematic investigation into the properties and effects of cannabis was conducted in Calcutta by W.B. O'Shaughnessy, who declared it a pain-killer and anti-convulsive. Some doctors in India, however, linked the drug with insanity, reflecting the controversial reputation that it was to attract in subsequent decades. But the Government of India was more interested in its taxable qualities than its medical ones. There were doubts about its hallucinogenic side effects and concern from the ranks of the anti-opium lobby, though in 1893 the Indian Hemp Drugs Commission failed to find a link between cannabis and mental illness. In the 1940s the British government's Drug Requirement Advisory Committee said that the Second World War had demonstrated Britain's reliance on drug imports, and that sources in the Empire should be identified and exploited to make Britain self-sufficient in drugs and prevent a repeat of wartime shortages:

> *A strong and progressive industry will prove essential to the new NHS [National Health Service], assure against repetition of war shortages, make a valuable contribution to the trade of the UK [and] offer useful opportunities to British and Empire farmers in the cultivation of vegetable drugs.*

Imperial advertising

Back in Britain, Empire produce was regularly advertised. In 1937 an elephant was hired for the opening of London's new tea auction rooms, carrying chests of tea from St Katherine's Dock to Plantation House in Mincing Lane. Adverts for

'Three Nuns' Empire Blend was made by the Imperial Tobacco Company based in Glasgow. According to the advert above, which appeared in a 1930s edition of Evelyn Waugh's novel *Black Mischief*, it was 'a blend of the finest tobacco of Nyasaland (where they speak Tumbuka) with Rhodesia's finest. Remember – EMPIRE TOBACCO AT ITS BEST. And don't forget the pleasingly low price made possible by the preferential Empire duty', referring to the imperial preference system (i.e. protection) that had been put in place at the 1932 Ottawa Conference.

A Queen's Honey Soap advert from the 1890s. Competition among soap manufacturers was intense. Soap, marketed to the masses in this period, was manufactured using West African palm products. By using the Queen as a brand name and in its advertising images, Queen's Honey Soap sought to appeal to buyers by associating itself with monarchy, empire and the military.

Turkish cigarettes and Astrakhan coats played on the exotic origins of the products. Imperial and national imagery proclaimed many other household products. 'Rule for Britannia' declared a Bovril advert, showing a glamorous housewife in a Britannic pose, a jar of Bovril in place of her shield, a teaspoon as her sceptre. Queen's Honey Soap was graphically associated with Victoria and her successors, and soldiers drawn from Australia, India, Africa and elsewhere.

The Empire Marketing Board was set up in 1926 under the chairmanship of Leo Amery (Secretary of State for the Dominions), a response to the Depression affecting imperial and world markets. Its publicity campaigns – using posters, leaflets, films, lectures, radio broadcasts and exhibitions – were aimed at encouraging people to buy Empire goods. This was at a time of revival for those seeking 'imperial preference' – protection for the Empire as a distinct international economic and trading community. In 1924 Prime Minister Stanley Baldwin established the Imperial Economic Committee, which organized a national movement to increase Empire buying, which, it was believed, would stimulate employment in Britain and relieve unemployment in colonies hit by the depression and the world-wide downturn in the price of primary produce. This reflected belief in the complementary nature of the Empire's economies. As much as possible was done to promote imperial produce, and housewives in particular were targeted. In 1930, for instance, 200 'British Empire Shopping Weeks' were organized in 65 towns.

A vital source of raw materials

Raw materials had always been one of the Empire's main attractions, from Burmese teak to North American furs. Gold rushes in places such as Bendigo, the Witwatersrand and the Klondike were well-publicized features of British imperial expansion. The Empire produced many raw materials in great demand around the world, including rubber, tin, sisal, bauxite, oil, pyrethrum, oilseeds, copper, gold, pyrites and sea-island cotton. According to Raymond Dummet, the Empire was responsible for producing a significant share of the world's total output of certain key raw materials: 15.6 percent of the bauxite; 37.6 percent of the chrome ore; 24.8 percent of the coal; 29.8 percent of the copra; 17 percent of the cotton; 12.9 percent of the iron; 98.9 percent of the jute; 35.9 percent of the lead ore; 36.1 percent of the manganese; 87.9 percent of the nickel ore; 42.5 percent of the palm oil; 51.9 percent of the rubber; 39.2 percent of the tin ore; 25.2 percent of the tungsten ore; 34.8 percent of the vanadium ore; 45.7 percent of the wool; and 29 percent of the zinc ore.

Many famous companies made their names through imperial business and survived the end of Empire and continue to thrive. Firms such as BP, Unilever and Tate & Lyle remind us that although the 'High Noon' of the British Empire passed many decades ago, its legacies are still to be found all around us, a subject that will be covered in the final chapter.

LEFT Pennant Kerosene was produced by Shell and sold in places such as Africa and Australia. This advert from the early 1930s shows a tropical night illuminated by a Pennant Kerosene-fuelled lantern.

ABOVE In 1870 a Scottish businessman won a contract to supply Napoleon III's faltering French army with tons of canned beef. Out of the attempt to meet the order, 'liquid beef' was invented, which from 1889 became known as Bovril (from *bovis*, the Latin for cow, and *vril*, a life-giving elixir popularized in a novel of 1870). Soon the company had vast estates in Argentina, grazed by over 1.5 million head of cattle, as Bovril became a national and international best seller.

Legacies of Empire

A GLOBAL LINGUA FRANCA, THE RUGBY WORLD CUP AND AFTERNOON TEA are among the many legacies of British imperialism that litter the world today. The British Empire left such giant footprints that they can easily be overlooked, because many of the Empire's legacies have simply become part of the furniture of the modern world.

Countries such as Australia, Canada, India, Malaysia, and Nigeria are in fact quintessentially imperial constructions that would not exist had it not been for the unifying, federating power of British imperialism. British names – of cities, mountain ranges and lakes – proliferate on every continent. Eastern beacons of capitalism and commerce, such as Hong Kong, Shanghai and Singapore stand as testament to Britain's imperial encounter with the wider world. Patterns of global trade and financial links pioneered by British imperialism persist to this day, as do norms of international diplomacy, political organization and 'universal' concepts such as the freedom of the seas and the rule of law. So successful was the British Empire, and so deep was its structural power, that the world has largely developed in Britain's own image, emulation and independent national development in an emerging international system indicating the highest form of flattery, and of success.

The British Empire, then, created much that is familiar in today's world. As well as physical manifestations, its legacy is cultural and psychological. Indeed the world-view illustrated in *Mad Dogs and Englishmen* is not as moribund as it might at first appear. America's brush with an idealized imperial mission is a key feature of the modern world, as is a less stridently-proclaimed, but no less controversial, version of the 'civilizing mission' as Westerners still seek to recreate the world in their own image, believing that non-Western societies should become more like their own, both for their own good and for the good of humanity.

The balance sheet of empire is an emotive issue; some will always point to the continued tension over Kashmir, to the conflict over the Falkland Islands and to the failure of the nation state in places such as Iraq and Nigeria. They will highlight legacies of violence and racism, of dispossession and marginalization, and the clash between traditional cultures and modernity that is an important part of the work of authors such as Sir V.S. Naipaul (a Trinidadian of Indian extraction, educated at Oxford) and Salman Rushdie (born in Bombay, brought up in England, educated at Cambridge). Others will always defend the imperial record in the round and talk of international law, the English language and the spread of

India's imperial legacy is much in evidence in this scene from Mumbai (Bombay), where cricketers battle it out in the shadow of the university's imposing neo-Gothic clock tower. The Rajabai Tower was designed by George Gilbert Scott (architect of St Pancras Station and the Albert Memorial); during the British Raj, its chimes used to play a selection of tunes, including 'Rule Britannia', 'God Save the Queen/King', 'Auld Lang Syne' and 'Home! Sweet Home!'

> WHATEVER THE EMPIRE'S EARLY CRIMES, AND THERE WERE
> MANY, THE BRITISH SUCCEEDED, BEFORE THE EMPIRE'S DEMISE,
> IN ATONING FOR MOST OF THEM AND TRANSFORMING THE
> INSTITUTION INTO WHAT IT BECAME: A COMMONWEALTH FOR
> THE COMMON WEALTH … SHOULD THE BRITISH BE PROUD OF
> THE EMPIRE THEY LEFT BEHIND? OF COURSE THEY SHOULD …
> IN MY CHILDHOOD, THE BRITISH EMPIRE WAS COMMONLY
> COMPARED IN IMPORTANCE WITH THE EMPIRE OF ROME –
> AS ELGAR DID IN *CARACTACUS*.
>
> *– John Keegan*, **Daily Telegraph** *(1997)*

democracy as shining, if sometimes tarnished, achievements. Despite the manifold legacies of empire, however, not everyone believed that imperial rule would have a lasting, or particularly significant, impact. Observing Aden's independence in 1967, a British diplomat told the Defence Secretary, Denis Healey, that the Empire's main legacies would be 'Association Football and the phrase "Fuck Off".'

Home and colonial: Legacies in Britain and beyond

As well as leaving its mark on the wider world through centuries of vigorous international action, Britain itself remains indelibly marked by its imperial past. Its foreign policy and self-image speaks of its imperial heritage. Obvious legacies include Britain's racial composition – largely the result of post-war immigration from major regions of the former Empire such as South Asia and the Caribbean – its uniquely globalized economy, the financial clout of the City of London, and the ethos, training and global deployments of its armed forces. The main foreign policy-making department of state is the Foreign and Commonwealth Office, denoting the merger in the 1960s between the Foreign Office and the then Commonwealth Office, successor to the Colonial and Dominions offices. The English language is laced with innumerable words and phrases directly imported from foreign tongues, or that were developed as hybrids. Many of them come from Hindi, Swahili and Urdu. Words include khaki, bungalow, chutney, verandah, juggernaut, bandanna, dinghy, zebra, punch, cummerbund, pundit, safari, barbecue and cannibal. British museums are full of treasures from all over the world, and the return of precious cultural artefacts housed in places such as the Ashmolean and the British Museum remains a sensitive issue, as the governments of former colonies demand to have them returned. British culture remains heavily influenced by pageantry and splendour associated with the height of empire. The Last Night of the Proms, Trooping the Colour, and state occasions, such as the Royal Wedding of 1981 and the funerals of Princess Diana and the Queen Mother, remain magnificent spectacles. The Royal Family retains its position in British society and politics, and the Queen continues the tradition of touring overseas.

IMPERIAL FOOD

Imperial foodstuffs are central to what might loosely be termed British cuisine. Curry houses first opened in Britain in the late 18th century, and from their long association with India and Southeast Asia the British gained a taste for curry-style dishes and a line of spicy sauces including ketchup, Worcestershire sauce and mint sauce. Chutney, kedgeree and mulligatawny soup became staples of the British table. In the 19th century Victorian stodge combined with exotic spices from the East – cinnamon, saffron, mace, nutmeg, pepper and ginger – to enliven the British diet.

Sugar was a quintessentially imperial commodity, rare and expensive before the development of cane sugar in British plantations in the Indian Ocean and the West Indies. The British adopted tea from China and exported the habit of tea-drinking all over the world. During the Second World War Winston Churchill wanted to grow tea in Britain itself, but as it would take five years from first planting to first harvest, tea from Assam and Ceylon was stockpiled throughout Britain instead.

Companies such as Tate & Lyle, manufacturers of a famous brand of cane-sugar golden syrup, had their roots in the colonies and survive to this day. Brooke Bond, producer of famous tea brands such as PG Tips, was founded in Manchester in 1930. Kenco Coffee originates from the Kenya Coffee Company, established in London by former coffee planters in 1923.

A silver spoon from the huge cutlery service of the Royal Yacht *Britannia*, which was decommissioned in 1997. Bearing the Admiralty crest, this cutlery set is now in use at the Joint Services Command and Staff College.

The British economy remains unusually globalized in a way that, for example, the German economy is not. This is a direct result of Britain's imperial heritage. The City of London and institutions such as Lloyd's of London remain central to British national wealth, institutions that grew alongside British commercial and maritime enterprise. Britain today is the leading overseas investor in many former imperial territories, including America. Many of today's multinational companies have distinctly imperial roots, such as British American Tobacco, Lonrho (the London and Rhodesian Mining and Land Company), Unilever and Cable and Wireless. Jardine Matheson, founded in 1832, is still a major player in the world of Asian trade and business, as is its great rival, the Swire Group. Tate and Lyle, with its roots deep in the West Indies sugar trade, is Europe's biggest sugar cane refiner. BP (formerly Anglo-Persian) and Shell, are among the world's five 'super major' oil companies and to this day are embedded in the oil and gas producing regions of Africa and the Middle East. HSBC began life in 1865 as the Hong Kong and Shanghai Banking Corporation (the 'Honkers and Shankers', as it was known), representing Britain's deep

WE IN EUROPE TOO ARE BEING DECOLONIZED: THAT IS TO SAY THAT THE SETTLER WHICH IS IN EVERY ONE OF US IS BEING SAVAGELY ROOTED OUT … IT WAS NOTHING BUT AN IDEOLOGY OF LIES, A PERFECT JUSTIFICATION FOR PILLAGE; ITS HONEYED WORDS, ITS AFFECTATION OF SENSIBILITY WERE ONLY ALIBIS FOR OUR AGGRESSIONS.

– Jean-Paul Sartre, preface to Frantz Fanon's **The Wretched of the Earth** *(1961)*

By the time this book was published in 1957, references to the 'Empire' were increasingly being supplanted by 'Commonwealth'. This term expressed the new sense of equality and independence among former colonies, ranging from Pakistan to Ghana. Though the emerging new Commonwealth was not an organization that the British could dominate in an imperialistic manner (as some British politicians had hoped), Britain still remained a significant player on the international stage.

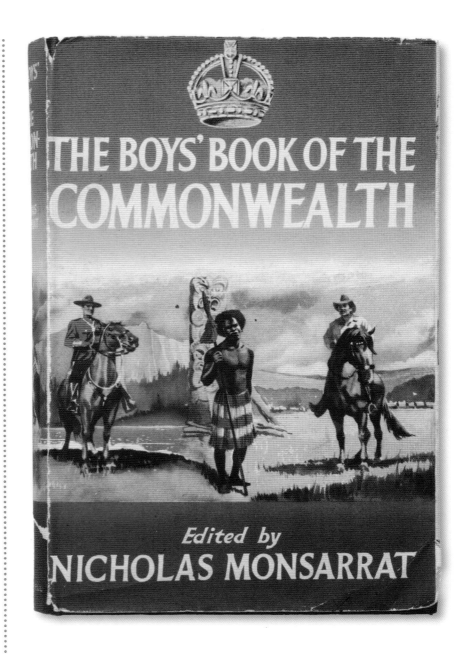

commercial and financial involvement with China and the Far East. In 1925 Barclays founded its overseas arm with the creation of Barclays Bank (Dominion, Colonial and Overseas), resulting from a merger of the Colonial Bank, the Anglo-Egyptian Bank and the National Bank of South Africa. Barclays thus gained a great deal of overseas business, particularly in Africa, the Middle East and the West Indies, and its presence overseas remains strong to this day.

Another legacy of the British Empire and the wanderlust of people from the British Isles is the British diaspora. The most obvious manifestation of this is the existence of 'Western' nations far beyond Western Europe, a result of overseas settlement. Because of Empire, countries such as America, Australia, and Canada share political systems, language, architecture, and culture with Britain. Today there is a diaspora of around 10 million Britons living overseas. Strong ties of family and fascination continue to link Britain to former settler colonies such as New Zealand and South Africa, and Britain's diplomatic and cultural presence throughout the world – surprisingly large for a small island off the European mainland – is a powerful legacy of the days when Britons were to be found in every corner of the world, and millions aspired to the culture of the world's most prestigious nation.

Martial and sporting prowess

P&O ships continue to sail from Portsmouth and Southampton, including among their fleet some of the largest passenger liners ever launched. The clientele of globetrotting planters, army officers and district commissioners on furlough has long since departed, though their successors – holidaymakers and the retired – are often in search of an echo of that vanished world. The Brigade of Gurkhas remains embedded within the British Army, a legacy of Britain's long association with Nepal and the magnificent Indian Army. It remains the case that Commonwealth citizens can join the British military (though not Americans, Germans or anyone from a non-Commonwealth country). Many British battalions have New Zealanders, South Africans, or Zimbabweans in their ranks, and there are currently 2000 Fijians serving with British regiments. At the time of writing, there are 7000 Commonwealth citizens in the British forces.

Juvenile literature continued to find themes of adventure in exotic lands popular with readers. The Canadian-born writer Willard Price's novels, like this one published in 1972, set the zoological activities of two brothers against the backdrop of a familiar view of the non-Western world. In this case, New Guinea is portrayed as a primitive land inhabited by headhunters and cannibals.

Providing a permanent legacy of the British Empire's martial endeavours, the Commonwealth War Graves Commission cares for over 925,000 graves in 2500 cemeteries located in 150 countries. The Scout Movement continues to flourish, with over 28 million members worldwide. The Anglican Church retains a global communion by virtue of the spread of missionaries around the world, and schisms between Anglican churchmen and women in Western countries and those in non-Western countries, where liberal attitudes to things like homosexuality and women priests are frowned upon, attract regular and unwanted publicity.

The British Empire bequeathed a global sporting community symbolized by events such as the Commonwealth Games and the Rugby World Cup (dominated by European and Southern Hemisphere – usually former imperial – lands). Cricket test nations include Australia, Bangladesh, England, India, Kenya, New Zealand, Pakistan, South Africa, Sri Lanka, the West Indies, and Zimbabwe. The BBC remains a truly global organization, disseminating news and culture through its World Service and its regional networks.

The Commonwealth and a continuing global outlook and presence

The Commonwealth is a highly visible legacy of the British Empire, and one of the most important international organizations. Its 54 member states profess attachment to shared values, and Commonwealth Heads of Government summit meetings are held every two years. The Commonwealth, with its Secretariat in London, provides a dense web of connections and professional associations throughout the world through agencies such as the Commonwealth Press Association and the Association of Commonwealth Universities. The monarch continues as head of state in 16 other countries, and the House of Lords remains the highest court of appeal for some of them. The honours system continues to have overseas reach, and the Queen's head still appears on currency in places such as Australia, and postage stamps are minted for Britain's remaining dependent territories.

Part of the British Empire still exists today, and the fact that the defence of these colonies remains a primary British military commitment has helped preserve the global posture of Britain's armed forces, as has Britain's continuing possession of global intelligence and security services such as GCHQ and MI6. The remaining British colonies, known today as Overseas Territories, are Anguilla, Ascension Island, Bermuda, British Antarctic Territory, British Indian Ocean

The vast output of material associated with the Empire during a period characterized by the rise of consumer culture has left a legacy of ephemera and a vogue for 'collectables'. Mugs, souvenir books, posters, toy soldiers, children's annuals, stamps, and even board games fill charity shops, antique fairs and flea markets all over the world. The illustration shows 'The Boer War Game', a revealing insight into attitudes at the time of the Second Anglo-Boer War (1899–1902). Players progressed towards the Boer capitals (Bloemfontein and Pretoria) and the beseiged towns of Ladysmith and Mafeking.

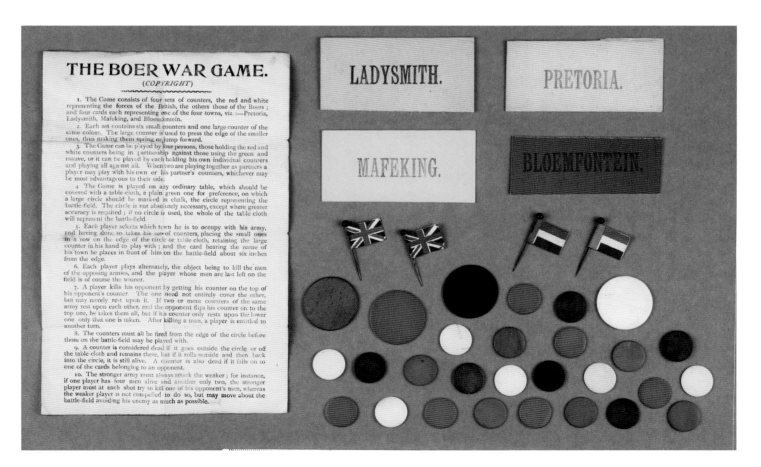

Territory, the British Virgin Islands, the Cayman Islands, the Falkland Islands, Gibraltar, Montserrat, Pitcairn, Henderson, Ducie and Oeno Islands, St Helena, South Georgia and the South Sandwich Islands, Tristan da Cunha, and the Turks and Caicos Islands. Some of these territories have a military use for Britain and its allies, or require garrison forces, such as Ascension Island, British Indian Ocean Territory, the Falklands and Gibraltar. Britain also has two Sovereign Base Areas in Cyprus, which support permanent British military establishments.

Today, British forces are committed in Africa, the Caribbean, Central Asia, the Mediterranean, and the Middle East, as well as in European locations such as the Balkans, several former Soviet states, Germany and Northern Ireland. In 2005, according to the then Chief of the Defence Staff, General Sir Michael Walker, in addition to British warships, air squadrons, and regiments serving in Afghanistan, the Balkans, Brunei, Cyprus, the Falklands, Gibraltar, Iraq and Sierra Leone, Britain had small detachments of service personnel in 74 countries and maintained 84 defence attaché sections around the world. The fact of Britain's continuing commitment to a global military presence and global military deployments – irrespective of decolonization, the Cold War and the downsizing of the armed forces – should come as no surprise; for the defence of British overseas interests and overseas territories has always been of paramount importance in British foreign and defence policy. Despite relative decline and imperial contraction, Britain's financial, commercial, diplomatic, and cultural links with the wider world remain substantial.

Empire was always just one among a number of different measures of national power, and the shrinkage of red on the map never signalled a disengagement from far-flung regions, any more than it signalled an end to British attempts to exercise power and influence overseas. Even when scaling down its territorial possessions or defence establishment, the British authorities time and again evinced a desire never to withdraw completely, and to retain a strategic culture associated with a global presence, global intervention and the export of British institutions and values. The former US Secretary of State, Dean Acheson, once said – to be paraphrased by many thereafter – that 'Great Britain has lost an empire and has not yet found a role'. On the contrary, in substance as well as in policy, Britain never in fact entirely lost that empire, and certainly never lost the appetite and capacity to perform a world role, despite the turn towards Europe that Acheson approvingly discerned, and the relative contraction of British economic, political and military power in the post-war decades. Britain's global interests never vanished, and even though the Cheshire Cat of Empire slowly faded, the grin remained.

Bibliography

Period pieces

Captain Bernard Acworth and Frank Mason, *The Navy's Here!* (London: Raphael Tuck & Sons, n. d., *c.* 1941)

Adventures Round the World (London: Strahan & Company, n. d., *c.* 1890)

Robert Baden-Powell, *Scouting for Boys* (London: C. Arthur Pearson, 1961), 33rd edition

_____, *African Adventures* (London, n. d., *c.* 1937)

Ernest Baker, *Arnot A Knight of Africa: A Stirring Account of the Life of an Intrepid Explorer, a Zealous Missionary, and a Knight-Errant in the Best Sense of the Term, Re-Told for Young People* (London: Seeley Service, 1932)

Martin Ballard, *The Speaking Drums of Ashanti* (London: Longman, 1970)

Lieutenant Colonel A. E. Bethell (ed.), *'Blackwood' Tales from the Outposts* series

(London: William Blackwood and Sons Ltd, 1944-46)

    i Frontiers of Empire
    ii Small wars of the Empire
    iii Tales of the borders
    vi Pioneering
    v Jobs of work
    vi Tales of the sea
    vii Soldiers' tales
    viii Jungle tales
    ix Tales of Africa
    x Shikar
    xi From strange places
    xii In lighter vein

Enid Blyton *The Queen Elizabeth Family* (London: Lutterworth, 1951)

Boy's Own Paper (May 1958)

Boy's Own Paper (July 1958)

Boy's Own Paper (August 1958)

Boy's Own Paper (September 1958)

A. R. Buckland (ed.), *The Empire Annual for Australian Boys* (London: The Religious Tract Society, 1917)

H. M. Buller, *Macaulay's Essay on Warren Hastings* (London: Macmillan and Co., 1923)

J. Burnett Knowlton, *The Empire Annual for Girls* (London: 'The Girl's Own Paper' Office, n. d., *c.* 1930)

S. E. Burrow, *Noodle* (London: Pickering & Inglis, n. d.)

Aubrey Buxton, *The King in His Country* (London: Longman Green & Co., 1955)

C. E. Carrington, *An Exposition of Empire* (Cambridge: Cambridge University Press, 1947)

Mollie Chappell, *Rhodesian Adventure* (London: The Children's Press, n. d.)

Seton Churchill, *General Gordon: A Christian Hero* (London: James Nisbet, n. d.)

Brigadier D. H. Cole, *Imperial Military Geography* (London: Sifton Praed & Co., 1924)

Chatterbox 1910 (London: Wells Gardner, Darton, and Co., 1910)

Chums, 1,215, XXIV (December 1915)

Chums, 1,216, XXIV (January 1916)

Chums, 1,217, XXIV (January 1916)

Chums, 1,218, XXIV (January 1916)

Chums, 1,219, XXIV (January 1916)

Chums, 1,229, XXIV (April 1916)

Chums, 1,230, XXIV (April 1916)

Chums, 1,231, XXIV (April 1916)

Chums, 1,232, XXIV (April 1916)

Chums, 1,237, XXIV (May 1916)

Chums, 1,238, XXIV (June 1916)

Chums, 1,239, XXIV (June 1916)

Chums, 1,240, XXIV (June 1916)

Winston Churchill, *My African Journey* (London, 1908)

Collins Book for Boys (London: Collins, n. d., *c.*1942)

Commonwealth and Empire Annual 1954 (London: The Gawthorn Press, 1954)

Commonwealth and Empire Annual 1956 (London: The Gawthorn Press, 1956)

Commonwealth and Empire Annual 1957 (London: The Gawthorn Press, 1957)

Rawdon Crawley, *Billiards: Its Theory and Practice* (London: C. H. Clarke, 1857)

John R. Crossland and J. M. Parrish, *The Boys and Girls Adventure Book* (London: Odhams Press, 1935)

David Scott Daniell, *Flight Five: Africa, Ladybird Book of Travel Adventure* (Loughborough: Wills & Hepworth, 1961)

Rev. C. S. Dawe, *King Edward's Realm: Story of the Making of the Empire* (London: The Educational Supply Association, 1902)

R. O. Dennys, *Flags and Emblems of the World* (London: Brooke Bond, n. d., *c.* 1968)

Frank Dodman, *The Observer's Book of Ships* (London: Frederick Warne & Co., 1966)

John Fawside (ed.), *The Flag of England: Ballads of the Brave and Poems of Patriotism* (London: Eveleigh Nash, 1914)

W. H. Fitchett, *Fights for the Flag* (London: Smith, Elder, & Co., 1910)

Sir Vivian Fuchs, *Antarctic Adventure: The Commonwealth Trans-Antarctic Expedition, 1955–58* (London: Cassell, 1959)

Stanley Gibbons Limited, *Priced Catalogue*, part i, *Stamps of the British Empire 1931)*, 37th edition (London: Stanley Gibbons, 1931)

Major Charles Gilson, *Mystery Island* (London: Partridge Publishers, n. d.)

Harry Golding (ed.), *The Wonder Book of the Navy for Boys and Girls* (London: Ward, Lock, & Co., [n. d.], *c.*1924)

_____, *The Wonder Book of Children of All Nations* (London: Ward, Lock, & Co., [n. d.], *c.*1924)

_____, *The Wonder Book of the Wild: The Romance of Exploration and Big Game Stalking* (London: Ward, Lock, & Co., [n. d.], *c.*1924)

Edwin Gomes, *Children of Borneo* (London: Oliphants Ltd, n. d.)

Major J. T. Gorman, *George VI: King and Emperor* (London: W. &. G. Foyle, 1937)

James Grant, *Cassell's Illustrated History of India*, volume I (London: Cassell, Petter, and Galpin, n. d.)

W. A. Green and E. G. Green, *Looking at the World: A Geography Course for Juniors*, book ii, *Our Neighbours and Their Work for Us* (London: Blackie & Son Limited, 1946)

I. & J. Havenhand, *The Airman in the Royal Air Force* (Loughborough: Wills & Hepworth, 1967)

H. Rider Haggard, *She* (London: Hodder and Stoughton, n. d.)

Herbert Strang's Book of Adventure Stories (London: Henry Frowde, n. d., *c*.1908)

Herbert Strang's Annual (London: Oxford University Press, n.d.)

Herbert Strang (ed.), *The Great Book for Boys* (London: Oxford University Press, 1928)

Herbert Strang (ed.), *The Splendid Book for Boys* (London: Oxford University Press, 1931)

Hergé, *Tintin in the Congo* (Paris: Editions Casterman, 1946)

Alfred Horn, *Trader Horn in Madagascar* (London: The Readers Library, n. d.)

E. C. T. Horniblow, *Wonderful Travels in Wonderful Lands* (London: The Grant Educational Co., 1951)

Charles Hose, *The Field-Book of a Jungle-Wallah: Shore, River, and Forest Life in Sarawak* (London: H. F. & G. Witherby, 1929)

A. E. Housman, *A Shropshire Lad* (London: The Richards Press, 1942)

John C. Hutcheson, *The Penang Pirate* and *The Lost Pinnace, Or, Dhow Chasing on the East African Coast* (London: Blackie & Son, n. d., *c*.1899)

Ideal Book for Boys (London: Dean & Son, n. d.)

Edward Joslin, *The Observer's Book of British Awards and Medals* (London: Frederick Warne & Co., 1974)

W. H. G. Kingston, *Our Sailors* (London: Henry Frowde Hodder and Stoughton, 1910)

Rudyard Kipling, *Land and Sea Tales for Scouts and Guides* (London: Macmillan and Co., 1923)

Andrew Lang, *Tales of King Arthur and the Round Table* (London: Longmans, Green and Co., 1923)

David Livingstone, *Travels and Researches in South Africa* (London: The Amalgamated Press, 1905)

Look and Learn, 581, 3 March (1973)

Look and Learn, 582, 10 March (1973)

Look and Learn, 583, 17 March (1973)

Look and Learn, 586, 7 April (1973)

Look and Learn, 587, 14 April (1973)

Look and Learn, 588, 21 April (1973)

Look and Learn, 589, 28 April (1973)

Look and Learn, 590, 5 May (1973)

A. B. Lloyd, *Uganda to Khartoum* (London: Collins, n. d., *c.* 1905)

Nicholas Monsarrat (ed.), *The Boys Book of the Commonwealth* (London: Cassell & Co., 1957)

Patrick Montague-Smith, *The Country Life Book of the Royal Silver Jubilee* (London: Hamlyn, 1976)

Rev. J. B. Myers, *The Congo for Christ: The Story of the Congo Mission* (London: S. W. Partridge & Co., n. d., *c.* 1896)

Leslie Norman, *Sea Wolves and Bandits* (Hobart, Tasmania: J. Walch & Sons, 1946)

Cecil Northcott, *My Friends the Cannibals – John Holmes of Papua* Eagle Books No. 5 (London: The Cargate Press, 1949)

Philips' Visual Contour Atlas (London: George Philips & Son, n. d., *c.* 1948)

J. Reason, *Bold Smuggler – Lian A-Fa* Eagle Books No. 56 (London: Edinburgh House Press, 1948)

H. Rider Haggard, *Hunter Quatermain's Story: The Uncollected Adventures of Allan Quatermain*, edited by Peter Haining (London: Peter Owen, 2003)

Sir Charles Grant Robertson, *Chatham and the British Empire* (London: Hodder & Stoughton, 1946)

Sir J. R. Seeley, *The Expansion of England: Two Course of Lectures* (London: Macmillan and Co. Ltd, 1899)

Walter Carruthers Sellar and Robert Julian Yeatman, *1066 And All That: A Memorable History of England, Comprising All the Parts You Can Remember, Including 103 Good Things, 5 Bad Kings and 2 Genuine Dates* (London: Methuen & Co. Ltd, 1936)

D. C. Somervell, *The British Empire* (London: Christophers, 1945)

St Dunstan's, *The Prince of Wales' Book: A Pictorial Record of the Voyages of HMS* Renown, *1919–1920* (London: Hodder and Stoughton, n. d., *c*.1921)

St Dunstan's, *The Prince of Wales' Eastern Book: A Pictorial Record of the Voyages of HMS* Renown, *1921-1922* (London: Hodder and Stoughton, n. d., *c*.1923)

Stanley and Africa (London: Walter Scott, n. d.)

Robert Louis Stevenson, *Treasure Island* (London: Collins, 1957)

The Boy's Own Annual 1917–18 (London: BOP Office, n. d.)

The Country Life Picture Book of Britain (London: Country Life Ltd, 1937)

The Golden Book of Children's Hymns (London: Blandford Press, 1952)

The Hawk and Other Stories (London: Blackie and Son, 1936)

The Queen Elizabeth Coronation Souvenir (1953)

The Tree of Empire: A Book of Readings in Prose and Verse Illustrative of the History and Development of the British Empire (London: Edward Arnold, n. d.)

T. F. Tout, *An Advanced History of Great Britain From the Earliest Times to the Death of Edward VII* (London: Longmans, Green, and Co., 1912)

B. Underhill, *Unarmed Among Outlaws – Theodore Pennell of the N.-W. Frontier*, Eagle Books No. 6 (London: The Cargate Press, 1937)

The Wide World: The True Adventure Magazine for Men (April 1938)

The Wide World: The True Adventure Magazine for Men (September 1957)

The Wide World: The True Adventure Magazine for Men (January 1959)

The Wide World: The True Adventure Magazine for Men (July 1959)

The Wide World: The True Adventure Magazine for Men (June 1961)

Geoffrey Willans and Ronald Searle, *Back in the Jug Agane* (1959)

The Wonder Book of the Army, second edition (London: Ward, Lock, & Co., n. d., *c*.1954)

The Wonder Book of the Royal Air Force

The Wonder Book of Ships London: (Ward, Lock, & Co., n. d.)

Sir Donald Mackenzie Wallace, *The Web of Empire: A Diary of the Imperial Tour of Their Royal Highnesses the Duke and Duchess of Cornwall and York in 1901* (London: Macmillan and Company, Limited, 1902)

Edgar Wallace, *Sanders of the River* (London: Ward, Lock, & Co., n. d.)

Warlord Book for Boys 1988 (London: D. C. Thomson, 1987)

J. A. Williamson, *Builders of the Empire* (Oxford: Clarendon Press, 1931)

W. J. Wintle, *Victoria R. I. and Albert the Good: The Story of Their Lives* (London: The Sunday School Union, n. d., *c.*1911)

Walter Wood (ed.), *The Boys' All-Round Book of Stories, Sports, and Hobbies* (London: Thomas Nelson, n.d.)

William Harrison Woodward, *Expansion of the British Empire, 1500-1924* (Cambridge: At the University Press, 1924)

Modern

Charles Allen (ed.), *Plain Tales from the Raj: Images of British India in the Twentieth Century* (London: Futura, 1976)

_____, *Tales from the Dark Continent: Images of British Colonial Africa in the Twentieth Century* (London: Futura, 1981)

_____, *Tales from the South China Seas: Images of British South-east Asia in the Twentieth Century* (London: Futura, 1984)

Patrick Brantlinger, *Rulers of Darkness: British Literature and Imperialism, 1830–1914* (London, 1988)

Bartle Bull, *Safari: A Chronicle of Adventure* (London: Penguin, 1988)

David Cannadine, *Ornamentalism: How the British Saw their Empire* (2002)

Martyn Connell, 'Hodgson's Brewery, Bow and the Birth of IPA', *Journal of the Brewery History Society*, 111 (2003)

David Cordingly, *Life Among the Pirates: The Romance and the Reality* (London: Abacus, 1999)

Helen Davies, *For the Record: James Bennell's Buildings in Early Launceston* (Launceston, Tasmania: Terrace Press, 2006)

Klaus Dodds, *Pink Ice: Britain and the South Atlantic Empire* (London: Tauris, 2003)

Raymond Dumett, 'Africa's Strategic Raw Materials during World War Two', *Journal of African History*, 26 (1984)

Rupert Faulkner (ed.), *Tea: East and West* (V&A Publications,)

Trevor Fishlock, *Conquerors of Time: Exploration and Invention in the Age of Daring* (London: John Murray, 2003)

_____, 'The Beasts Who Bore the White Man's Burden', Weekend Review, *The Times*, 31/1/04.

Robert Giddings, 'Delusive Seduction: Pride, Pomp, Circumstance, and Military Music', Mack, 26)

Catherine Hall and Sonya Rose (eds.), *At Home with the Empire: Metropolitan Culture and the Imperial World* (Cambridge: Cambridge University Press, 2006)

Richard Hall, *Empires of the Monsoon: A History of the Indian Ocean and its Invaders* (London: HarperCollins, 1996)

Jessica Harland-Jacobs, *Builders of Empire: Freemasons and British Imperialism, 1717–1927* (University of North Carolina, 2007)

C. W. Hill, *Picture Postcards* (Princes Rosborough: Shire Publications, 2007)

Bevis Hillier, *John Betjeman: The Biography* (London: John Murray, 2006)

Steve Holland (ed.), *Unleash Hell: 12 of the Best* War Picture Library *Comic Books Ever!* (London: Prion, 2007)

Anne Hugon, *The Exploration of Africa: From Cairo to the Cape* (London: Thames and Hudson, 1993)

Ronald Hyam, *Britain's Imperial Century*

_____, 'Concubinage and the Colonial Service: Silberrad and the Crewe Circular' (1909)

David Killingray, '"A Swift Agent of Government": Air Power in British Colonial Africa, 1916–1939', *Journal of African History*, 25 (1984)

A. H. M. Kirk-Greene, *On Crown Service: A History of Colonial and Overseas Civil Services, 1837–1997* (London: I. B. Tauris, 1999)

_____, *Britain's Imperial Administrators, 1858-1966* (Basingstoke: Palgrave Macmillan, 2000)

Ashley Jackson, 'Governing Empire: Colonial Memoirs and the History of H. M. Overseas Civil Service', review article, *African Affairs*, 103, 412 (2004)

Chandrika Kaul (ed.), *Media and the British Empire* (Basingstoke: Palgrave, 2006)

V. G. Kiernan, *The Lords of Humankind: European Attitudes towards the Outside World in the Imperial Age* (1969)

Ian Lace, 'Elgar and Empire', *The Elgar Society Journal* 10, 3 (1997)

D. A. Low, 'Empire and Christianity', in Low, *Lion Rampant*

George Low (ed.), *The Dirty Dozen: The Best 12* Commando *Comic Books Ever!* (London: Carlton Books, 2005)

Alan Macfarlane and Iris Macfarlane, *Green Gold: The Empire of Tea* (London: Ebury,)

John Mackenzie, (ed.), *Popular Imperialism and the Military, 1850–1950* (Manchester: Manchester University Press, 1992)

_____, *Orientalism: History, Theory, and the Arts* (Manchester: Manchester University Press, 1995)

_____, 'The Popular Culture of Empire in Britain', in Judith Brown and William Roger Louis (eds.), *The Oxford History of the British Empire*, volume iv, *The Twentieth Century* (Oxford: Oxford University Press, 1999)

J. A. Mangan (ed.), *Benefits Bestowed? Education and British Imperialism* (Manchester: Manchester University Press, 1988)

Philip Mansel, *Sultans of Splendour: Monarchs of the Middle East, 1869–1945* (London: Parkway, 1988)

Microsoft Encarta Encyclopaedia 2004.

James Mills, *Cannabis Britannica: Empire, Trade and Prohibition, 1800–1928* (OUP)

Stephen Mills, *The History of the Muthaiga Country Club, Volume I, 1913–1963* (Nairobi: Mills Publishing, 2006)

Jan Morris, *Farewell the Trumpets*

Roy Moxham, *Tea: Addiction, Exploitation and Empire* (London: Constable,)

John Newsinger, *The Blood Never Dried: A People's History of the British Empire* (London: Bookmark, 2006)

Harry Pearson, *Achtung Schweinhund! A Boy's Own Story of Imaginary Combat* (London: Abacus, 2008)

Michael Pearson, *The Indian Ocean* (London: Routledge, 2003)

Tom Pocock, *Battle for Empire: The Very First World War, 1756–63.*

Bernard Porter, 'Elgar and Empire', *Journal of Imperial and Commonwealth History*, 29, 1 (2001)

_____, *The Absent Minded Imperialists: Empire, Society and Culture in Britain* (2004)

Terence Ranger, 'The Invention of Tradition in Colonial Africa', in Eric Hobsbawm and Terence Ranger (eds.), *The Invention of Tradition* (Cambridge: Cambridge University Press, 1993)

_____, 'Making Northern Rhodesia Imperial: Variations on a Royal Theme, 1924–1938', *African Affairs*, lxxix, 316 (1980)

P. J. Rich, *Chains of Empire: English Public Schools, Masonic Cabalism, Historical Causality, and Imperial Clubdom* (London: The Regency Press, 1991)

_____, *Elixir of Empire: English Public Schools, Ritualism, Freemasonry, and Imperialism* (London: The Regency Press, 1993)

David Roach (ed.), *Aarrgghh!! It's War: The Best War Comic Cover Art* (London: Prion, 2007)

Anthony Sattin, *The Gates of Africa: Death, Discovery and the Search for Timbuktu* (London: HarperCollins, 2003)

Patsy Smith and Max Angus, *Hobart Sketchbook* (Adelaide: Rigby Limited, 1968)

_____, *Tasmania Sketchbook* (Adelaide: Rigby Limited, 1971)

Richard Symonds, *Oxford and Empire: The Last Lost Cause?* (Oxford: Clarendon Press, 1993)

Richard Tames, *The Victorian and Edwardian Sportsman* (Princes Risborough: Shire Publications, 2007)

Jacqueline Toovey (ed.), *Tigers of the Raj: Pages from the Shikar Diaries – 1894 to 1949 - of Colonel Burton, Sportsman and Conservationist* (Gloucester: Alan Sutton, 1987)

P. A. L. Vine, 'By Train to War in Abyssinia', *The Railway Magazine* (February 1973)

Other resources

John Johnson Collection of Printed Ephemera
Printed resources and images from the Bodleian Library, Oxford:

Empire and Colonies Box 1
Australian Life: Arrival at Sydney
Australian Life: Kangaroo Hunting (p.28)
Edward II illustrated message 'To My People Beyond the Seas', 4/2/01 (p.86)

Empire and Colonies Box 2
Cole's First Book for Little Australians: With Hundreds of Pictures

Canada's Confederation Diamond Jubilee 1867–1927 (p.6)

New Zealand: Scenic Playground of the Pacific (p.9)

Empire and Colonies Box 5
Stanley in Africa, Heroes in Africa (p.66)

Empire and Colonies large folder
United South Africa political poster (p.10)
Illustrated London News, 22/5/58: Sale of English goods in Canton (p.217)
Pictorial Times 1846, picture of Maori chief and wife (p.102 [top])

Games folder
A Tour of the British Colonies and Foreign Possessions (p.24)
The Siege of Sebastopol: A New and Amusing Game

Recruiting for Kitchener's Army
Diamond Jubilee Skittle Pool

Exhibition Catalogues 24
Empire of India Exhibition Earl's Court 1895 (p.166)
Palestine Pavilion Handbook and Tourist Guide, Empire Exhibition, Wembley 1924
Adelaide Jubilee International Exhibition Programme (p.5)
The Stanley and Africa Exhibition Catalogue (p.67)
Palestine in London Official Guide, Royal Agricultural Hall, Islington, June/July 1907
District Railways Guide to the Colonial and Indian Exhibition, South Kensington 1886

Exhibition Catalogues 20
Empire Exhibition Scotland 1938
Greater Britain Exhibition Earl's Court 1899 (p.188) – Empress Theatre twice

daily showing 'Savage South Africa'; Australian Theatre Elysia showing 'Jesse Jewell's Australian Marionettes'
Scotland Empire Exhibition 1938 Official Guide

Temporary Box
The Boer War Game (p.230)

Jaques Countries of the Empire: The New Educational Game

Festival of Empire Exhibition 1911 postcards

1924 Empire Exhibition postcards

Bodleian Map Room
1900 Map of the British Empire (B 1 (133))

Sri Lanka National Archives, Colombo
War propaganda and recruitment poster (p.127)

Opie Collection, Bodleian Library
Geography of the British Colonies, India etc, Royal School series (London: Nelson, n. d.)

E. Burrows, *Our Eastern Empire: Stories from the History of British India* (London: Griffith and Farrar, 1857)

Emily Huntley, *The Book of Little Black Brother* (London: Church Missionary Society, n. d., *c.*1913)

Stella Mead, *Through the British Commonwealth: In Ceylon, Burma, Singapore* (n. d., *c.*1947)

Violet Methley, *Seeing the Empire* (London: Raphael Tuck and Sons, n. d., *c.*1935)

Thomas Moscrop, *Children of Ceylon* (London: Oliphant, Anderson, Ferrier, 1911)

Nelson's Panorama Book for the Young: The Polar Seas and Regions (London: Nelson, n. d.)

The Bengal Peasant, number 1, *Life in the Empire* (London: British Youth Peace Assembly, n. d.)

The Children of Africa, Written for All English-Speaking Children (London: Hodder and Stoughton, 1886)

Imperial War Museum
'Our Allies the Colonies' (p.121 [top])

Pitt Rivers Museum, Oxford
Yoruba wooden caricature of the District Officer of the Ondo Province (p.101)

Index

Note: page numbers in **bold** refer to illustrations and captions.

A

abolitionists 31, 57
   see also Anti-Slavery Society
Abyssinia 158–9
Acheson, Dean 231
Aden **88–9**, 147, 226
Admiralty 17, 71
advertising **145**, **190–1**, **214–15**, 221–2, **221–3**
Africa 18–19, 28, 37, 88
   architecture 159–60
   armed forces in 127
   and colonial administration 100–4, **101**, 107, 112–14
   durbars 95
   explorers in 65–71, 73–4
   films based on 177–9, **178**
   hunting 197–8, **198–9**
   King Khama 55–7
   missionaries in 45, 46–7, 57
   and popular culture 177–9, **178**, **183–4**, 184, 186, 187
   railways 157, 158
   royal tours 93
   and the slave trade 57
   touring 107
   trade 216, 218
   see also Southern Africa
African Association 65, 68
Age of Curiosity 63
age of steam 144–8, 156
Ainley, John 105, 110
air mail **143**, 150
Air Ministry 150
air travel 149–51
Airman, The (Ladybird book, 1967) 134, **134**
Alcock, John 149
alcoholic beverages 219–21
Alert (ship) 72
Alexander, General Sir Harold 23
Alexandra, Queen **95**
'All-Red Route' 13
Allen, Charles 112
Allen, Geoffrey 107
Almásy, Count László 73–4
America 26–7, 43, 225
   see also United States
American War of Independence 27, 36
Americas 36
Amery, Leo 222
Amundsen, Roald 72
Anglican Church 229
Anglo-Portuguese alliance (1662) 34
Anglo-Zanzibar War **40–1**
animals 70, **70**
annuals **53**, 186, **195**
Antarctic exploration **70**, 72, 73, **73**, 77
Anti-Slavery Society 50, 68
   see also abolitionists
apartheid 30
Arab horses 171
Arabia 27–8
Arabs 57, 74, 104
architecture 155, 158–65, **224–5**
Arctic exploration 71, **71**, 72, 73
armed forces 13–14, 114–15, 117–41, 229, 230–1
   global commitments 123–4

as guarantor of security 117–18, 120
   heroes of the 118–20, 121–2, 136–7
   and infrastructure 157–8
   martyrs 119–20
   military literature **118**, **122**, **133–5**, 136–7, **136–7**, **137–8**
   military music **136**, 137
   military pageants 117, 128, **129**, 134
   pomp and ceremony 117, 126–7, 128, **129**, 134
   recruitment 127, **127**, 185
   see also British Army; Royal Air Force; Royal Navy
Army Game (TV series, 1950s) 183
Arnold, Dr 164
Arracan, Treaty of 40
Aston, Richard 186–9
Atkins, Tommy (fictional character) 118–19, 122
Aurangzeb 34
Australia 27, 28, 191–2
   railways 157
   royal tours 88, 93–4, 96
   Victoria state 163
   'white Australia' policy 30
Australian Aboriginals **28**

B

Bab el Mandeb straits 19
Baden-Powell, Colonel Robert **10–11**, 18–19, **18**, **139**, 140–1, 186
badminton 191
Bagyidaw, Emperor 40
Baines, Thomas 69–71, **69**
Baker, Ernest 53
Baker, Florence 66
Baker, Sir Herbert 160
Baker, Samuel 66
Baldwin, Stanley 222
Balfour Declaration (1926) 21
Ballantyne, R.M. 199
Bangs, Bill 151
Banks, Edward 106
Banks, John 206
Banks, Sir Joseph 65
Barclays 228
Baring, Evelyn, Earl of Cromer 112
Barnado, Thomas 30
baronial splendour 158–60
Barth, Heinrich 68, **68**
Bass 219, 221
Bathoen II 96, **102**
battleships 129
Baxter, John 105–6
BBC Empire Service 177
BBC World Service 229
Bechuanaland 55–7, 96, 102, 149
Bell, Sir Gawain 87
Bell, Sir Hesketh 204
benign feudalism 101, 102–3
Bennell, James 164–5
Benson, A. C. 175
Bentinck, Lord William Cavendish 144
Bentley, Mr and Mrs Holman **56**
Beresford, Lady 176
Beresford, Lord Charles 176
Betjeman, John 163, 188
bicycles 194
Bigglesworth, Squadron Leader James 'Biggles' (fictional character) 117, 134, **138**, 185

billiards 193–4
Birdwood, Vere 113, 126
Biscoe, Captain John **73**
Black & White whisky **145**
'blackbirders' 48
Blixen, Karen 213
Blunt, Lady Anne 171
Blunt, Wilfrid Scawen 171
board games **24–5**, **63**, **230**
Boer War Game, The **230**
Boer Wars 124–5, 140, 164, 196
Bombay 173
   see also Mumbai
Boorman, John 15
Borneo 34–5
Bosanquet, Admiral 92
Boston Gazette (newspaper) 27
botanical gardens 74–6
Bourdillon, Sir Bernard 112–14
Bovril **223**
Bowder, Cuthbert 107
Bowles, Sir Robert 62
Boxer Rebellion 182
boxing 195
Boy Scout movement 18–19, 50, 53, 139–41, **139**, 229
Boys' Book of the Commonwealth, The **228**
Boys' and Girls' Adventure Book, The (1935) **135**
Boys Own Annual **195**
Boys Own Paper 105, 117, **118**, 120, **130**, 185–6, 189, 205
bridges **156**, **159**
Britannia (Royal Yacht) **227**
British, as 'civilizers' of the world 43, 44, 51, 53, 225
British Army 117, 118
   brutality 123
   Christmas Fund **141**
   cigarette cards **120**, **121**
   commands 123
   global commitments 123
   in India 125–7
   and irregular warfare 121
   medals 123
   mess **124**
   pomp and ceremony 126–7
   recruitment 127, **127**, 185
   reputation 121–3
   sport 193–4, 195
   Armies, Fourteenth ('Forgotten') 124
   Brigades, Brigade of Gurkhas 108, 229
   Regiments and Battalions
      Berkshire Yeomanry **168–9**
      Buckinghamshire Yeomanry **168–9**
      Dorset Yeomanry **168–9**
      Gloucestershire Regiment **140**
      Royal Engineers 149, 158
British Broadcasting Corporation (BBC) 80, 110, 177, 229
British Colombia 163
British diaspora 228–9
British Empire 11–23
   armed forces 13–14, 114–15, 117–41
   colonial administration 19, 99–115
   communications 141, 143–53
   defining the 19–20
   duration 25
   early 25–7
   evil of 99
   expansion 25–41

   see also explorers; missionaries
   explorers 41, 57, 59–77
   first 27
   geographical commands 18
   God and the 53
   greatest extent **15**
   'informal empire' 23
   infrastructure 153, **153**, 155–65
   institutions of the 199, 201–13
   justification myths 18–19, 31, 56
   last hurrah 22–3
   legacy 223, 225–31
   maps 11–14, 11–18, 15, **15**, 16–18, **16**, 23, 71–2, 231
   migration 29–31, **29**, 226, 228–9
   missionaries 41, **42–4**, 43–57
   personal recollections of 186–9
   popular culture 163, 167–89
   and the power of the sovereign/monarchy 19–20, 77, 79–97
   satirical accounts **22**
   scaling down of 231
   second 27
   settlement 29–31
   special cases 21–2
   and sport 191–9, 229
   statistics 13
   terminology of the 20–1
   and trade 29, 32–5, **32–3**, 143–4, 156–7, 213, 215–23, 225
   world-view 209, 225
British Empire Exhibition, Wembley (1924) 92, 175, 176, 177, 188
British Empire Medal 90
British India Steam Navigation Company 146–7
British national identity 169–70
British South Africa Company 55, 57
British 'superiority' 163–4
Brooke Bond 218, **218**, 227
Brooke, James 34–5, 76, 90
Broome, Richard 110
Brown, Arthur Whitten 149
Brown, Cecil 151
Brownrigg, Sir Robert 62
Bruce, James 69
Brunel, Isambard Brunel 144
Buchan, John 180
Bull, Bartle 198
Buller, H.M. 206
Bülow, Bernhard von 11
Burke's Peerage and Gentry 90
Burma 27, 40, 124
Burma Office 21
Burnaby, Colonel Fred 137
Burroughs, Edgar Rice 177
Burton, Charles 73
Burton, Sir Richard 60, 61, **61**, 66, 68–9
Butler, Lady 167
Butler, Ralph 173
Butt, Clara 175
Buxton, Sir Thomas Fowell 50
Buxton, Victor 52

C

cables, underwater 13, 143
Cabot, Henry 215
Cabot, John 59
Calcutta, 'Black Hole' incident 35

campaign chests 145
Canada **29**, 163
Canadian Pacific Railway 159, **159**
Canadian troops 125
cannabis 221
Cannadine, David 11, 61, 82, 88, 104
Caribbean 26–7
Carry on Up the Khyber (1968) 179–82
Carter, Sir Howard 77
Cassell 60, **60**, 184, 185
Central Asia 27
Ceylon 40, 101, 105, 108, 158, **160–1**, 162, 177
Challenger (ship) 72
Chamberlain, Joseph **10–11**, 216–17
Chamberlain, Colonel Sir Neville Bowes 194
Chappell, Mollie, *Rhodesian Adventure* 181, **181**
Charles, Hughie 173
Charles II, King of England 34
chartered companies 32–4
China 28
   missionaries in 45
   tea 74, 76
   trade with 216, 228
Chinese labourers **30**
Christianity 204–5, 229
   at home 50–3
   conveying the message 53–5
   spread of 43–50, 53–7
Chums (comic) 184–5, **184**
Church Lads Brigade 50, 53
Church Mission Society 46, 50
Church of Scotland missions 57
Churchill, Seton 53
Churchill, Winston **30**, 70, 80, 83, 101, 113, 125, 129, 134, 156, 174, 195, 197, 204, 216, 227
cigarette cards 220
   Armed forces **120**, **121**, **128**
   bridges **159**
   exotic places 220, **220**
City of London 215–16, 226, 227
'civilizing mission' 43, 44, 51, 53, 225
Cleopatra's Needle 84, **215**
Clifford, Sir Hugh 90
Clive, Robert 33, 35, 136
Clunies-Ross, John 34, 35
Cobham, Sir Alan **17**, 149
Cobham, Lady Gladys 17, **17**
cock fighting **192**
cocoa 217–18, **219**
Cocos (Keeling) Islands 35
Cody, Samuel 149
coffee 227
Colombo, Captain, maps of **12**, 13
'colonels' 103
colonial administration 19, 99–115
   career plans 100–1
   children of the service 114
   concubines 108
   District Commissioners 99, 104–6
   drawbacks 99–100
   fatalities 100
   fresh recruits 109–10, 113
   and 'home' 114
   imperial proconsuls 111–12
   kit 108–9
   perks 99–100
   power 112–14

preparation for 108–9
protocol 113
recruitment and interviews 106
ruling by proxy 104
social life 110–11, 113
touring 107
use of force 114–15
wives 109, 113
'colonial empire' 21
Colonial Office 21, 23, 84, 90, 106
Colonial Service 100, 101, 104–6, 192
colonies 26–7, 230–1
comics 183–5, **184**
military 136–7, **137**
Commando (comic) 136, **137**
Commonwealth 20–1, 83, **228**, 229, 230–1
Commonwealth War Graves Commission 229
communications 141, 143–53
and the age of steam 144–6
flight 149–51
postal service **143**, 146–7, **147**, 148, 150, 151–2
sea voyages **142–3**, 143–9, 229
and technological innovation 143–4
Conan Doyle, Arthur 69–71
concubines 108
Condominiums 22
Connell, Martyn 219
'Conquest of Africa, The' (board game) 63
Conrad, Joseph 101
consumer goods 215, 219
Cook, James 17, 59, 61, 62, 64–5, 64, 68, 70
coronations **79**, 81, **82**, 83, 87, 88, 94, 95, **95**, 151, 171
Cory, Johnson 203
Cotton, John 43
Coubertin, Baron Pierre de 194
Coward, Noël 174
Crawley, Captain Rawdon 194
Crean, Tom **70**
Crewe, Lord 108
cricket 110, 191–2, 195, **195**, **224–5**, 229
Cripps, Sir Stafford 114
croquet 191
cross-cultural influence 114, 170–1, **170**
Crown
authority of the 20
see also monarchy
Crowther, Rev. Samuel Ajayi **44**
cultural stereotypes 171
Cunard, Samuel 144
Cunard Steamship Company 146, 148–9
Cunyngham-Brown, Sjovald 105, 145
Curzon, Viceroy Lord 37, 90, 94, **95**, 112, 198, 203

D

Daily Mail (newspaper) 120, 167
Daily Telegraph (newspaper) 226
Dalai Lama 37
Danakil Desert 74
Darton's *Heroes in Africa* **66**
Darwin, Sir Charles 59
Davis, Windsor 183
Dawe, Revd C.S. 81
King Edward's Realm 14–18, **14**

De Havilland (aircraft) 149–50
Deavin, C.H. 81
deep-sea exploration 71–2
Deere, Al 169
Delaware people **26**
Delhi Durbar (1911) 94, **95**
Deolali 195
Depression 222
Deputy Commissioner's house, Jullundur **111**
desert exploration 73–4
Diana, Princess 226
Dinky toys 185
Discovery (ship) 72
Disraeli, Benjamin 146
District Commissioners 99, 104–6, 109
Dominions 20–1, 23, 30, 31
Dominions Office 21
Downie, J.M. 180–1
Drake, Dawsonne 35
dreadnoughts 128–9
drugs 221
Duke of York (1923) 80
Dummet, Raymond 223
Duncan, Sir David 159
Dunlops 193
Dupleix, Joseph-François 35
durbars 94–5
Dutch 37
Dutch East India Company 59

E

East India Company 27, 29, 32–5, 37, 203, 209
beer consumption 219, 221
cohabitation 108
diwani 36
docks **32**
exploitation 99
hunting 199
sea transport 144
tea 74
East India Company College, Addiscombe 194
East India Docks **32–3**
Easter Island **64**
economy 227
education, imperial 14–18
see also schools, public
Edward VII, King of England 13, 81, 82, **86–7**, 87
coronation 83, 87, 94, **95**, 171
durbars 94, **95**
imperial honours 90
and music 175, 176
Edward VIII, King of England **88–9**, 92–3, 96, **105**
Edwardes, Sir Herbert 52
Egypt 16, 22–3, 73–4, 77, 112, 151
Elgar, Alice 175, 176
Elgar, Edward 174–6, **175**, 219
Eliot, John 43
elites, global 25, 90, 101, 102–3
Elizabeth I, Queen of England 26, 33, 209
Elizabeth II, Queen of England 87, **116**, 163, 170, 230
coronation **82**, 83, 87
royal tours 88, 96, **96–7**, 226
Elizabeth, Queen Mother 81, 93, 226
Ellesmere Island 72
Ely, George Herbert 186
see also Strang, Herbert
Empire Annual for Australian Boys, The (1917) **53**
'Empire Christmas Pudding' recipe **170**

Empire Day 81, 188, 207
Empire of India Exhibition (1895) **166–7**
Empire Marketing Board **215**, 222
Endurance (ship) 73
engineering 155–9
English language 226
Enigma Variations (Elgar) 175
ennoblement 90
Erebus (ship) 71, **71**
Eton 203
evangelicals 43, 44, 45, 57
Everest, George 16, **16**, 34, 83
Everest, Mount **16**, 60, 61, **62**, 71, 76
exhibitions 67, **166–7**, 188, **188**
see also British Empire Exhibition, Wembley (1924)
explorers 41, 57, 59–77
in Africa 65–71, 73–4
and botanical gardens 74–6
dangers faced by 61
desert 73–4
and museums 61–3
Polar **70**, 71, **71**, 72–3, **73**, 77
public interest in 63–4

F

Faisal II, King of Iraq 102, **104**
Falkland Islands **73**
Falkland War 146, 225
Fanon, Frantz 227
Far East 28
Farmer, Chris 197
Fawside, John, *Flag of England* 182, **182**
Fenn, George Manville 136
feudalism, benign 101, 102–3
Field, The 110
Fiennes, Ranulph 73
film 177–82, **178**
First World War 23
Fishlock, Trevor 70
Fleet Reviews **116–17**
flight 149–51
Flight Five: Africa (Ladybird book, 1960s) **183**
Flinders, Matthew 70
food
'Empire Christmas Pudding' recipe **170**
trade 217–18, 227
football 191, 195, 226
Foreign and Commonwealth Office 226
Foreign Office 22, 57, 67, 68, 106
Forgotten Patrol, The **122**
Formby, George 173
Forster, Reinhold 62
Fortune, Robert 74–6
A Journey to the Tea of China **74–5**, 76
Four Feathers, The (1939) 179
France 35–6, 37
Franklin, Sir John 71, **71**
Fraser, George MacDonald 31
Fraser, Simon 163
free trade 216–17
Freemasonry 201, 210, 212–13
Fringes of the Fleet 176
Fuchs, Sir Vivian 60, 73, 76–7
Furse, Sir Ralph 104, 192

G

Galle Face Hotel, Colombo, Ceylon **160–1**, 162
gentleman's clubs 210–13, **211**

geography 207–8, **208**
geology 155
George, King of Greece 112–14
George II, King of England 83
George III, King of England 11, 101
George IV, King of England (formerly Prince Regent) 62, 90, **162**
George V, King of England 188
coronation 87
durbar 94
and football **80**
imperial honours 90
royal tours 88, 92, 93, 96
Silver Jubilee 13, **83**, 88, 152
and stamps 152, **152**, 153
on trade 216
George VI 82
coronation **79**, 81, 83, 87, 88, 94, 95
durbar 94, 95
imperial honours 90
royal tours 92, 93
and stamps **43**, **152**
George VI: King and Emperor (1937) **81**
George, St 53
Germans 11
Germany 37, 189
Gibbons, Edward Stanley 153, **153**
Gibraltar 27
Gibson desert 73
Giddings, Robert 80–1, 137
Gilbert, Sir William 171
Giles, Ernest 73
Giraffe Manor 159
Girl Guides 140, 163
global elite 25, 90, 101, 102–3
God 53
Godfrey, Fred 173
Godley, John Robert 44
Golden Book of Children's Hymns, The (1952) 53
Golledge, E.J. 206
Gomes, Edwin 53
Gordon, Arthur Hamilton 101
Gordon, General Sir Charles 53–4, **54–5**, 63, 112, 122, 124, 175–6, 209
Gore-Brown, Sir Stewart 159–60
Government House, Nigeria 112–14
Graham, Gerald 39
Grant, James, *Cassell's Illustrated History of India* 60, **60**
Grant, James Augustus 60, 66
Graphic, The **125**
Great Trigonometrical Survey 16, **16**, 34
Greater Britain Exhibition (1899) **188**
Griffiths, Katherine 109
Guinness **190–1**
Gunga Din (1939) 179

H

Haggard, Sir Henry Rider 199
Haidar Ali 36
Haining, Peter 180
Hall, Richard 146
Hamed, Sultan 41
Hannay, Richard 180
Hannington, Bishop James 46, 47–8
'Happy Valley set' 213
Harding, E. J. 147
Hardy, Thomas 123
Harrison, Bill 104

Hart, Peter 173
Hasan, Sayyid (the 'Mad Mullah') 135
hashish 221
Hatton, Denis Finch 213
Hawkins, William 33–4
Hayward, Archdeacon 81
Headrick, Daniel 156–7
Healey, Denis 226
Hemingway, Ernest 198
Hendon Air Pageant 134
Henry, Prince 213
Henry VII, King of England 59
Henty, G.A. 136, 180
Hergé 184
Hill, Rowland 151
Hillary, Sir Edmund 60, 76, 83
Himalayas 16
Hindus **49**
Hinkler, Bert 149
history lessons 208–9
HMS Pinafore (1878) 171, **172**
Hobart, Lord 164
Hobart, Tasmania 164
hockey 195
Hodgson's Brewery 219–21
Hong Kong 28
Hong Xiuquan 45
Hood (battleship) **38–9**
Hope and Glory (1984) 15
Horn, Alfred, *Trader Horn in Madagascar* (1928) **57**
Hornblow, E.C.T. 207–8
Horse Guards 84, **84**
Hose, Charles 76, 144
hotels 160–2, **161**
House of Lords 230
Huddleston, Revd Trevor 45
Hudson, Henry 59
Huessler, Robert 202
Hugon, Alice 67
humanitarians 43–4
hunting 197–9, **198–9**
Hussein I, King of Jordan **104**
Hutchins school 164
Hyam, Robert 108
hymns 53

I

I Only Arsked! (1958) 183
Ideal Book for Boys **199**
Idris, Sultan 90
Il Papagallo (magazine) **22**
Illustrated London News 84, **84–5**, 113, 122
immigration 226, 228–9
Imperial Airways **139**, 149, 150, 151
Imperial British East Africa Company 47, 50, 146
Imperial Crown of India 94
Imperial Economic Committee 222
Imperial Federation 14
imperial honours 90
Imperial March (Elgar) 175
Imperial Order of the Crown of India 90
imperial proconsuls 111–12
India 27
architecture 160
armed forces in 125–7
British control of 36–7
and British popular culture **166–7**, 170, 173, 179–82
cannabis use in 221
colonial administration **98–9**, 99–101, **100**, 104, 107–8, 110, 112–14
communications 146–7
concubinage 108

durbars 94
Empress of 88
films based on 179–82
food 227
gentleman's clubs 211–12, **211**
Great Trigonometrical Survey 16, **16**, 34
hunting 198, 199
imperial honours 90
maharajahs **90–1**
mapping 16
missionaries in 44, 45, 52
railways 157
Seven Years War 35–6
sport 191, 192, 193–4, 195–6
status in the British Empire 21
suttee 49, **49**, 50
tea 74, 76
touring 107
Viceroy 21
India Office 21
India Pale Ale 219, 221
Indian Army 37–9, 124–6, 229
cigarette cards **128**
sport **196**
Armies, Bombay **125**
Regiments and Battalions, Bengal Lancers 126, **126**
Indian Civil Service (ICS) 100–1, 210–11
Indian Imperial Police 99, **100**
Indian migrants 30, 31, 158
Indian Mutiny (1857) 45, 119
Indian princely states 22, 104, 124
Indirect Rule 104
infrastructure 153, **153**, 155–65
institutions of the British Empire 199, 201–13
Freemasonry 201, 210, 212–13
gentleman's clubs 210–13, **211**
public schools 197, 201–9
Iraq 23, 102, 135, 138, 139, 225
Ismail, King of Egypt 66
It Ain't Half Hot Mum (1974–81) 183
Italy 18–19

J

J&P Coats **215**
Jahangir 33–4
Jamaica 27, 169–70
James, I King of England 26, 33–4
Johns, Captain W.E. **138**
Johnson, Amy 149–50
Jones, Pitcairn 164
Jones, Terry 183

Kaiser-i-Hind 90
Kandy, Ceylon 40, 62, 124, 157
Kashmir 225
Kaunda, Kenneth **46**, 110
Keegan, John 226
Kenya 30, 45, 197, 213
Khama 55–7, **55**
Kikuyu 45, 93
Kipling, John 176
Kipling, John Lockwood 163
Kipling, Rudyard 117, 144, 176, 180, 210
Just So Stories 170–1
poetry 182
Stalky and Co 194–5
The Jungle Book 170, 179
'The White Man's Burden' 51

'Tommy Atkins' character 118–19, 122
Kitchener, Lord 123–4, 136, 157–8
Knight Grand Commander 90
Korda, Zoltán 177, 179
Kuala Lumpur 212

L

La Martiniere College, Lucknow **204**
Lace, Ian 175
Ladybird books 134, **134**, **183**
Lake Albert Nyanza 66
Lambton, Colonel William **16**
Land of Hope and Glory 175, 176
Lander, John 68
Lander, Richard 68
Last Night of the Proms, The 171
Launceston, Tasmania 164–5, **165**
Lawrence, Sir Henry 206
Lawrence Memorial Royal Military School (LMRMS) 206
League of Nations, Covenant 22, 23
legacy of the Empire 223, 225–31
Leighton, Lord 162
León, Juan Ponce de 60
Leopold II, King of Belgium 57, 67
L'Estrange, Charles James 186
see also Strang, Herbert
Lhasa 16, 37
Libya 16
liners **142–3**, 144–5, 146, 147–9
Linlithgow, Lady of **98–9**
Linlithgow, Marquess of **98–9**
Lipton's 92
literature 134, 170, 180–1, **180–3**, 199, **199**, **228–9**
military **118**, **122**, **133–8**, 136–7
missionary **42–3**, 53–5
Livingstone, David 44, 45, 48, 55, 57, 61, 63, **63**, 66–**7**, **69**, 70
Lloyd, Revd A.B., *Uganda to Khartoum* 52, **52**
London 84, 215–16, 221–2
London Company 26
London Conference **20**
London Missionary Society 55, 56, 57, 66
Longford, David 107
Look and Learn (magazine) **185**, 186
Louis XIV, King of France 34, 36
Lucy, Peter 192
Lugard, Frederick 104
Lutyens, Sir Edwin Landseer 160
luxury goods 32–3
Lyne, Philip 27
Lytton, Lord 94, 162

M

Macdonald, Connie 169–70
Mackenzie, Charles 45
Mackenzie, John 56–7, 120, 140, 160, 162, 171, 177, 207, 208
Mackinnon, Sir William 146
Macmillan, Harold 106
Macnaghten, Melville 203
'Mad Dogs and Englishmen' (Coward) 174
Madoc, Guy 110

Madrid, Treaty of (1670) 26
magazines **77**, 183–4, 185–6, **185**, **187**
maharajahs **90–1**
Mallory, George Leigh 60, 61
Mandates 22–3
Manila 35
Manning, Sir William Henry 177
Maori people **102**
maps
coastal 71–2
'red' 11–18, **15**, **16**, 23, 231
Marathas 36
Margaret, Princess 170
Markham, Beryl 213
Marryat, Frederick 40
martyrs
military 119–20
missionary 46–8, 53–4, **54–5**
Mary, Princess **141**
Mary of Teck **83**, 90, 92
Masekela, Hugh 45
Masonic lodges 201, 210, 212–13
Matthews, B.J.A. **101**
Mauritius 158
Mayo College 195
Me and My Girl (1937) 168
Mediterranean 27
Mehmet Ali 84
Mercator projection map 15
Merchant Navy 13, 32–4, 35, 146, 207, 218
Mid-Atlantic Range 72
Middle East
colonial administration 102, 104
horses 171
Mandates 22–3
migration 29–31, **29**, 226, 228–9
Mikado, The (1885) 171
military pageants 117, 128, **129**, 134
Milligan, Spike 114, 126
Milner, Sir Alfred 112
'mini-Englands' 163–5
Minorca 27
missionaries 41, **42–4**, 43–57
against slavery 57
at home 50–3
dangers faced by 46–8
educating function 45–6
health services of 46
martyrs 46–8, 53–4, **54–5**
and the outlawing of 'uncivilised' practices 49, 50
Protestant 45, 48
public interest in 63–4
publishing industry **42–3**, 53–5
Roman Catholic 46
and the slow process of conversion 48–50
Mitchell, Henry 106
Mogambo (1953) **178–9**
monarchy 19–20, 77, 79–97
coronations **79**, 81, **82**, 83
durbars 94–5
imperial honours 90
imperialization 87–8
importance of 87
royal tours **88–9**, 89–96, **96–7**
Montgomery, Bernard 125
Mornington, Lord 36, 37
Morris, Jan 176, 212
Morrisby, Sergeant Frank 164
Most Eminent Order of the Indian Empire 90

Most Exalted Order of the Star of India 90
Most Excellent Order of the British Empire 90
Mountbatten, Admiral Lord Louis 23, 110, 114, 162, 174
multinational companies 227–8
Mumbai **224–5**
museums 61–3, 226
music 168, 171–6
Mussolini, Benito 18–19
Mutesa I 46, **47**
Mutesa II (Sir Edward 'Freddie') 102–3, **103**, 204
Muthaiga Country Club 213
Mwanga II 46, 47
Myers, Revd John Brown, *The Congo for Christ* **42–3**
Mysore 36

N

Naipul, Sir V.S. 225
Nairobi 213
Napier, General Sir Charles 49
Napier, General Sir Robert **136**, 157–8
Napoleon Bonaparte 36
Napoleonic Wars 27, 36, 90
Nares, Sir George 71–2
Nash, John **162**
Nasser, Colonel 22
National Anthem 87
unofficial 175
national identity 169–70
nationalism 103
Native Americans **26**, 43
Ndebele 55, 57
Nehru, Jawaharlal **202**
Nelson, Horatio 13
New Delhi 94, 160
New Zealand 28, 169
Newbolt, Sir Henry 194, 202
Newman, Robert 171
news services 110, 143, 170
newspapers 170
Nigeria 197, 225
Nile, source of the 66, 67, 68
Nimrod expedition 73
'noble savage' myth 44
North-West Passage 71
Northern Rhodesia 57, 95, 110, 159–60, **214–15**
Noyes, Alfred 176
Nyasaland **214–15**

O

Oates, Captain 72
Oceanic Steamship Company **142–3**, 148
oceanic surveys 17, 71–2
Olympic Games (1896) 1994
Omdurman, battle of 123–4
Ootacamund Club 193, **211**, 212
Opium Wars 216
Order of St Michael and St George 90
orders of merit 90
Ordnance Survey 11
Orwell, George 99, **100**, 184, 211
O'Shaughnessy, W.B. 221
Ottoman Empire 37
Our Neighbours and their Work for Us (geography textbook) **208**, 217–18, **219**
Our Sailors (1910) **39**
Owen, Captain William 17
Oxford movement 44, 45, 48

P

P&O 145, 146, **148**, 229

Pacific region 28, 64, 65, 68
Palestine 23
Palin, Michael 183
Paris, Treaty of (1763) 36
Park, Mungo 68
Parker, Ross 173
patriotism 13, **14**
Patteson, John Coleridge 48
Pearson, Michael 144
Peary, Robert 185
Penang Club 212
Penn, William **26**, 27
Pennant Kerosene **223**
Penny Black 151
personal recollections, of Empire 186–9
Peterloo massacre (1819) 122
Philip III, King of Spain 34
Philip, Prince 96, **96–7**, 162, 163
Pictorial Review **102**
pig-sticking 140, **193**
piracy 27
Pirates of Penzance, The (1879) 172
pith helmet 115, **115**
Pitt, William 13, 34
Pitt Rivers, General Augustus Lane Fox 62
Pitt Rivers Museum, Oxford 62–3
place names 11, 44, 72, 164, 225
Players **120–1**, **128**, 220
Pocock, Tom 34
poetry 182, **182**
Polar exploration **70–1**, 71–3, **73**, 77
polo 195–6, **196**
pomp and ceremony 117, 126–7, 128, **129**, 134, 226
popular culture 163, 167–89
annuals 186
comics 183–5, **184**
cross-cultural influences 170–1, **170**
film 177–82, **178**
literature 180–3, **180–3**
magazines 183–4, 185–6, **185**, **187**
music 168, 171–6
personal recollections of Empire 186–9
poetry 182, **182**
radio 177
television 183
Port Said 18
postage stamps **73**, **143**, 151–3, **152–3**
postal service **143**, 146–7, **147**, 148, 150, 151–2
Powell, Enoch 21
Prester John 59
Price, Willard, *Cannibal Adventure* **229**
Prince Regent *see* George IV, King of England
Prince of Wales' Eastern Book, The **88–9**
protectionism 216
Protestants 45, 48
protocol 113
Punch magazine **154–5**
Purity Campaign 108

Q

Qing government 45
Quakers 43
Quatermain, Allan (fictional character) 199
Queen Elizabeth (liner) 147, 148–9
Queen Mary (liner) 147, 148–9
Queen's Honey Soap **222**

R

radio 170, 177
Radio Ceylon 177
Rae, John 70
RAF Habbaniya 135, 138–9
Raffles, Stamford 34
railways 156, 157–8, **157**, 159, **159**
Raj 21, 90, 112, 160, 179
Raleigh, Sir Walter 26
raw materials 222–3
regional appellations 11
Reith, Lord 177
religion 204–5
Rendall, Montague **207**
Renown (battlecruiser) 92–3, 96
Resolution (ship) 65
Rhodes, Cecil 55, 57, **154–5**, 158, 181, 197, 210, 217
Rhodesia 30, **157**, 158
  see also Northern Rhodesia; Southern Rhodesia
Rhodesian Adventure 181, **181**
Rich, P.J. 201, 203, 205, 212
Rider Haggard, H. 179, 180
Ridgeway, Sir West 92
Ripping Yarns (1970s) 183
Roberts, John 194
Roberts, Lord **10–11**, 140, 203
Roderick, Jean 81, 82
Roman Catholicism 46
Rommel, General Erwin 74
Roosevelt, Teddy 198, **198**
Rosebery, Lord 203
Royal Air Force 117, 120, 127, 134–9, **134–5**, 150–1, 185
  see also RAF Habbaniya
Royal Flying Corps 120
Royal Geographical Society 66, 68, 71, 72
Royal Mail 151–2
Royal Marines 115, 118
Royal Military School of Music 137
Royal Naval Air Service 173
Royal Navy 12–13, 17, 35–41, 65, 117–18, 127–34, **130**, **132–3**
  Christmas Fund **141**
  commands 130–1
  dreadnoughts 128–9
  exploration 71, 72, 73
  Fleet Reviews **116–17**
  importance of 37–9, 127–9
  and the monarchy 87
  naval charts 17
  recruitment **130**, 185
  ship names 131
  strength 129
  The Navy's Here! propaganda 131–4, **132**
  Fleets
    First Fleet 27
    Home Fleet 130
    Mediterranean Fleet 130–1, 176

Royal Pavilion, Brighton **162**
Royal Society 65, 72
Royal Titles Act (1876) 88
Royal Tournament **129**
Royal Victorian Order 90
Royal West African Frontier Force **121**
rubber 193, 194, 219
rugby 193, 195, **200–1**
Rushdie, Salman 225
Russia 37

S

safari 107, **190–1**, 197–9, **198–9**
St Kitts 26
St Thomas' College, Ceylon 203
Salmon, Captain E. 107
Salote, Queen of Tonga 90
Sanders of the River (1935) 177–9
Sarawak 34–5, 106
Sartre, Jean-Paul 227
Savoy Operas 171–2, **172**
Sayid Khalid 41
schools, public 169
  curriculum 206–9
  fostering the imperial elite 197, 201–9
  and Freemasonry 210
  sports 194–5
science 155–7
Scott, Paul 205
Scott, Captain Robert 60, 61, 72
Scouting for Boys (1908) 139, 140, 141
Sea Pictures (Elgar) 175
sea voyages **142–3**, 143–9, 229
Second World War 74, 114, **121**, 189
  Army recruitment posters **127**
  infrastructure 158
  military requisition of sea transports 146, **148**
  music 173
  Navy propaganda 131–4, **132**
  and the Royal Air Force 134, 150, 151
Seeley, Sir John 31
Selangor Club (Spotted Dog) 212
Seven Years' War 35–6, 64
Shackleton, Ernest 73
Shaw, Captain Frank 185
sheep 70
shikar (tiger hunting) 198, 199
Shiwa House 159–60
Short Singapore I flying boat 17, **17**
Short Sunderland flying-boat 150–1
Short S.23C 'Empire' class flying boat 149, 150, **150**
Simpson desert 73
Singapore 27, 34, 145, 151, 212
Sitwell, Edith 172–3

slavery 26, 29, **30**, 31–2
  abolition 31, 50, 57, 68
Slim, General 124
Smith, Ian 21
smuggling 217
snooker 193–4
Social Darwinism 119, 120
Somaliland 135
Somaliland Camel Corps **106–7**
South Africa **10–11**, 30
South Asia 27
Southeast Asia 27
Southern Africa 21
Southern Rhodesia 21, 30, 55
Southon, Arthur Eustace, *Khama the Conqueror* (1930) 55, **55**
Spain 35
Spectator (magazine) 112
Speke, John Hanning **58–9**, 60, 61, 66, 68–9
sport 191–9, 229
Stanley, Henry Morton 60, 63, **63**, 67
Stanley and African Exhibition, London 67
State Forces of India 124
Statute of Westminster (1931) 21
steam boats 144–8, 156
Steevens, G.W. 120
stereotypes, cultural 171
Strang, Herbert 180, **180**, 186, **200–1**
Strathallan (liner) 148
Strip, Captain 107
Stroyan, William 61
Stuart, John 73
Sturt, Charles 73
Sudan 22, 63, 123–4, 197
Suez, east of 29
Suez Canal 18–19, 22, 144–6
sugar 26, 31, 227
Sullivan, Sir Arthur 171
Sultan of Zanzibar, palace of the 40–1, **40–1**
suttee 49, **49**, 50
Sydney Harbour Bridge **156**
Symington, David 107
Symonds, Richard 205

T

Taiping Rebellion 45
Takoradi Air Route 151
Tames, Richard 193, 194
Tarzan series 177
Tasmania 164–5, **165**
taxation 32, 216–17
tea 74, 76, 217, 221–2, 227
tea cards 218, **218**
technology 155–7
  hard 155
  soft 155–6
  and sport 194
  wireless 177

telegraphy, global (the 'All-Red Route') 13
television 183
Tenko (1970s TV series) 183
tennis 194
Terror (ship) 71, **71**
Tewodoros (Emperor of Abyssinia) 40, 158
theatre 168, 170
Theophilus, John 193
Thesiger, Sir Wilfred 60, 74
Thomson, James Anderson **140**
Three Nuns Empire Blend **221**
Tibet 37
timber 215
Times, The (newspaper) 41, 108, 122
Times Weekly Airmail Edition 110
tin 219
Tintin (fictional character) 184
Tipu Sultan 36
'Tipu's Tiger' **36**
tobacco 26, **214–15**, 220, **220–1**
  see also cigarette cards
Tomb of the Unknown Solider, Westminster Abbey **118–19**
'Tour through the British Colonies and Foreign Possessions' (board game) 24–5
touring 107
  royal **88–9**, 89–96, **96–7**
Tout, T.F. 209
Townshend, Arthur 81, 82
trade, global 29, 32–5, **32–3**, 143–4, 156–7, 213, 215–23, 225
Trade Horn (1931) 179
Trans-Jordan 23
Trooping of the Colour 84
tropical disease 100, 155
Tshekedi Khama 96, 102
Turkmanchai, Treaty of 37
Tutankhamun, tomb of 77
Tutu, Archbishop 46
Twain, Mark 149
Twining, Sir Edward 95, 112

U

Uganda 46, 47, 95, 102–3, 197
'uncivilized' practices, abolition of **49**, 50, 55
underwater cables 13, 143
Union-Castle Mail Steamship Company 148
United States 27, 51
  see also America
Universities' Mission to Central Africa (UMCA) 45

V

Venus, transit across the sun 65
Vernede, Nancy 114
Viceroy's House, Delhi 110, 112

Victoria, Queen 25, 40, 55
  birthday 81
  coronation 151
  Diamond Jubilee **78–9**, 93, 94, 164, 175
  as Empress of India 88
  funeral **87**
  Golden Jubilee 51, 94, 175
  and imperial honours 90
  and the imperialization of the monarchy 87–8
  and music 175
  political posters **10–11**
Vincent, Colonel Sir C.E. Howard 13–14, 19

W

Walker, General Sir Michael 231
Walker, Patrick Gordon 101
Wallace, Sir Donald Mackenzie 92
Wallace, Edgar 177, 179, 184
Walton, William 172–3
Warren, Sir Charles 55
Watson, William 182
Waugh, Andrew 16
W.D. & H.O. Wills 220, **220**
Wellesley, Arthur 36, 39
Western Desert 73–4
Western Desert Air Force 151
Wheeler, Major **62**
'White Man's Burden, The' 51, **51**
'white supremacy' 61, 90, 112, **191**
Wide World, The (magazine) **77**, **187**, **190–1**
Wilberforce, William 31, 50
William IV, King of England 87
Williams, Mike 111
Wilson, General Sir Henry Maitland 23
Winchester, Simon 212
Wingate, Orde 16
wireless technology 177
Wolfe, General James 36
Wolseley, Captain E. J. 196
Wolseley, Sir Garnet Joseph **115**, 136, 149
Wonder Book of the Navy, The **133**
Wood, Sir Henry 171
Woodward, William 209
world-views, imperial 209, 225

Y

'yellow peril' 30, **30**
Yellow Raiders, The **181**
Yeomen of the Guard, The (1888) 171–2
Younghusband, Sir Francis 16, 37

Z

Zanzibar 40–1, **40–1**

Acknowledgments

In preparing the manuscript I have had cause to be thankful for information and assistance provided by Jodie Adanac, Tom Cosgrove, Henry Gunston, Lynda Hobbs, Ronald Hyam, Lisa Footitt, Tom Norman, Andrew Stewart, Victoria Syme-Taylor, David Tomkins and Mark Winwood. I have been particularly appreciative of books written by Charles Allen, David Cannadine, John Mackenzie and P. J. Rich. Richard Aston deserves special thanks for allowing me to use his masterful essay on imperial memory, 'The Empire too, what does it mean to you?', reproduced in Chapter 10. Julie Anne Lambert of the John Johnson Collection, Bodleian Library, Oxford, and the staff of the Special Collections Reading Room, rendered invaluable assistance during the hugely enjoyable picture research. Stuart Ackland and John Mackerell of the Bodleian Library Map Room provided patient assistance. The Director of the Sri Lanka National Archives, Colombo, kindly granted permission to use images from their collections, and for the research trip to Sri Lanka that enabled these images to be gathered, grateful thanks are due to the British Academy for funding. Malcolm Barrett, keeper of the mess silver at the Joint Services Command and Staff College, Defence Academy of the United Kingdom, provided friendly access to his treasure trove. Lieutenant Colonel Bruce Pennell gave kind assistance in procuring images of paintings hung at the Joint Services Command and Staff College, images that are reproduced by kind permission of the Commandant, Joint Services Command and Staff College, who retains copyright (no further reproduction permitted). Peter Lewis has provided expert advice and suggestions whilst copy-editing the text and discovering wonderful images, offering the most skilful, sympathetic, efficient, and speedy assistance and direction imaginable. Patrick Nugent has worked wonders of visual presentation in arranging the page layouts. Tony Morris provided a key connection early in the book's genesis. My greatest debt is to Richard Milbank, publishing director at Quercus, the most urbane, scholarly and personable publisher that one could wish to work with, and who took to this project with enthusiasm and drive from our first meeting.

Picture credits

All images in the book are taken from the author's own collection of memorabilia, except for those listed separately on p. 235 (under 'Other resources') and those reproduced by kind permission of the following lenders:

The Bridgeman Art Library

12 Royal Geographical Society, 16 Royal Geographical Society, 20 Archives Charmet, 22 Bibliothèque Nationale, Paris/Archives Charmet, 32–33 Guildhall Library, City of London, 36 Victoria & Albert Museum, London, 44 The Stapleton Collection, 47 Private Collection, 49 Stapleton Collection, 54 Leeds Museums and Galleries, 58 Royal Geographical Society, 61, 62 Royal Geographical Society, 63 Archives Charmet, 69 Royal Geographical Society, 75 Archives Charmet, 150 Stapleton Collection, 162 Stapleton Collection, 198 Edinburgh University Library

Corbis

2–3, 17 Underwood & Underwood, 18 Michael Nicholson, 26 PoodleStock, 46 epa, 64 Stapleton Collection, 71 Bettman, 106–7 Bettman, 113, 139 Hulton-Deutsch Collection, 159 Blue Lantern Studio, 161 Paper Rodeo, 178 Photo B.D.V., 196 Hulton-Deutsch Archive, 215 Swin Ink2, 224 Christophe Boisvieux

Getty Images

40–41 Hulton Archive, 51 Hulton Archive, 98 Popperfoto, 103 Time & Life Pictures, 157 Hulton Archive

Topfoto

68 The Print Collector/HIP, 70, 80, 91, 95, 100 The British Library, 105 The Print Collector/HIP, 111 The British Library/HIP, 115, 118, 125 The Print Collector/HIP, 136 Ann Ronan Picture Library/HIP, 154, 165, 170 National Archives/HIP, 172 Michael Diamond/ArenaPAL, 175, 192 Art Media/HIP, 193 The Board of Trustees of the Armouries/HIP, 202, 204 The Print Collector/HIP, 207, 211 The British Library/HIP, 214 National Archives/HIP

Every effort has been made to credit the source of materials used in this book and to discover any existing copyright holders. The author and publishers apologize if any have been missed and invite anyone claiming ownership not identified above to contact Quercus Publishing.

Editor and project manager   Peter Lewis
Designer Patrick Nugent
Picture researcher   Mary Jane Gibson
Indexer Lisa Footit

Endpapers by kind permission of Jonathan Potter Ltd
'British Empire Throughout the World Exhibited In One View'

From: Bartholomew's The Royal Illustrated Atlas, Edinburgh, c.1860. Steel engraving, 440 x 530 mm

The world in Victorian times is shown in this engraving, with the British Empire marked in red.
Both above and below the map are representations of the different dress of British subjects on five continents. There are Africans; Europeans include a Scot in a kilt, a guardsman wearing his bearskin and Greeks from the Aegean islands; Americans include Canadian Indians and Eskimos; Chinese and Indians represent the Asians; and Aborigines and Maoris the Australians. This is a symbolically happy montage of the supposed blessings and benefits brought by British rule.

This book is dedicated to two very special Australian ladies. To my beautiful wife, Andrea, and to her grandmother in Launceston, Tasmania, Edna Bennell.